SORTING SEXUALITIES

SORTING SEXUALITIES

Expertise and the Politics of Legal Classification

STEFAN VOGLER

The University of Chicago Press
Chicago and London

The University of Chicago Press, Chicago 60637
The University of Chicago Press, Ltd., London
© 2021 by The University of Chicago
Published 2021
Printed in the United States of America

30 29 28 27 26 25 24 23 22 21   1 2 3 4 5

ISBN-13: 978-0-226-76916-5 (cloth)
ISBN-13: 978-0-226-77676-7 (paper)
ISBN-13: 978-0-226-77693-4 (e-book)
DOI: https://doi.org/10.7208/chicago/9780226776934.001.0001

Library of Congress Cataloging-in-Publication Data

Names: Vogler, Stefan, author.
Title: Sorting sexualities : expertise and the politics
of legal classification / Stefan Vogler.
Description: Chicago : The University of Chicago Press, 2021. |
Includes bibliographical references and index.
Identifiers: LCCN 2020051230 | ISBN 9780226769165 (cloth) |
ISBN 9780226776767 (paperback) | ISBN 9780226776934 (ebook)
Subjects: LCSH: Sex and law—United States. | Sexual
minorities—Classification—Social aspects—United States. |
Gay political refugees—United States. | Sex offenders—United
States. | Classification—Social aspects—United States. |
Evidence, Expert—United States. | Justice,
Administration of—United States.
Classification: LCC KF9325 .V64 2021 | DDC 345.73/025336—dc23
LC record available at https://lccn.loc.gov/2020051230

♾ This paper meets the requirements of ANSI/NISO
Z39.48-1992 (Permanence of Paper).

For Kellen,
without whom none of this would have been possible

CONTENTS

INTRODUCTION

In 1985 the US government faced a new challenge. For the first time, a gay man attempted to seek political asylum based on persecution he had faced in his home country due to his sexual orientation. Given the requirements of asylum law, the US government was put in the position of determining the man's sexuality—that is, whether he was truly gay or simply trying to find a way to stay in the United States rather than being deported. Because of the immense stigma that homosexuality carried in 1985, state representatives appeared mostly unconcerned with the possibility that the man could be lying. Instead, government attorneys argued that he could not receive asylum because homosexual behavior was illegal in the United States. After a five-year appeal process, the man ultimately was allowed to remain in the country. But as more lesbian, gay, bisexual, transgender, and queer (LGBTQ) people sought asylum over the course of the 1990s and 2000s, the government faced the prospect of sorting the truly queer from the fraudulent. How was it to do so?

In a very different, though I argue related, setting, state governments faced a similar hurdle. In 1990 Washington State became the first of what would eventually be twenty-one jurisdictions to enact a "sexually violent predator" (SVP) statute allowing for the indefinite civil commitment of sex offenders after their criminal sentences. But, as with asylum seekers, government adjudicators faced the challenge of determining what an individual's sexual identity was—that is, should a particular offender actually be labeled a pedophile, a sadist, an exhibitionist? Or did his past sexual behaviors not, in fact, indicate an inner sexual essence? Second, the government had to sort those whose sexualities posed a significant risk from those whose did not. Although states could draw on past experiences with similar "sexual psychopath" laws from the mid-twentieth century, many of those procedures had been discredited, forcing those statutes into disuse or repeal. How, then, was the state to discern a sex offender's true sexuality?

Though these two settings present similar questions—namely, how do we *know* someone's sexuality—the measurement and classification techniques, what I term "epistemic logics," that have taken shape in these two legal complexes are dramatically different. *Sorting Sexualities* argues that in these two very different contexts, how we come to *know* sexuality undergirds myriad governance decisions regarding sexual others. I show how, through efforts to render sexual subjects legible to and thus manageable by state institutions, legal and scientific actors work together to coproduce sexuality as a regulatory category. I draw particular attention to ways by which "the state" depends on non-state actors—particularly various kinds of experts—to carry out and legitimate the day-to-day practices of classification and categorization of individuals.[1] Through its exercise of symbolic and coercive power, the state acts as a dominant force in the reification of sexual identities and naturalization of difference along the lines of sexuality, much as it has done with race.[2] As with race, however, many cultural, institutional, and political factors influence precisely how such classification efforts take shape and what effects they have.

Through this analysis, I argue that sexuality is more central to state power than we have recognized. As sexualities scholar Jyoti Puri asserts, "The mandate to regulate sexuality helps reproduce states and ... cares and considerations related to sexuality impact the spaces, discursive practices, and rationalities of governance."[3] Yet, to the extent that sociologists have recognized these connections, they have been in historical and postcolonial contexts. There has been little consideration of the ways by which sexuality continues to structure state governance and power in the contemporary West. Even as sexuality appears to be more liberated than ever—as evidenced by such developments as the legalization of same-sex marriage—sexuality continues to authorize state regulation and intervention and even to serve as a vector for the expansion of state authority. Indeed, with the advancement of various kinds of sexual science and the state's enrollment of such scientific experts, the state has expanded its capacity to govern via sexuality. This is true not only because sexuality grants the state a reason to expand its oversight to more and new areas of social life, but also because it allows the state to penetrate deeper into individual bodies and lives. The state quite literally probes the bodies of sexual deviants, hoping to peer inside the bodies, to look at the brains, the genes, the hormones of those it hopes to regulate, perhaps even eradicate.

The state accomplishes this remarkable feat through two interrelated processes. First, sexuality must be constituted as a multidimensional, polyvalent phenomenon that can uniquely signal a subject that is either risky or at risk. Through this process—which, in reality, plays out through numerous small-scale interactions that aggregate to create a larger regulatory apparatus—sexuality is rendered a risk object, of sorts. A sex offender's sexuality becomes a source of danger that can only be divined and controlled by the state and its experts. Or the queer asylum seeker becomes a particularly vulnerable subject because of his sexuality. In both instances, sexuality becomes a source of risk—though in very different ways—either to the individual or to the nation. Constituting sexuality as a risk object in need of state oversight allows the state to expand its reach both through overtly punitive and apparently benevolent means. Put another way, sexuality itself is a technology with immense power to shape the social world, an insight I develop throughout this book, particularly in the conclusion.

This first process depends on a second: the enrollment of non-state actors that serve to legitimate these new and/or expanded forms of regulation and relief. New forms of social control require new kinds of knowledge, and new knowledges engender a perceived need for new forms of social control. Indeed, this process offers yet another, subtler, way by which the state expands its reach via sexuality. That is, it partially sets the terms by which we come to know sexuality, the disciplines that will wield expert authority on the topic, and the kinds of knowledge about sexuality we will get. This is especially true when new laws give rise to completely new research agendas, as is the case for sex offenders. Because of its close relationship with the law, the field of forensic psychology has been guided in many ways by the advent of new regulations aimed at sex offenders, whether it is evaluating the effectiveness of residency restrictions and public registries or concocting new ways of identifying individuals' sexual preferences and propensities for sexual danger. The law proffered such questions, and forensic psychology responded by building entire research agendas around them. Indeed, a cottage industry centered around the identification, control, and treatment of sexual offenders has arisen since the early 1990s in the wake of new laws aimed at regulating them. However, the state not only creates the need for new forms of knowledge, but it also enrolls non-state experts into its regulatory schemes in order to legitimate its expanded power. In this way, the state both anoints those who will be recognized as experts on sexuality and then offers up those experts as proof that its chosen methods are sanctioned by those with the most knowledge on the subject.

This is not to discount the agency of non-state experts and other social actors to mutually shape state classification schemas and resist state classification efforts. We see this most clearly in the asylum case, where a coalition of lawyers, human rights activists, and academics successfully pushed back against the use of things like gendered stereotypes by state actors as criteria for determining if asylum seekers were truly queer. Through their interventions, the criteria for determining asylum seekers' sexualities have moved away from strictly bodily indicators to include more narrative evidence, illustrating how non-state expert actors can shape classification criteria, even when facing resistance from state actors. Even forensic psychologists, who largely support the goals of the sex offender legal complex, maintain some autonomy in such endeavors as crafting diagnostic categories and therefore act back on state institutions. Thus, this is not just a top-down story of state institutions imposing their will onto powerless actors. Rather, this is a story about how "the state" and "the social"—a largely fictional dichotomy I will return to in chapter 2—are mutually imbricated and dependent. *Sorting Sexualities* demonstrates that state classification schemas result from both cooperation and conflict between state and non-state actors and that various social actors, including experts, are vital for the creation and functioning of state classification efforts. A glimpse into the two settings that constitute the focus of this book will begin to illustrate my argument.

OBSERVING CLASSIFICATION IN ACTION

The Chicago Immigration Court for detained claimants is housed in a nondescript government building downtown, a few blocks away from the main immigration court for the city. It is easy to miss if you don't know where to go, as I learned the morning I arrived to observe my first asylum hearing. Once I found the right building, I passed through security with a few other visitors and proceeded to the security desk near the entrance, where I told the guard that I was there for an asylum hearing. The guard pointed me to a US flag in the corner where I was to wait. Soon another guard approached and unlocked the door next to the flag, directing me to follow. We passed through another checkpoint attended by two more guards and down an elevator to the basement of the building, where he showed me to a hallway lined with a handful of chairs. This whole process struck me as rather circuitous to get to an ostensibly public courtroom. I was the first to arrive, so I took a seat and waited for Sarah, the lawyer I was shadowing.

After everyone arrived, a clerk unlocked the courtroom. It wasn't much like what I was expecting to see. It looked more like a conference room than a courtroom. There was a table with six chairs in the center of the room. On one side was a computer, which I soon learned was where the Department of Homeland Security lawyer (representing the government) sat. Sarah and her intern sat on the other side. The observation area where I was seated had only about eight chairs. An area to my left, against the wall, looked to be for a court reporter, perhaps, but none was present. There were microphones at each spot at the table to record the proceedings (there is no written record of immigration proceedings, only the recording, which is controlled by the judge). There was an elevated judge's bench, also with a computer, which I would come to see as quite fitting: immigration judges are in many ways as much administrators as they are adjudicators. Judges often take extensive notes during hearings that they later use to deliver extemporaneous oral opinions at the conclusion of proceedings.

Soon after 9:00 a.m. the judge entered the courtroom. I would later learn that she was considered by the immigration lawyer community to be one of the "better" judges in the Chicago Immigration Court, particularly when it came to LGBTQ claims. Unlike many judges, she insisted on conducting most hearings with detained claimants in person rather than via televideo, a technology that has received considerable criticism from immigrant advocates.

Soon after the judge arrived, the asylum seeker, Kofi Addai[4]—a soft-spoken nineteen-year-old—entered, escorted by a bailiff. He wore the tan jumpsuit of the Kenosha County Detention Center and was in handcuffs. To my surprise, Addai's handcuffs were left on for the entire hearing, despite the fact that this was a civil proceeding, and he was neither convicted nor accused of a crime, a stark reminder of the increasingly criminalized status of immigrants. After a bout of trouble with the translator—a not uncommon occurrence—Addai elected to proceed in English, despite his relatively limited grasp of the language. This can present a significant obstacle for asylum seekers, who are expected to be able to recount details of their lives and persecution coherently and with "proper" emotion. In any event, Andrea, Sarah's intern, began the questioning, essentially constructing a "coming out" narrative. When did you realize you were gay? When was your first sexual experience? Did you ever have a boyfriend? Have you ever told anyone in your family that you are gay? The testimony proceeded to cover questions of Addai's persecution claims, and he concluded by stating that if granted asylum, he wanted to "lead a good life as an openly gay man." Addai's sexual orientation narrative seemed basically straightforward, consistent, and genuine. However, the government attorney on cross-examination latched on to one particular detail: Addai had tried to date a woman for a short period. "Did you ever have sex with a girl?" Addai responded that he had when he briefly tried to date a woman to conceal that he was gay. "Did you have sex through to completion?" the lawyer persisted. Addai replied that the encounter stopped before either of them climaxed and that neither of them enjoyed it. He claimed that she could tell that he didn't know what he was doing and told him that he acted "like a woman" in bed. At the end of the hearing, the judge asked the final question: "To verify, the only gay sexual experience you had was when you were eleven or twelve? And the only other was with a woman last year?" Addai answered yes to both. Nevertheless, the judge ultimately found Addai to be credibly gay and rejected the government argument that he had not proven his sexual orientation. She found it plausible that a gay man in Ghana would try to have a relationship with a woman to conceal his sexuality and that having sex with a woman didn't necessarily mean that Addai wasn't gay. His asylum petition was granted.

Unlike the clandestine immigration court, the Cook County Criminal Court on the South Side of Chicago is unmistakable. Along with the attached Cook County Jail, it occupies a huge swath of an area that has otherwise been left to deteriorate. On the morning I arrived to observe my first "sexually violent person" (SVP) civil commitment hearing, I passed through security and found my way to the courtroom. Despite civil commitment hearings being civil, they are often held in criminal courts, as they are in Cook County. Again unlike immigration court, this courtroom was much more like the ones you expect, that is to say, the ones you see on television. Large wooden doors gave way to a gallery of rows of benches with a grand judge's bench at the front of the courtroom. There was an actual court reporter this time, seated in front of the judge's bench. A jury box was situated to the left, and the tables for the defense and prosecution were situated just in front of the railing partitioning the gallery from the area where the "action" happens, so to speak.[5] I found a seat among the crowd packing the room. Though court ostensibly convenes at 9:00 a.m., the judge did not enter until 10:15, at which time he began hearing a number of motions for criminal cases, disposing of most in only a few minutes each. By 11:30 the docket was complete except for the SVP hearing, and the gallery crowd was gone, leaving only me being eyed suspiciously by a bailiff who would intermittently insist that I wasn't allowed to write anything down during court (that's not true, and I would surreptitiously resume my note-taking after she moved on). After a short recess, the jury filed in followed by the defendant, Jordan Lowe, led by a bailiff and in handcuffs. He remained restrained throughout the trial, but unlike Addai, Lowe had been allowed to don street clothes and was wearing khaki slacks, a button-up shirt, and tie.

The trial began with the assistant attorney general's opening statement, during which she explained for the jury the requirements of declaring someone an SVP, that Lowe had committed two sexual assaults, and that they would be hearing testimony from two doctors. Both diagnosed him with paraphilic disorder, antisocial personality disorder, and alcohol and cocaine abuse, and would give their opinion that Lowe is a sexually violent person. Next, Lowe's defense attorney presented his opening remarks, highlighting for the jury that they must determine not just that Lowe has a mental disorder but that his mental disorder must predispose him to future acts of sexual violence. Moreover, he continued, even though they would be hearing from psychologists, it was the jury's job to "put them to the test"; just because they are psychologists does not mean they are "infallible." Each of the psychologists then testified over the course of the two-day trial. Unlike the asylum hearing where Kofi was the primary witness and source of information about his sexuality, Lowe never testified himself, and our only knowledge of his sexuality came from the two expert witnesses. Also different from the asylum case, testimony about Lowe's sexuality concentrated heavily on acts and fantasies, which were used to deduce an underlying sexual preference for coercive sex—"other specified paraphilic disorder: nonconsenting females"—that was presented as akin to any other sexual orientation. The psychologists recounted in detail exactly what had happened during the two sexual assaults for which Lowe had been convicted, and, moreover, they discussed how he talked about those incidents in therapy. SVP trials allow many things into evidence ordinarily not allowed, including certain types of hearsay evidence and normally confidential information obtained during psychological treatment.

Notably, during an extensive sidebar conversation during which the jury was dismissed, it came to light that one of the psychologists had partially based his diagnosis on a technology not usually allowed in Illinois courtrooms: the penile plethysmograph (PPG).[6] This device is widely used among sex offender treatment providers and works by placing a silicone ring around a man's penis and gauging the extent of his erection (or lack thereof) in response to different types of stimuli. Advocates assert that the process measures sexual arousal, attraction, and orientation. Despite its prohibition as direct evidence, the judge felt no need to inform the jury that the technology underwrote part of the psychologist's testimony, and nothing of its use was ever mentioned in the jurors' presence. Nevertheless, in a rare turn of events, the jury ultimately found Lowe not to qualify as an SVP. Though juries do not have to state reasons for their decisions, according to the prosecutor who tried the case and spoke with the jurors briefly after their pronouncement, it seemed that they were uncertain of the validity of the expert testimony because the evaluations had been completed more than a year and a half before the trial. They appeared to wonder whether Lowe's sexuality was really still a danger or if treatment had substantially changed it or at least allowed him to control it.

As these vignettes begin to show, different ways of knowing sexuality have been institutionalized in these two legal complexes. Where asylum adjudications favor narrative evidence of sexuality contextualized within specific cultural settings, SVP trials lean more heavily on technologies meant to read the body or otherwise "objectively" measure or quantify sexuality. Asylum hearings tend to draw on anthropological and sociological expertise while SVP trials depend on psychological and psychiatric knowledge. Whereas asylum decisions depend on assessing the risk a petitioner may face *from* his home country, SVP determinations depend on assessing the risk an offender poses *to* his community.

This book traces precisely how these practices have taken shape and been institutionalized, which I show has been the result of contestations between both state and social actors and between rival networks of expertise vying for authority. Though it can appear at first blush that these two areas of law come to divergent conclusions about sexuality and how to measure it because they are concerned with different aspects of sexuality, that is only superficially true. As these vignettes illustrate, although asylum law may purport to assess sexual identity and sex offender law to evaluate sexual behaviors, in practice these are often distinctions without a difference. The law is not uniform in its operationalization of sexuality, nor in its slippages. Behaviors frequently become identities; fantasies are taken to determine behaviors, and identities may be assigned that fail to accurately describe individuals. Or perhaps the differences are because asylum seekers are viewed as more honest and forthcoming than sex offenders. But constant cries to beware of fraudulent asylum claims—particularly for things like sexuality that are difficult to objectively ascertain—belie such an easy answer. Maybe the explanation can be found in the differing perceptions of danger associated with each group. Yet our current political climate, the increasing criminalization of migrants, and the equating of many immigrant groups with terrorists again calls this explanation into question. Facile explanations for these different approaches thus begin to fall apart upon deeper inspection.

Yet we also have strong reasons to think that both legal domains would approach the classification of diverse sexual subjects in similar ways. Even today many sexuality researchers search for clues to the etiology of homosexuality, pedophilia, and other non-normative sexualities in the same areas of the brain or the same genes, or look for bodily clues in the same places. Both gay men and pedophiles, for instance, purportedly are more likely to be left-handed. Likewise, many lab scientists use the PPG in experiments with both pedophiles and gay men. Given the continuing use of similar scientific methods for a range of sexualities, then, we might expect the law to also approach the measurement of diverse sexualities in comparable ways.

Sorting Sexualities puts our cultural common sense about sexuality under a microscope in order to, as the old anthropological axiom goes, make the familiar strange. I ask how commonsensical our assumptions actually are. Rather than accepting them at face value, I uncover the cultural, historical, and political contingencies that have created our current legal conceptions of sexuality. This, therefore, is a study of how different notions of sexuality and sexual identity have come into being through contestations over legal and scientific knowledge-making. But beyond that, this study is about how those knowledge-making practices become institutionalized and affect how we govern. Who wields expertise in relation to sexuality? Who decides? What counts as evidence of sexuality? How should we classify and categorize individuals' sexualities? Who is a proper sexual citizen? I show that in the legal domains of LGBTQ asylum law and sex offender law, different knowledge practices undergird decisions about what constitutes sexuality and how we should manage different sexual populations, including defining the boundaries of sexual citizenship and what types of sexual subjects should be part of the polity.

In both cases, sexuality works as a mechanism for sorting the moral from the immoral subject, the benign from the dangerous, the potential citizen who can be brought into the national fold from the permanent non-citizen who must be excluded at all costs. Where the LGBTQ asylum seeker is welcomed (if only lukewarmly) as an acceptable sexual subject, the sex offender is banished to the margins of civil society or excluded altogether.

Though our cultural common sense may lead us to believe that the differences in classification practices can be explained by the apparent fact that homosexuality and sexual criminality are very different things, it is only very recently that such a distinction has appeared in legal, scientific, and popular discourses. In the epistemic paradigm that predominated in the United States for most of the twentieth century, there was little to no conceptual distinction between homosexuality and various forms of sexual criminality, such as pedophilia, sadism, or exhibitionism.

Yet today it is such strong cultural common sense that being gay is *not* the same as being pedophilic or sadistic that many readers may balk at the juxtaposition. But that is precisely why comparing institutional responses to these two categories is so illuminating. Until 2003, for example, consensual same-sex sexual relations were still criminalized in fourteen US states. Until 1990 gay people were barred from entering the United States because they were deemed "psychopathic personalities." Before 1973 "homosexuality" was considered a paraphilic disorder, categorized in the same section of the *Diagnostic and Statistical Manual of Mental Disorders* (*DSM*) as pedophilia, voyeurism, and other criminal sexualities. Through the mid-twentieth century, homosexuality and pedophilia were considered similar disorders of the male sexual impulse, while rape was considered a natural outgrowth of male sexual aggression; now we are more likely to categorize rapists and pedophiles together.[7] The penile plethysmograph was used in the "treatment" of gay men and pedophiles alike into the 1980s and continues to be used on sex offenders today. Yet ways of legally classifying sex offenders are no longer acceptable methods for use on gay people. But this is a historically recent development.

By tracing the divergent ways that state institutions make sense of non-normative sexualities, I show that this seismic cultural shift is anchored to institutional changes that are the product of collective action. The state works as a powerful force for naturalizing social difference along the lines of sexuality and for reifying cultural changes around sexuality. Specifically, the state imports lay notions of sexuality and renders them "natural" by co-opting the expert authority of scientific disciplines that support those views. Through selectively drawing on scientific expertise, state institutions avoid the appearance of governing by cultural common sense and instead purport to offer objective truths about sexuality. In this way, cultural changes around sexuality become reified in institutional practice and have both material and symbolic effects. *Sorting Sexualities* unpacks the political, institutional, and cultural factors that guide these state decision-making processes. In essence, I contend that how we culturally define sexual subjects dictates how we legally classify and interrogate their sexualities. If we define subjects as a priori deviant or abnormal, then procedures for determining their sexualities will follow in the historical footsteps of studying deviance, which has often meant looking for defects in or on the body. Conversely, if sexual subjects have been culturally normalized, as gay and lesbian people generally have been in the United States, it is far less likely that we will subject them to similarly invasive procedures. Of course, it's not quite that simple because we see the same procedures applied to "normal" and "deviant" sexual subjects outside the domain of law. This is why institutional settings and imperatives, as well as the type of expertise adjudicating one's sexuality, are paramount.

In explaining these processes, I develop the heuristic of "epistemic logics," explaining how these epistemic logics become institutionalized, how they affect understandings of sexuality, and how they shape risk determination processes. In doing so, I aim to illuminate the centrality of expertise—and in particular, non-state epistemic actors—in state legibility projects. But I also seek to show how law, science, and the state draw on cultural notions of sexuality to legitimate governance decisions and, in the process, simultaneously authorize certain views over others. Though chapter 2 fully fleshes out the theoretical scaffolding of the book, here I want to introduce the concept of epistemic logics.

Epistemic Logics

Epistemic logics are institutionalized ways of knowing that guide action in organizational settings and vary based on institutional, cultural, and political factors. In the cases analyzed here, institutional actors draw on different cultural framings to make sense of sexuality and to legitimate their approaches to measuring it. Though they are part of a broader cultural tool kit, epistemic logics are not reducible to cultural schemas of interpretation.[8] They are more precise, guide action more directly, and take shape through the interplay of extant cultural, institutional, and political factors, on the one hand, and expert actors, on the other. For instance, a predominant cultural schema regarding sexuality is that it is inborn, unchanging, and locatable within the body in some biological substrate—perhaps our genes or hormones. This cultural framework suggests a particular epistemic logic. If sexuality is a bodily phenomenon, then we should measure it via the body, by looking for clues in our brains, genes, or even on the body itself or in how the body reacts. This epistemic logic predominates among forensic psychologists and, in turn, sex offender law, where psychology is the institutionalized form of expert knowledge. A competing cultural schema suggests that sexuality is culturally and historically specific and that bodies are socialized into particular sexual behaviors and identities; it is not inherent in individuals. This schema calls for a different epistemic logic, one that looks more to cultural and historical context than to individual bodies to understand sexuality. This is the epistemic logic that sociology and anthropology bring to asylum law. Thus, epistemic logics will vary depending on which schema predominates in a given institutional setting, and they will produce independent effects distinct from broader cultural schemas. They give rise to different legal conceptions of sexuality, what counts as evidence of sexuality, and how sexuality will be measured and assessed, and they naturalize distinct sexual ontologies and identities.

The concept of epistemic logics borrows from the ideas of both institutional logics and epistemic cultures, but is not reducible to either one. In their classic statement defining institutional logics, Roger Friedland and Robert Alford write, "Each of the most important institutional orders of contemporary Western societies has a central logic—a set of material practices and symbolic constructions—which constitutes its organizing principles and which is available to organizations and individuals to elaborate. . . . These institutional logics are symbolically grounded, organizationally structured, politically defended, and technically and materially constrained, and hence have specific historical limits."[9] This definition is similar to what I have described as epistemic logics, though it differs in important ways. First, institutional logics are supra-organizational. Conversely, I suggest that epistemic logics are unique to particular organizational settings. We might consider them to be more specific elaborations of broader institutional logics. Friedland and Alford offered five primary institutional logics—those of capitalism, the state, democracy, family, and religion/science—that may structure individual and organizational activity and cognition. The logic of capitalism can travel from one organization to another and maintain its central logic of accumulation and commodification of human activity. In this sense, institutional logics are much broader than epistemic logics. Epistemic logics are specific to particular interstitial organizational contexts and would look different if they traveled to a different setting. The institutional logics of the state and science characterize both the asylum and sex offender legal complexes, but because of their specific constellations of institutional, cultural, and political constraints, each of their epistemic logics looks different. Thus, even though both complexes evince the same *institutional* logics, they approach the measurement and classification of sexual subjects very differently because their *epistemic* logics are distinct.

Second, although institutional logics are concerned with meaning-making and cognition, the concept does not foreground knowledge-making as does the notion of epistemic logics. In this regard, I draw from Karin Knorr Cetina's idea of epistemic cultures. She defines epistemic cultures as "those amalgams of arrangements and mechanisms—bonded through affinity, necessity, and historical coincidence—which, in a given field, make up *how we know what we know*."[10] Again, this definition comes close to the concept of epistemic logics. But where Knorr Cetina seeks to describe the "machineries of knowing" for scientific fields, my goal is to understand how specific hybrid spaces come to know sexuality. That is, epistemic logics do not describe entire fields but only specific organizational spaces where different epistemic cultures come together to form unique and hybridized ways of knowing. In other words, even though anthropologists often provide expert testimony in asylum hearings, the epistemic logic of the asylum complex that I describe would not apply to anthropology as an entire field. Rather, when anthropologists testify in asylum proceedings, they know that they may have to adapt their practices to suit the setting in a way that may be very different from what they would do when talking to other anthropologists. Similarly, the epistemic logic dictating understandings of sexuality in SVP hearings would not apply to psychology as an entire discipline. The organizational cultures and institutional needs of science, law, and state administration come together in these two spaces to create distinct ways of knowing. In short, epistemic logics refer to the hybrid ways of knowing formed at the zones of intersection between the broader institutional logics that span social domains and the broader epistemic cultures that span scientific fields.

Epistemic logics themselves are shaped by cultural, political, and institutional factors. But once epistemic logics become institutionalized, they take on a life of their own in defining what counts as empirical evidence of sexuality and how sexuality should be measured. Forms of expertise are therefore a mediating force between larger structural factors and ultimate state understandings of sexuality. But because understandings of sexuality are inevitably constrained by larger structural forces, I want to summarize some of the most salient factors that shape these distinct epistemic practices.[11]

Cultural Frames

Sex offenders are considered a particularly heinous type of criminal in our culture, and these cultural frames inevitably find their way into state institutions.[12] The popular (and legal) trope of the sexual predator serves to dehumanize sex offenders. Moreover, the cultural frame of medicalization powerfully structures how we view sex offenders and particularly sexual predators. Deviant sexualities have a long history of being pathologized, and whereas homosexuality has moved out of this frame, paraphilias such as pedophilia and sadism have not.

Unlike sex criminals, LGBTQ people are no longer viewed through the lenses of criminalization or medicalization. Rather, LGBTQ people are increasingly accepted in society, and this is reflected in the legal sphere where they are granted considerably greater agency than pathologized sex offenders. This, I would argue, also means we increasingly recognize the nuance of their sexualities and sexual identities. Thus, cultural currents around ideas of sexual fluidity and the variability of sexual expression can more easily penetrate the legal complex of LGBTQ asylum law, where the subjects under scrutiny are seen as more fully human and complex than the sexual predator, who remains more a cultural stereotype than a human subject. Regardless of our personal feelings of the horrible acts that some offenders commit, the failure to see sex offenders as complex humans is analytically problematic and also legitimizes anomalous, unique, and disproportionate treatment, such as indefinite confinement.

These frames affect how legal and scientific actors view the subjects under scrutiny and, in particular, their trustworthiness. Perhaps because LGBTQ asylum seekers are seen as more trustworthy than convicted sex offenders, there is not a perceived need to be as invasive with techniques of interrogation for asylum seekers. Notably, however, concerns with fraudulent asylum seekers have been voiced continuously over many years and have even been the basis for changes in asylum law, such as the enactment of a one-year filing deadline in 1996. The logic goes that any "real" asylum seeker would lodge their claim within a year of arriving in the country, a view that, of course, fails to account for any number of factors that might prevent such an outcome. The increasing criminalization of all migrants also adds some doubt to the possibility that completely different cultural frames apply to criminals and immigrants, especially since 9/11, and even more so since the 2016 election of Donald Trump, with his continuous equating of the two groups in his public comments and policy agenda, including his labeling of whole groups of immigrants as "rapists."[13]

Finally, cultural frames may be pivotal in determining our collective level of acceptance for false positives and false negatives. The analogous

TABLE 1. False negatives and positives in asylum and SVP law

	False Negative	False Positive
Asylum	Finding someone to be not gay when they actually are.	Finding someone to be gay when they are not.
SVP	Finding someone to be not an SVP when they actually are.	Finding someone to be an SVP when they are not.

situations here are false negatives for asylum seekers and false positives for SVPs and vice versa (see table 1). A false *negative* for an asylum seeker (not believing someone is gay when they are) would likely result in deportation and possibly future harm in their home country, whereas a false *positive* for an SVP (finding someone to be an SVP when they aren't) would result in someone being indefinitely deprived of freedom. Conversely, a false *positive* for an asylum seeker (believing someone is gay when they aren't) may allow someone into the country who otherwise would not be, and a false *negative* for an SVP (finding someone to not be an SVP when they are) would result in his release from custody even though he shouldn't be freed. In both cases, most social actors probably have lower tolerance for false negatives in both cases (freeing a dangerous offender or deporting someone who is likely to be harmed) and may, in fact, care very little about the potential for false positives. So what if an immigrant who has been well-vetted is admitted to the country, even if they lied about their sexual orientation to do it? Likewise, given widespread cultural views of sex offenders, many would care little if an already-convicted sex offender is further punished. It should come as no surprise, then, that the forms of expertise institutionalized in both legal arenas are more likely to produce false positives than false negatives. These decisions are, of course, political, as well.

Political Pressures

SVP laws arrived on the heels of the satanic ritual abuse panic of the 1980s in the midst of an acute sex panic over crimes against children. The first of these laws was enacted in Washington State in 1990 in direct response to a particularly heinous sexually motivated abduction and mutilation of a boy by a recently released sex offender. An outraged public demanded a response, and the Washington legislature obliged, passing the nation's first SVP law within months of the crime. This story fits with the wider "governing through crime" paradigm ascendant during this period, and scholars have pointed out the "popular punitiveness" of sex crimes legislation indicative of this political strategy.[14]

The form of SVP laws was also constrained by the downfall of the earlier generation of "sexual psychopath" civil commitment statutes. These laws faced heavy criticism due to the subjective nature of dangerousness predictions that opponents contended resulted in many false positives. The new SVP laws, by contrast, outlined more explicit criteria for assessing risk, and clearer diagnostic guidelines, and the advent of quantitative actuarial risk tools by forensic psychologists granted greater scientific and legal legitimacy to this new generation of civil commitment statutes and provided political cover.

Asylum for LGBTQ people likewise arose in a particular political context. Fidel Toboso-Alfonso, a Cuban man who arrived as part of the Mariel Boatlift, lodged the first sexual orientation–based asylum claim in 1985. Though the McCarran-Walter Act made it officially illegal for homosexuals to enter the country, it was not politically expedient to deport a Cuban man in the midst of the Cold War when the United States maintained a policy allowing Cubans who made it to the US to stay. The politically expedient move appeared to win out, and Toboso-Alfonso was granted withholding of removal, though the Immigration and Naturalization Service (INS) appealed the decision. However, the Board of Immigration Appeals (BIA) ultimately sided with Toboso-Alfonso in 1990. Subsequently, in 1994 Attorney General Janet Reno declared Toboso-Alfonso's case precedential, meaning gay people were officially recognized as a "particular social group" eligible for asylum. This declaration also arose out of a political compromise. In an effort to assuage his gay supporters during the "Don't Ask, Don't Tell" controversy, Bill Clinton offered asylum as an olive branch.

Institutional Constraints

Institutional mandates enable and constrain courses of action within each legal complex. Overarching institutional goals, for instance, partially structure the kinds of knowledge drawn upon by legal actors. The institutional goal of the asylum complex is to provide humanitarian relief and to determine those eligible for such relief, and the types of knowledge and expertise used are therefore geared toward that goal. Similarly, the institutional goal of SVP law is to regulate and contain those deemed sexual dangers, and knowledge deployed in that arena thus aims for clear assignations of individual risk. Greater needs for communication across organizational boundaries and greater internal and external oversight in SVP law compared to asylum law likely also leads to different knowledge practices, such as the more frequent reliance on quantitative information in SVP trials.[15] Table 2 contains a summary of salient institutional factors.

Legal infrastructures—such as governing statutes, rules of evidence,

TABLE 2. Institutional variables

	Asylum	SVP
Institutional Goals	Determining eligibility for humanitarian relief	Determining individual dangerousness
Standards of Proof	Varies by type of relief: "well-founded fear" to "more likely than not"	Varies by jurisdiction: "substantially probable" to "beyond a reasonable doubt"
Legal Infrastructure	Broad governing statutes; mostly precedent and some agency guidelines	Detailed, specific laws dictate procedures; some precedent
Communication Needs	Limited mostly to immigration system	Significant communication across organizational and institutional contexts
Oversight/ Accountability	Limited; low public visibility; immigration judges have considerable autonomy; decisions appealed infrequently	High public visibility; decisions frequently appealed multiple times
Decision-maker	Judges; asylum officers	Varies by jurisdiction: judge or jury

and required levels of proof—also shape the kinds of knowledge deployed. Laws governing asylum are broad and have allowed activists to take advantage of considerable legal ambiguity. LGBTQ asylum law has therefore been shaped mostly by legal precedent and, more recently, agency guidelines and policies. Though common law jurisprudence has also considerably shaped SVP law, including determining whether technologies like the PPG are allowed as evidence, statutes more directly dictate the type of expertise that courts call upon by requiring things like diagnoses of mental abnormalities.

Taken together, these cultural, political, and institutional variables create divergent epistemic logics that support competing interpretations of sexuality itself. Ultimately, these logics provide powerful cultural legitimacy for governance decisions.

STUDYING LEGAL COMPLEXES

In studying asylum and sex offender law and the forms of expertise that inform them, I have attempted to avoid personifying both "law" and "science." "Law," as Mariana Valverde points out, is the "mother of all legal fictions," an abstract idea impossible to grapple with empirically.[16] The same could be said of the nebulous "science." Rather, people interact with concrete "legal complexes": "ill-defined, uncoordinated, often decentralized sets of networks, institutions, rituals, texts, and relations of power and of knowledge."[17] Legal complexes, unlike "law," can be empirically studied. By examining the actors, networks, institutions, and practices constituting the legal complexes around asylum and sex offender law, I can offer fine-grained analysis of how the epistemic practices of deploying expertise, evidence, and technologies of knowing in legal settings constitute sexuality and legitimate social control techniques.

Similarly, I have sought to disaggregate "the state" in order to analyze whether and how governance practices vary across different state domains, and have therefore tried to avoid reifying the idea of a monolithic state or, indeed, a concept of "the state" as a concrete entity that exerts independent force upon a distinctly separate entity called "society."[18] The state/society divide is largely artificial and continuously permeable, and, as much scholarship has attested, the state is a thoroughly cultural phenomenon.[19] Thus, I view the state as a complex and historically changing configuration of discourses, people, and institutions that sometimes have conflicting goals, interpretations, and approaches to a variety of issues. Rather than existing as an agentic entity detached from society, the state provides a "scheme of intelligibility for a whole group of already established institutions and realities."[20] In line with this theoretical orientation, I view state institutions as anchor points for cultural practices, including knowledge creation, and therefore adopt a middle-range analysis that focuses on specific organizations as powerful "machineries of knowing" that configure the knowledge-making process.[21] Organizations constrain action, create opportunities, make certain trajectories more tenable, and render particular arrangements unthinkable, resulting in institutionalized patterns of action.[22] Furthermore, organizations require "classification systems and standardized documents that regiment, restrict and reduce experience and understanding into easily digestible and communicable abstractions from more complex, dynamic interactions and situational logics."[23] The asylum and SVP legal complexes offer two organizational settings to observe these processes in action in relation to sexuality and, specifically, where state officials are charged with determining individuals' sexualities.

Moreover, as historian of sexuality Regina Kunzel has argued, "One way to subject the social process of normalization and the categories of identity and experience defined as normal to historical scrutiny is to examine responses to what might be considered their border problems."[24] As I describe extensively in chapter 1, homosexuality and sexual criminality have historically been tightly linked. However, in recent years homosexuality, and especially monogamously coupled "respectable" gays and lesbians, have arguably crossed the line to become part of what Gayle Rubin has called the "charmed circle" of acceptable sexual expressions and have become delinked from criminality and pathology.[25] Sexual offenders, conversely, remain strongly stigmatized. The comparison therefore allows me to analyze the ways by which (de)criminalization and (de)medicalization contribute to the constitution of sexual identities and the role that state institutions, in conjunction with non-state actors, play in naturalizing and reifying sexuality-based distinctions.

As a final point, I want to note that although I analyze epistemic practices that are drastically different and represent sexuality in very different ways, I avoid declaring one way "true" and another "false." I critique some aspects of the measurement and classification practices in both asylum and sex offender law, but in accord with the principle of symmetry drawn from the sociology of scientific knowledge, I attempt to scrutinize both domains through a similar analytic lens.[26] The divergent ways that sexuality is understood are equally real in their respective institutional contexts and have material consequences, regardless of whether we as observers subscribe to those belief systems.

This methodological premise applies similarly to the fact that I am comparing institutional practices around sex offenders and LGBTQ people. Although I discuss this comparison in-depth in chapter 1, it bears reiterating here that I am not equating the two groups but rather using them as cases that illustrate how state institutions differentially define and govern sexuality. I also refrain from making moral judgments about the character of individuals I discuss in this study. My purpose here is not to further entrench a particular moral view of sex offenders or asylees, but to analyze how it is that we have come to understand these figures in the way we do today.

To empirically study these legal complexes, I draw on over four hundred legal decisions, forty-one semi-structured interviews with legal and scientific actors in the fields, and multi-sited ethnographic observations. Triangulating multiple sources of data works as a robustness check for my findings and guards against the shortcomings inherent in any single method. Because both the letter of the law and its implementation vary across jurisdictions, multiple sources of data allow me to speak to different levels of analysis. Asylum law, for instance, is promulgated by the federal government, and agency policies regarding asylum officers and immigration judges affect the entire national system. However, federal appellate court decisions are only binding on immigration courts in that circuit (though in practice the courts mostly follow their sister circuits' precedents), and research shows that asylum grant rates vary widely between federal circuits and even between immigration courts in the same circuit.[27] Conversely, sex crimes laws are mostly enacted and enforced at the state level. But the federal government has also threatened to withhold federal law enforcement funds from states that do not comply with its desired guidelines, resulting in sex crime policy that looks relatively similar across states. The federal government also has its own sex crimes laws, including a civil commitment statute.

In order to cover this patchwork of laws, I sampled legal decisions that cover many jurisdictions, selected interviewees from across the nation, and conducted observations in multiple locations. I collected 184 LGBTQ asylum decisions from federal appellate courts in addition to relevant pub- licly available decisions by the Board of Immigration Appeals (BIA) and various NGO and government documents, and I interviewed immigra- tion lawyers, activists, adjudicators, and expert witnesses from across the United States—all data that allow me to examine asylum practices across the country. Additionally, I conducted two years of fieldwork with Midwest Immigrant Rights Advocates (MIRA), a nonprofit legal organization in Chi- cago that has a national presence on queer immigration issues. Through MIRA, I observed twelve asylum hearings in the Chicago immigration court, which allowed me to witness the real-time workings of the asylum process, though in only one locale.

Data for the sex crimes legal complex came from over two hundred legal decisions sampled from an archive of several thousand cases (see "Appendix 2: Methodology" for a full discussion) that covered both state and federal courts. Interviewees, particularly psychological experts, were similarly drawn from across the country. I also conducted ethnographic observations at the professional meetings of the Association for the Treat- ment of Sexual Abusers (ATSA) and the International Association for the Treatment of Sex Offenders. These data allow me to speak to sex crimes policy across the nation. However, because sex crimes statutes are largely governed by states, I also conducted an in-depth case study of Illinois, selecting an additional thirty-two state legal decisions, over-sampling evaluators from Illinois, attending the biannual meeting for the Illinois chapter of ATSA, observing the bimonthly meetings of the Illinois Sex Of- fender Management Board for two years, and witnessing two sex offender civil commitment trials in Chicago.

Thus, I have sought to collect data on both legal domains in a way that allows me to examine the institutions, actors, and practices at all levels of the legal complexes. For both legal complexes, I concentrated analysis on the years from approximately 1990 (the year the first gay asylum case was granted and the first SVP law was enacted) to 2015. This period also roughly tracks the dramatic success of the LGBT movement in gaining legal protections and public favor and the simultaneous increase in scope and punitiveness of sex crimes laws.

PLAN OF THE BOOK

As an inquiry into the techno-legal classification of sexuality, *Sorting Sexualities* addresses issues that exist at the boundaries of traditional academic fields and thus draws on a variety of disciplinary approaches and literatures that have not often been in conversation. My analysis offers an interdisciplinary perspective that speaks to three broad strands of scholarly inquiry with resonance across academic fields: (1) knowledge formation (how state institutions, in conjunction with non-state expert actors, measure, classify, and know sexualities); (2) state power (how state and legal organizations use different forms of knowledge to govern individuals and populations); and (3) cultural boundaries and identity formation (how legal and scientific practices and technologies reify sexual identities and reinforce cultural distinctions, including the boundary between citizen and noncitizen). The next two chapters assemble the theoretical and historical tool kit needed to tackle these issues. But first I offer a brief overview of what is to come.

The first chapter traces the historical emergence of the "sexual deviant" in late nineteenth- and early twentieth-century sexology and medicine. Notions of both homosexuality and sex crimes took shape during this period, and at the time both were considered part of the same phenomenon. The same body of laws targeted homosexuals, pedophiles, and rapists alike. Though some early thinkers argued that homosexuality was "benign variation" and advocated for the decriminalization and depathologization of homosexuality, it was not until the mid-twentieth century that conceptualizations of homosexuality and other categories of sexual deviancy began to diverge significantly. The removal of homosexuality from the *DSM* helped this process, but stereotypes of the "homosexual pedophile" continue even today. This chapter therefore contends that it would be wrong to see no enduring relationship between the legal and knowledge politics of queerness and sexual crimes today. Indeed, twenty-first-century approaches to studying sexuality—attempts to "locate" pedophilia and homosexuality in the same areas of the brain, for instance—keep this specter alive.

Chapter 2 develops the theoretical backdrop of the book. Drawing on ideas from sociology, legal studies, science and technology studies, and queer studies, I offer a framework for analyzing the techno-legal classification of sexuality within state institutions. I bring sociologist Robin Stryker's notion of "technocratization" into conversation with work on state classification and the legal regulation of sexuality to suggest that particular institutional settings give rise to hybrid forms of knowing social phenomena that result from the alchemy of political constraints, cultural frames, and expert claims-making. By drawing on the cultural legitimacy of non-state expert actors, I contend that legal institutions both legitimate new forms of social control aimed at sexuality and naturalize sexual identity categories. The ultimate result is to expand state power and capacity via sexuality, even as such developments may engender new forms of resistance and claims-making.

Chapters 3 and 4 ask how different networks of expertise formed in each legal complex. I use the idea of epistemic logics to explore how historically contingent arrangements of actors, institutions, technologies, and knowledges have crystallized as temporarily stabilized ways of knowing sexuality in each legal domain. Why is forensic psychology the predominant form of expertise informing sex offender law? Historically, psychiatrists have outnumbered psychologists in the penal management of sexual deviance, but this has changed since the enactment of new civil commitment laws for sex offenders in the 1990s. In chapter 3, I show that this change was the product of a professional and legal skirmish between psychiatry and forensic psychology, particularly around each field's stance on how the term "mental abnormality" should be applied to sex offenders. Whereas organized psychiatry, represented by the American Psychiatric Association (APA), viewed the term as ill-defined and opposed its use in legal settings, forensic psychology, represented most prominently by the Association for the Treatment of Sexual Abusers (ATSA), believed the term was workable in practice. Ultimately, the Supreme Court sided with ATSA in two landmark decisions. By conceding some of its epistemic authority in defining the framework within which it would work, ATSA secured itself professional jurisdiction and authority in the legal management of sex offenders. Additionally, forensic psychologists were able to capitalize on prevailing concerns with the subjectivity of psychiatric clinical assessments by offering greater "mechanic objectivity" in the evaluation process.

Unlike forensic psychologists, asylum advocates faced no entrenched expertise that had to be dislodged. Rather, their expert network formed contemporaneously with the development of queer asylum law. However, they did contend with adjudicators' "commonsense" approach to determining sexualities and had to find creative ways to shift these erroneous ways of understanding sexuality. Chapter 4 shows that asylum advocates accomplished this by cobbling together a network consisting of lawyers, activists, academics, and "lay experts" that was able to bridge the distance between their own ideas about adjudicating LGBTQ asylum claims and those of state officials. These mostly lay experts—often lawyers who trained themselves in social scientific conceptions of sexuality—brought novel legal arguments that put forward nascent social constructionist accounts of sexuality in language that registered with state adjudicators. Eventually, this expert network inserted itself into the very workings of the immigration system, providing trainings to asylum officers and immigration judges, and even institutionalizing their epistemic authority through a training module about adjudicating LGBTQ claims that all new asylum officers must complete.

Once established, epistemic logics significantly affect what counts as empirical evidence of sexuality in legal proceedings. Chapters 5 and 6 take up this issue to demonstrate how competing social scientific views of sexuality result in different forms of evidence predominating in each legal arena and ultimately result in divergent interpretations of sexuality. I argue that this is due to epistemic stances suggesting either that sexuality can be directly assessed via the body, as in sex offender law, or that sexuality must be determined through indirect indicators, as in asylum law. Chapter 5 shows that the epistemic logic at play in asylum proceedings values narrative evidence of claimants' sexualities over physical indicators. When LGBTQ asylum law started forming in the early 1990s, adjudicators often resorted to gendered stereotypes of the effeminate gay man or butch lesbian or asked invasive questions about sex acts to confirm subjects' sexualities. As the network of expertise described in chapter 4 gained ground, however, it began shifting evidentiary standards away from bodily evidence and toward developmental narratives of asylum seekers' sexual identities or "coming out" stories. I argue that this evidentiary preference reflects an epistemic logic that views sexuality as discernible only through indirect indicators that must be placed in a particular context to make sense.

Chapter 6 takes an in-depth look at the forensic assessment of sex offenders' sexualities. One step in this process is determining exactly *what* the offender is sexually attracted to and whether that attraction warrants a diagnosis from the *Diagnostic and Statistical Manual (DSM)* that will legally brand him with a pathological sexual identity. This chapter considers how forensic psychologists and, ultimately, courts make such decisions. I argue that determining the sexuality of a potential "sexually violent predator" depends on an epistemic logic that suggests sexuality is directly discernible through bodily measures, such as those provided by polygraphs and penile plethysmographs, and other technologies meant to distill one's subjective state into objective indicators. As one neuropsychologist I spoke with stated, his ideal goal is to never have to "talk to the guy at all—just plug his brain and penis into a machine."

Chapters 7 and 8 analyze the risk assessment processes in asylum and sex offender decision-making. To receive asylum, an adjudicator must find that a claimant faces a "well-founded" risk of persecution if returned to her home country. But what does "well-founded" mean? And how do adjudi-

cators decide if a country poses a well-founded risk? Chapter 7 takes up
these questions. Though the Supreme Court has given some guidance on
the former question, I show that risk determinations depend on a rather
subjective process of judgment. Furthermore, I argue that this risk assessment process resonates with the broader epistemic logic of the asylum
complex. Risk is determined through a process that involves assessing the
risk of a sociocultural setting for an individual. That is, risk is a structural
and cultural characteristic of a particular country. This approach resonates
with the asylum complex's ways of understanding sexuality, which revolve
around contextualizing sexual narratives within a specific cultural setting.

Chapter 8 shows that in sex offender adjudications, risk is determined
through a process of individualized assessment using tools that are universal, or understood to be anyway—actuarial tools, polygraphs, PPGs,
mental health diagnoses, and psychological testing. In other words, the
individual himself is seen as the source of risk. Structural or cultural factors are not considered, even though, for instance, more than 90% of sex
offenders are men, suggesting a strong gender socialization component.
Culture seems to be a factor only when it is *other* cultures, as in asylum
decisions. These risk assessment practices are clearly in line with the more
essentialist and individualized conceptualization of sexuality found in
the sex offender legal complex. Although actuarial tools are presented as
objective technologies that remove human judgment and bias from risk
adjudications, I show that subjectivity continues to find its way into these
decisions.

I conclude with a consideration of how these legal knowledge practices
shape social conceptions of sexuality and the boundaries of citizenship, as
well as how different forms of expertise contribute to the (de)legitimation
of state actions and policies. Bringing together insights from the various
parts of my analysis, I examine how sexuality and race are intertwined and
mutually constitute both each other and our collective notions of proper
citizens. Ultimately, I argue that we should reconceptualize sexuality and
begin to think of it not merely as an identity but as a technology that can
powerfully shape the social world.

Before proceeding, I must note a couple of things about my terminology.
While I generally refer to LGBTQ asylum or LGBTQ people, at times I use
"queer" as a broad catchall term for non-normative gender and sexual
expressions and identities. "Queer" was seldom used by the actors in my
research sites; rather my use of the word is purely as an analytical tool, both
to capture the range of gender and sexual identities that exist in the world
that cannot necessarily be reduced to "gay," "lesbian," et cetera, and to
signal my queer theoretical approach to understanding sexualities. Though
it may seem to be at odds with a queer theoretical lens, the reader will also

notice that I predominantly use male pronouns throughout this book unless I am explicitly discussing a woman or gender-nonconforming individual. This is conscious and deliberate and meant to reflect the fact that most of the subjects I encountered in my research sites were men. The vast majority of sex offenders are men, and most asylum seekers are men. This means that legal understandings of sexuality are often structured around male experiences and the male body. That being said, while I do think we must be cautious of generalizing studies of men to other genders, my work in these sites suggests that many of the findings I discuss would apply very similarly to these groups. As scholars of classification have shown, states often create general grids and fit people to them, even when they fit imperfectly. Thus, although they were developed for men, the classification schemes at work in LGBTQ asylum and sex offender law are often applied to people of other genders without many adjustments. I return to this schematic mismatch in the conclusion to consider how gender (in conjunction with race) organizes techno-legal conceptions of sexuality.

But first, I take up the historical relationship between homosexuality and sexual criminality and address a question likely on many readers' minds: Why compare the two?

1: KISSING COUSINS

QUEERNESS, CRIME, AND THE POLITICS OF KNOWING

Juxtaposing the legal management of sex criminals with that of LGBTQ people is sure to raise some eyebrows. Sociologists typically compare things that are similar in some ways and different in others. The phenomena must be similar enough for comparison to be possible but different enough to make comparison fruitful. Some may feel that sexual criminality and queerness are so different as to make comparison useless or even dangerous. But such concern is only warranted if one adopts a very narrow historical and theoretical scope. Though colloquially we tend not to think of these things as similar in kind, there are good reasons to think that the state might consider them similarly and therefore approach their measurement and classification similarly (though, of course, even dissimilar things may be managed in similar ways). First, there is the historical intertwining of homosexuality and sexual criminality that began in the nineteenth century, and until just over a decade ago, sex between consenting adults of the same sex remained illegal in almost half of the United States. In other words, gay people (who had sex, that is) *were* sex criminals until 2003 when the US Supreme Court struck down remaining anti-sodomy statutes. And until 1990, it was illegal for homosexuals to even enter the country. Rewind another couple of decades, and gay people were considered mentally ill, in the same vein as sadists and pedophiles. (Reverberations of this relationship continue even today as conservative commentators link homosexuality with pedophilia, bestiality, and other stigmatized and illegal sexual behaviors.) Go back a bit further, and we arrive at a time when the age of consent for girls was ten years old in most American jurisdictions, an age of sexual debut that we can only regard as pedophilic through a contemporary lens.

Some will shrug off these historical parallels and argue that science has corrected itself. We were wrong in the past, and now we know better. Being gay, we now know, is a qualitatively different thing than being a pedophile. But these past parallels are anything but history. While in mainstream public, expert, and legal discourse, gay people are no longer considered sex criminals, the professionals who work with sex offenders today *do* largely consider sexual deviations (or paraphilias, as the *DSM* calls them) to be akin to sexual orientations, and there is continued scientific fascination with determining the etiology and physiological correlates of non-normative sexual expressions. And again, while we may not even think of homosexuality and pedophilia as originating in the same biological or biosocial substrate, many scientists approach the (attempted) measurement of both in similar ways. They look to the same areas of the brain and genes. When lab scientists want to gauge homosexual arousal, they often employ the PPG, just as lab and forensic scientists alike do when attempting to determine if someone is a pedophile or sadistic rapist. Similarly, scientists continue to look for clues on the bodies of homosexuals and pedophiles—whether it is finger-length ratios, handedness, or otherwise—that will tell their sexualities. So, if scientists continue to conceptualize and try to measure all types of sexualities in similar ways, why would legal approaches to classifying sexual subjects differ so much? The dramatic differences that I detail in this book—and the fact that most people today would have a knee-jerk reaction against even mentioning sex criminals and LGBTQ people in the same breath—speak to the powerful ways by which social institutions and processes contour our conceptions of sexuality and then deploy those cultural notions of sexuality to shape the social.

The categories of queerness and criminality are closely linked in our cultural imaginary, and throughout much of the last century, there was no distinction at all between homosexuals and sex criminals. It is no surprise, then, that moral panics over sex crime and homosexuality have erupted at the same times throughout the course of the twentieth century. The "sexual psychopath" panic that began in the 1930s branded homosexuals and pedophiles alike as psychopathic and worthy of commitment in secure psychiatric facilities. In the 1950s and 1960s, children were warned that homosexuals *were* pedophiles, an equation that continued with Anita Bryant's "Save Our Children" campaign of the 1970s. The "satanic ritual abuse" panic of the 1980s cast particular suspicion on men who were around children.[1] As gay people began gaining cultural recognition as people and citizens rather than criminals and psychopaths, society started to conceptually decouple homosexuality and sexual criminality.

The sex panic of the 1990s that led to a new wave of civil commitment statutes aimed at sex offenders featured gay people much less and instead featured a new figure: the sexual predator. Most often a pedophile but often also a rapist, the sexual predator became the paradigmatic boogeyman, a danger to women and children everywhere. Yet the sexual predator continued to resemble the predatory homosexual of midcentury: dangerous, difficult to identify, insatiable, mentally unstable, and, most of all, requiring new techniques to identify and control.

Given such historical and conceptual similarities, we stand to learn much about cultural processes of classification through comparing the treatment of homosexuality and sexual criminality. How do different disciplinary perspectives and techniques of measurement affect how state actors "know" sexuality and make governance decisions? I argue that institutionalized classification methods are a mechanism for naturalizing social conceptions of sexuality, and following transformations in these techniques can help us understand how cultural change is anchored by institutional practices.

SEXOLOGY AND THE "DISCOVERY" OF SEXUALITY

The mid- to late nineteenth century witnessed an explosion of interest around sex and sexuality worldwide.[2] Much of this new concern for sex stemmed from the increasing visibility of new sexual subcultures in urban centers. As young men and women were freed from their traditional familial duties and increasingly migrated to more densely populated cities, they gained some anonymity away from the prying eyes of family and often found themselves in sex-segregated spaces, such as boardinghouses.[3] As historian John D'Emilio argues, these social changes allowed the creation of a collective gay identity for the first time. However, even before such a collective identity formed, these nascent communities drew the attention of sexologists and law enforcement alike. Indeed, law and medicine mutually reinforced each other's fascination with the topic of sexual deviance, as medical experts were increasingly called to evaluate the mental state of individuals charged with sexual "perversions."

One of the earliest studies of sexual deviance to gain widespread attention evinces this mutual constitution. German neurologist Richard von Krafft-Ebing published *Psychopathia Sexualis* in 1886, subtitling his controversial book "a medico-forensic study."[4] Many of the subjects featured in the book came to Krafft-Ebing's attention through the legal system, for which he often provided testimony regarding offenders' mental states and moral responsibility. Given his position as a medical doctor, it is perhaps no surprise that Krafft-Ebing's theory of sexual perversion centered on the body, as did most of the early sexological accounts of sexuality. Krafft-Ebing was particularly interested in the brain, nervous system, and hormones, and his general explanation for sexual pathology centered on degeneration. In other words, sexual deviants represented a kind of regression toward a less-developed stage of humanity, very much like scientific racism of the same era that viewed people of color as evolutionary throwbacks. Coupled with his theory of degeneration, Krafft-Ebing also believed, as most sexologists at the time did, that homosexuality was the result of gender inversion. Inversion and degeneration were integrated in Krafft-Ebing's theory, as he explained: "The secondary sexual characteristics differentiate the two sexes; they present the specific male and female types. The higher the anthropological development of the race, the stronger these contrasts between man and woman, and vice versa."[5] Thus, inverts exhibit signs of physical and psychic degeneration by adopting the mannerisms of the opposite sex or desiring the same sex. Other sexologists, such as Karl Ulrichs and Magnus Hirschfeld, took less pathologizing views but still generally agreed that homosexuality resulted from inversion and that homosexuals were therefore likely physically different from heterosexuals.

Despite their views, most European sexologists were sympathetic to homosexuals and believed that homosexuality should not be criminalized because it was an inborn abnormality, or if it was acquired, then it was nearly impossible to change. Curiously, however, they tended to see all sexual perversions as similar in kind. For example, Krafft-Ebing categorized homosexuality (or antipathic sexuality) in the same group of "parathesias" (perversions of the sexual instinct) as sadism, masochism, and fetishism, and all of these were classified as "cerebral neuroses."[6] Krafft-Ebing did, however, make some moral distinctions, as when he declared, "It is psychologically incomprehensible that an adult of full virility and mentally sound should indulge in sexual abuses with children."[7] Thus, despite painting sexual perversions with a broad brush, Krafft-Ebing and others did make some distinctions among the perversions, often singling out child molestation as particularly pathological. However, as sexology traveled to America, it also became more punitive, as experts rejected the more sympathetic European stance regarding homosexuality and uniformly targeted "sex perverts," often pursuing homosexuals with particular zeal.[8]

Although American authorities shared with their European counterparts a view that willful vice should be distinguished from irrepressible psychopathology and that the latter perhaps deserved some sympathy, unlike many European sexologists Americans generally did not advocate decriminalizing sodomy.[9] Indeed, homosexuality remained thoroughly intertwined with ideas of sexual criminality for most of the twentieth century in the United states. For example, in the 1940s, consensual sodomy with a person over the age of eighteen carried a maximum sentence of twenty years in prison in fifteen states, and until Illinois reformed its laws in 1961, all US jurisdictions enforced anti-sodomy statutes.[10] Rape, pedophilia, and "sex killings" also came under more scrutiny at the turn of the century, thanks in part to an outpouring of writings on sexual conditions engendered by the publication of Krafft-Ebing's *Psychopathia Sexualis*. Terms such as "homosexual," "pervert," and "pedophile" entered the English language shortly after the book's publication. Thus, although the justice system had dealt with sex crimes prior to the late nineteenth century, it was not until the 1880s that American medicine and psychiatry began to think of "sexual perversion" as an essential aspect of one's identity rather than a temporary lapse in behavior, which caused a critical shift in notions of sex crime.

Ideas of bio-criminality taking root at this time helped cement this view of sex offenders as particular kinds of people and led to calls for "treating" perverts like other people with diseases under the bio-criminal model—through methods such as sterilization and quarantine.[11] As historian Philip Jenkins explains, "The new positivist criminology was founded upon the radical principle that deviant acts were symptoms indicating underlying medical or biological flaws in the offender, conditions that demanded treatment or incapacitation."[12] Other methods of "treatment" and incapacitation during this time could range from quarantine to sterilization to castration and even execution.[13]

Because prisons were key sites for the early study of sexuality in America, researchers often believed that "perverts" were of a distinctly criminal bent and thus that criminality and perversion generally co-occurred. Homosexuality and criminality therefore became tautologically related. Historian Regina Kunzel further points out that "Oscar Wilde's well-publicized fate—his trials, conviction, and incarceration—ensured that, at this formative moment in the public recognition of this new sexual type, 'the homosexual' would become ineradicably affiliated with criminality and the prison."[14] Surprisingly, however, despite a new fascination with perversion and a dedication to the goal of protecting communities from its corrupting influence, sexual subcultures flourished at the end of the nineteenth century and beginning of the twentieth century.[15] This would change after World War I, when social anxieties escalated over sex offenses—including homosexuality, prostitution, voyeurism, indecent exposure, child molestation, and rape—giving rise to a more punitive stance toward sexual deviance.

THE BIRTH OF THE SEXUAL PSYCHOPATH

Arrests for homosexuality increased in the late 1920s as public sentiment turned against the perceived excesses of the "Roaring Twenties."[16] Because many such arrests were technically classified as sex crimes, it reinforced the impression that gay men and lesbians accounted for most violent sex criminals, when in fact their arrests were often merely for congregating in public spaces. Popular reporting about sex crimes around this time also promulgated the notion that homosexuals were child molesters

and lumped homosexuals in with violent offenders, rapists, and child molesters. This was reinforced by a common assumption that homosexuals
were trapped in an arrested stage of development that led them to seek
out children to satisfy their perversions.[17] Even the most sympathetic
commentators discussed homosexuality alongside other dysfunctions and
sexual crimes, ensuring that stigma was sure to attach.

These notions were amplified with the stock market crash of 1929 and
the subsequent Great Depression, which engendered widespread social
anxieties around the family and masculinity and brought a newfound
scientific concern for male sexuality. This, coupled with sensationalistic
coverage of atrocious sexual crimes against children, gave rise to a sex
panic, and the first iterations of "sexual psychopath" statutes were enacted in the late 1930s. Psychiatric authorities became concerned with
two general sexual subtypes over the course of the decade: one lacking in
masculinity, the effeminate homosexual, and one with an excess of masculinity, the hypersexual sexual predator.[18] The latter category included
pedophiles, rapists, and "active" masculine homosexual men. Both types
were linked via their psychological immaturity and maladjusted character,
which led them to prey on the innocent and to choose objects that could
substitute for the proper heterosexual objects or to engage in "immature"
acts, such as voyeurism, exhibitionism, or oral sex.

Curiously, whereas most sex crimes statutes previously specified the
protection of women as their purpose, sexual psychopath laws and psychiatric discourse of the 1930s focused predominantly on protecting children
and did little to prosecute violent crimes against women or even coercive
incest by male relatives against children in their families.[19] Rape was therefore mostly undiscussed in the psychiatric literature of the time, which
instead focused predominantly on the twin specters of the homosexual
and the child molester. As historian Jennifer Terry points out, "In much
of the discourse on sex offenses, the rape of women was deemed closer
to normal relations than homosexuality, since the perpetrator's sex object
was normal, and his aim, though excessive, conformed to a basic gender
ideology that positioned man as active agent and woman as receptive object."[20] In line with this observation, records show that most offenders sen-
tenced under sexual psychopath statutes were child molesters, gay men,
and noncontact offenders, such as exhibitionists and voyeurs, while rapists
were more likely to be sent to prison as "regular" criminals.[21] Although
such offenders were supposed to receive therapy and be rehabilitated, in
reality offenders deemed most like "useful citizens" were diverted from
prison while those who seemed more "harmful" were sent to prison,
though little therapy happened in either location.[22] Notably, those typically
deemed to be potential "useful citizens" tended to be White, while people

of color convicted of sex crimes continued to be treated as criminals and sent to prison.[23]

World War II brought an abatement of this sex panic, and by the late 1940s considerable quantitative evidence showed that claims by the media and FBI of a sex crime wave of massive scale were overblown and that rates might even be dropping.[24] Kinsey's studies in the 1940s also revealed that sexual practices in America were quite varied and that a large portion of the population could be considered sex criminals if laws were strictly enforced. Kinsey's findings, in particular, helped engender resistance as homosexuals used his studies to push back against the pathologization of gayness, instead embracing the label as a normal variant of human sexuality that was quite common among the US populace.[25] In spite of these new findings, highly publicized crimes against children ignited another sex panic in the late 1940s and 1950s. The specter of the pedophilic predator was at the center of the panic, and as with the panic of the late 1930s, homosexuals were particularly targeted, even though arrest records show that the vast majority of sex crimes against children were committed by men against girls.[26]

Many factors contributed to the notion that child molesters were homosexuals, including the assumption that homosexuals' psychosexual immaturity led them to prefer young partners and the insistence by psychoanalysts that homosexuals were compulsive, obsessive, and uncontrolled in their sexual impulses. The media frequently reported stories of child sexual abuse and child murder in the same stories that featured statistics on arrests of men involved in consenting activities with adults. Demonstrating this tight linkage, in the wake of a highly sensationalized pair of child murders in the early 1950s, California increased the penalty for consensual sodomy from ten to twenty years in prison.[27] Kinsey's findings about the prevalence of homosexual activity also stoked fears that such behaviors were occurring right under the noses of authorities, and a growing climate of homophobia was fueled by Cold War xenophobia and a "strangers in our midst" mentality.[28] Although homosexuals had been prohibited from entering the United States on various grounds since the late 1800s, it was during this time that homosexuals were officially barred from entering the country as "psychopathic personalities" with the passage of the McCarran-Walter Act of 1952. This postwar sex panic solidified psychiatrists' place in the criminal justice system, as twenty-one additional states and Washington, DC, passed sexual psychopath laws, and six states funded psychiatric studies of sex offenders.

The late 1960s saw the fragmentation of the term "sex crime," as various sexual behaviors, including homosexuality, became more accepted and were no longer viewed as on par with rape and pedophilia. Psychiatric and psychological experts began to change their views of homosexuality at this time, as well, thanks in part to research like Evelyn Hooker's demonstrating that homosexuals were generally as mentally well-adjusted as heterosexuals and did not suffer from psychopathology.[29] During this period, experts confidently reported remission and cure of deviant sexual desires and asserted that sentencing sex criminals to prison was therefore not productive and, moreover, that recidivism rates for sexual offenses were generally low.[30] By contrast, today "psych" experts generally do not speak of "curing" paraphilias but rather "managing" them. Pedophilia, in fact, cannot be classified as "in full remission" in the *DSM* and is widely considered to be similar to a sexual orientation, like gay or straight.

As gay activism gained traction after the Stonewall Riots in 1969, political pressure combined with considerable disagreement within the psychiatric discipline led to the removal of "homosexuality" from the *DSM* in 1973. Before this time, homosexuality was first classified as a "sociopathic personality disturbance" in the *DSM-I* and then a "sexual deviation," along with conditions such as pedophilia and sadism, in the *DSM-II*. However, even after homosexuality's removal, it was replaced with "sexual orientation disturbance" to appease opponents of de-medicalization.[31] The diagnosis legitimated conversion therapy by regarding homosexuality as an illness if one found their same-sex attractions distressing and wanted to change them.[32] "Sexual orientation disturbance" was replaced with "ego dystonic homosexuality" in the *DSM-III*, but this diagnosis was removed in the subsequent revision of the 1987 *DSM-III-R*. It was thus not until 1987 that the APA definitively recognized homosexuality as a normal form of sexuality. By contrast, paraphilic disorders such as pedophilia, exhibitionism, voyeurism, fetishism, sadism, and masochism remain in the latest version of the *DSM*.[33]

Despite the move toward de-medicalization, homosexuality remained criminalized in most jurisdictions, whether through prohibitions on sodomy, lewdness, or public congregating. Though the first state antisodomy statute was repealed in 1962, the majority of states did not repeal their sodomy laws until the 1980s and 1990s (see table 3). In California, which created the nation's first sex offender registry in 1947, gay sex was included as a dangerous and registerable offense, along with child molestation and rape. It was only in 1979 that the California Supreme Court ruled that the lewd conduct law permitted the police to be too repressive of gay social life and prohibited the use of the law in semi-private spaces, such as gay bars.[34] Subsequently, the 1983 California Supreme Court case *In re Reed* finally dropped the registration requirement for lewd conduct, deeming registration to be a punishment out of proportion to the crime. Homosexuality thus made incremental progress in its slow march toward decriminalization.

TABLE 3. Year of decriminalization of same-sex sodomy

1962	Illinois
1971	Connecticut
1972	Colorado, Oregon
1973	Delaware, Hawaii, North Dakota
1974	Ohio, Massachusetts
1975	New Hampshire, New Mexico
1976	California, Indiana, Maine, Washington, West Virginia
1977	South Dakota, Vermont, Wyoming
1978	Iowa, Nebraska, New Jersey
1980	Alaska, New York, Pennsylvania
1983	Wisconsin
1992	Kentucky
1993	District of Columbia, Nevada
1996	Tennessee
1997	Montana
1998	Georgia, Rhode Island
1999	Maryland
2001	Arkansas, Arizona, Minnesota
2003	Alabama, Florida, Idaho, Kansas, Louisiana, Michigan, Mississippi, Missouri, North Carolina, Oklahoma, South Carolina, Texas, Utah, Virginia

However, the link between homosexuality and pedophilia reemerged in the late 1970s, thanks in large part to Anita Bryant's "Save Our Children" campaign, in which Bryant emphasized gay men's supposed predilection for child porn and involvement in organized pedophile rings. As historian Philip Jenkins asserts, pedophilia remained "central to antigay rhetoric until the mid-1980s, when it was largely replaced by the still more effective terror weapon of AIDS."[35] Still, homophobia has rarely been far below the surface of sex panics throughout the course of the twentieth century, including the satanic ritual abuse panic of the 1980s, which engendered homophobic attacks against male childcare workers.[36] Even the most recent wave of panic beginning in the 1990s and giving rise to the new generation of "sexually violent predator" statutes featured a pedophile who molested and mutilated young boys as a central catalyst.[37]

Given the historically tight linkage between queerness and criminality, how (and to what extent) have the two become decoupled? Measurement and classification practices are one key way to track this change, as they offer a crystallization of many cultural assumptions about sexuality. The remainder of this book will consider in detail the divergence in contemporary techno-legal classification practices around sexuality. But in the final section of this chapter, I want to first provide a bit more historical context for thinking about measuring sexuality.

MEASURING SEXUALITY

Historically, there have been two predominant methods of measuring human sexuality: bodily measurement and subjective reporting. Early sexology drew on both of these techniques, soliciting life histories and narrative accounts of sexual "deviants" as well as searching for physical differences between the bodies of "perverts" and "normal" people. Psychoanalysis moved more firmly into the "confessional" mode of sexual inquiry, as described by Foucault.[38] Midcentury behaviorists shifted back toward a focus on bodily measurement and response, using technologies such as the polygraph and the recently invented penile plethysmograph. More recently, new technologies, such as fMRI machines and DNA analysis, have allowed researchers to assess sexuality in novel ways that still view the body as providing an unmediated view into one's "true" sexual identity but attempt to bypass any subjective elements to one's sexuality. Today all of these methods continue to coexist as accepted ways of measuring sexuality, though their acceptability varies across institutional settings and academic disciplines and by the kind of sexual subject being evaluated.[39] In what follows, I briefly consider these different approaches and their underlying epistemological and ontological assumptions about sexuality.

The body has long been viewed as the most reliable source for ascertaining information about one's sexuality. Although early sexologists encountered many of their subjects as patients and recounted details of their lives in lengthy narrative accounts in their publications, their theories—whether degeneration, inversion, or otherwise—centrally revolved around the body. For instance, nineteenth- and early twentieth-century sexologists often suggested that homosexuals, or inverts, constituted a physically distinct "third sex," different from either males or females. Part of this argument relied on comparative anatomy, an approach, as Siobhan Somerville points out, that was drawn directly from scientific racism of the same era.[40] Havelock Ellis believed that the genitals of homosexuals were generally less developed than the norm, and Magnus Hirschfeld thought that homosexual men had wider hips and pelvises than heterosexual men. Krafft-Ebing posited that homosexuality was a sign of physical and psychic degeneration. Sexologists further proffered that the voices, hair growth patterns, hair textures, musculature, and skin tone of homosexuals differed from those of heterosexuals. Early sexologists also pursued lines of inquiry that look more familiar to us today, including attempts to trace the heredity of homosexuality and to analyze hormones, which they hoped would prove the inborn nature of homosexuality.

Somatic theories remained popular into the 1940s, and "treatments" for perversion often focused on the body, including shock therapy, hormone therapy, sterilization, castration, and, rarely, lobotomy.[41] Opposition to such dramatic and dangerous therapies was a central point of contention between the older generation of asylum-based psychiatrists and the younger psychoanalysts, many of whom completely rejected all somatic and congenitalist theories of sexuality.[42] By the mid-1940s, most scientific authorities agreed that homosexuality resulted from a mixture of psychological factors and social conditioning and that homosexuality could not be detected merely by examining individuals' bodies.[43] Psychoanalytic theories gained ground after World War II. However, psychoanalytic ideas helped fuel the McCarthy witch hunts for homosexuals in the government because there was a fear that they couldn't be identified, producing considerable anxiety around homosexuals who appeared "normal."[44] Because it was difficult to identify homosexuals, and they were incentivized to lie, psychiatrists began employing "objective" tests—such as the Rorschach, Goodenough-Harris (Draw-a-Man), MMPI, Cornell Selectee Index, vocabulary, and Terman-Miles Masculinity-Femininity—to determine who was homosexual.[45] Hooker would show in the following decade that such tests were useless for distinguishing gay from straight people.[46] The Lavender Scare also gave rise to the use of the polygraph to search for homosexuals in the government.[47]

In addition to these new "objective" techniques, psychoanalysts continued their talk therapy approach, with the guiding assumption that all perversions were rooted in childhood development and early family dynamics. Patients were therefore compelled to discuss intimate details of their entire lives, including their sexual behaviors and fantasies. Discarding Freud's sympathetic stance toward homosexuality, American psychiatrists and psychologists of the 1950s and 1960s used this psychoanalytic approach to attempt to convert homosexuals into heterosexuals. New behavioral theories of sexuality were also emerging at this time.

Behaviorists approached sexuality in much the same way they did other phenomena—as learned behavior that could be conditioned. Thus, in the same way that Pavlov taught dogs to salivate at the sound of a bell through operant conditioning, behaviorists believed they could teach homosexuals and other sexual deviants how to respond to "proper" sexual stimuli. These "treatments" took the form of aversion therapy, using either drugs to induce nausea and vomiting or electroshocks, and often employed the penile plethysmograph (PPG) to gauge arousal and determine treatment efficacy. First developed by Kurt Freund in Czechoslovakia in the 1950s, the PPG made its way to the United States in the 1960s. The PPG understood male sexuality to be located within the body and to be a learned physiological response to visual stimuli. As sociologist Tom Waidzunas explains, "Within the rubric of behavior therapy, physiological arousal within a testing scenario was conceptualized as a form of behavior, regardless of one's ability or willingness to control it, given that consciousness was considered epiphenomenal to begin with."[48] Unlike psychoanalysis, then, behaviorism returned to the body as the ideal way to measure sexuality.

The PPG, in fact, is still in wide use and continues to be understood as the gold standard for ascertaining individuals' sexual orientations and preferences in some domains. As Waidzunas and Epstein suggest, phallometric testing may be considered as a kind of confessional technology that seeks to bypass the subject by forcing the body to speak for itself.[49] In this sense, phallometric technology follows in the scientific tradition that assumes sexual identity is inscribed on the surface or interior of the body. Today the PPG is considered to be ideal for measuring sexual arousal of many sex offenders and particularly for determining if individuals are pedophiles, though it is also used for rapists and sadists.[50] The PPG also remains in fairly wide use in academic research on sexual orientation within the discipline of psychology.

Researchers are also now pioneering approaches to studying sexuality that bypass the exterior of the body completely and instead look to the brains, hormones, and genes of subjects. Such research on homosexuality gained widespread attention with the publication of Dean Hamer's and Simon LeVay's research in the early 1990s, which found purported linkages between homosexuality and a small segment of the X chromosome in gay men and a cluster of cells in the brains of gay men that were smaller than those of straight men, respectively. Research of this kind is still in its infancy for sex offenders, but it is certainly underway. Unlike genetic studies of homosexuality, genetic studies of pedophilia have not yet generated significant findings.[51] Like neurological studies of homosexuality, however, studies of pedophiles' and rapists' brains have found varying and sometimes contradictory results. One finding that has been replicated concludes that pedophilic men have smaller amygdalae than non-pedophilic men.[52] Notably, brain research on sex difference has also found that women have smaller amygdalae than men and has suggested that gay men's brains more resemble heterosexual women's brains than they do heterosexual men's brains, harkening back to early sexological notions that gay men were women trapped in men's bodies.[53] In other words, both gay men and pedophiles have smaller amygdalae, according to some studies, which, regardless of intention, may promulgate the homosexuality-pedophilia link.

Other research continues to look explicitly at bodily differences between heterosexual and non-heterosexual, or "normal" and "deviant," individuals, some of which also fuels the purported homosexual-pedophile linkage. For instance, pedophiles have been found to have IQs that are ten to fifteen points below average, to be 2.3 centimeters shorter than the average male, and to be more likely left-handed.[54] Other work has suggested that homosexual men are also more likely to be left-handed.[55] Similarly, psychological studies attempting to identify how gay men's faces, voices, or walks differ from straight men's rest easily with notions of the embodied nature of (homo)sexuality and sexual non-normativity.

In the end, these various epistemological approaches to measuring sexuality implicitly (if not explicitly) suggest discrepant ontologies of sexuality, as well. On the one hand, behaviorist and other physiological methods assume that sexuality is largely an individual phenomenon that can be discretely located on or within the body. On the other hand, psychoanalytic and other approaches that rely on narrative and self-report suggest that sexuality may not be discernible from the body at all, but is instead a socially produced phenomenon that emerges through socialization, interaction, and learning. Rather than viewing sexuality as located, and thus detectable, within or on the individual body, such theories posit that sexuality can only be known indirectly through subjective accounts. This is somewhat consistent with the newest line of thinking regarding sexuality—social constructionism—which has been promulgated by critical humanist scholarship and disciplines such as anthropology and sociology. In this school of thought, sexuality cannot be known only through the body as physiological methods would suggest. It must be discerned by placing behaviors, identities, and subjective understandings within a particular historical and social context.

Whether one adopts one view over the other holds significant consequences for how research on sexuality will be conducted and, importantly for this study, how legal institutions will seek to measure and classify sexual subjects. As this chapter has shown, historical conceptions of homosexuality and sexual criminality have been tightly intertwined, and the methods that scientific, medical, and legal authorities have used to understand and control sexual non-normativity have been largely similar regardless of whether the deviation was called homosexuality, pedophilia, sadism, or otherwise. It was only in the 1970s—notably coinciding with the rise of an organized gay movement that consciously sought to separate homosexuality from other stigmatized sexual expressions—that approaches to studying and legally regulating these various forms of sexual non-normativity began to diverge. However, even today we can see echoes of this historical legacy. Although our cultural understandings of homosexuality and pedophilia generally no longer group them together, many psychological researchers and practitioners *do* consider pedophilia and other paraphilias to be sexual orientations.[56] There is no longer a strong belief that we can *change* pedophilic orientation, but treatment providers do use less drastic forms of aversion therapy and conditioning—such as having offenders sniff ammonia when they have deviant thoughts or desires and training offenders to masturbate to healthy fantasies—to try to recondition arousal. When it comes to measuring sexuality, many academic researchers do not distinguish different approaches for hetero-sexual, homosexual, pedophilic, or sadistic arousal. All are measured using the same techniques: plethysmography, fMRIs, EEGs, self-reports, and so on. This suggests that these sexual phenomena are not necessarily seen as ontologically distinct for researchers: they are all varieties of sexuality. Put another way, sexuality seems to be a multiplicity that still hangs together as a somewhat coherent biosocial phenomenon.[57] Culturally, we tend to see homosexuality and pedophilia as completely different things, yet their historical roots are intertwined to such an extent that they remain episte-mologically interwoven. They are part of the same biosocial phenomenon that we call "sexuality," but we have fractalized "sexuality" in our cultural imaginations such that colloquially speaking of homosexuality and sadism in the same breath makes little sense, even if both may be products of the same biosocial substrate. In other words, we might say that homosexuality is one thing on the streets and another in the lab.

But what happens when the streets and lab come together in the space of the courtroom? Will we try to ascertain one's homosexuality in the same way we do one's pedophilia? Why or why not? In the remainder of this book, I show that in everyday legal practice, when we seek to know one's sexu-ality, we do so in institutionally specific ways that reflect dominant cultural frames, political concerns, and the epistemological stances of the experts on which the law calls to adjudicate individuals' sexualities and legitimate state authority. Cultural attitudes that proclaim a strict differentiation be-tween homosexuality and things like pedophilia and sadism are strongly felt in the arena of law, and, as such, divergent conceptions of sexuality take shape within the law. Before proceeding to the main analytical chap-ters of the book, the next chapter completes the theoretical scaffolding for understanding how these processes develop in each legal complex.

2: SEEING SEXUALITY LIKE A STATE

Legal processes, including courtroom trials, are rituals meant to grant legitimacy to state decisions. Objectivity is therefore a central tenet of the law, and yet we know from studies on a range of topics—from policing to prosecutorial discretion to sentencing and beyond—that objectivity is often an aspiration of the law rather than a reality. In the face of such challenges to the legitimacy of legal outcomes, one way that courts have striven for greater objectivity—particularly on questions that go beyond law's usual expertise—is to draw on various forms of scientific and technical expertise. This might take the form of epidemiologists in toxic torts claims, economists in wage discrimination cases, or the development of algorithms and actuarial risk assessment tools.

Sociologist Robin Stryker has termed these multifaceted processes by which techno-scientific knowledges inform legal and policy decisions "technocratization."[1] Science, she points out, is often called upon by state actors to quell legitimacy crises or to bolster the capacity and authority of the state. Both asylum and sex offender policy were facing different kinds of legitimacy crises before outside experts lent their epistemic authority. These crises were diffused, in part, by incorporating these non-state epistemic actors—forensic psychologists in the case of sex offender law and a hybrid network of lawyers, human rights activists, and social scientists in the case of asylum—into the legal decision-making process. In addition to working to expand the state's capacity to regulate and punish, these different disciplinary perspectives also offered each area of law very different ways of classifying sexual subjects, and they were chosen for particular political and institutional needs.

Yet there's been little consideration of the ways by which technocratization might operate differently in relation to what Charles Camic, Neil Gross, and Michèle Lamont call social knowledge, or "descriptive information and analytical statements about the actions, behaviors, subjective states, and capacities of human beings," as opposed to the more clearly technical questions of causation in toxic torts and the like.[2] What is sexuality? Is this person gay? Are they sexually dangerous? What does Title IX mean when it says it protects gender? What *is* gender? How do we know? These are the kinds of questions that courts are increasingly being asked to answer and for which they are ill-equipped to do so. In these instances, courts often turn to science for the answers. But depending on the kind of science called upon, the court may receive starkly divergent interpretations. For example, sexuality is understood rather differently in sociology than psychology. Asking a biologist is likely to yield yet another interpretation. The same could be said about gender, race, and many other social categories and phenomena. These issues dovetail with those considered in the vast literature on state classification efforts.

Classification and categorization are ubiquitous to modern science, politics, and social organization, and numerous scholars have noted the importance of state classification and information-gathering practices for state-making and state administration.[3] Indeed, political scientist James Scott contends that "legibility" is a "central problem in statecraft."[4] Ranging from requiring permanent last names to standardizing language and land tenure practices, state legibility projects entail taking complex social phenomena and fitting them to standardized grids that allow states to record and monitor them. Such processes necessarily require simplification and the loss of local specificity. A prime example is the census.[5] Censuses take concepts that may be fluid and locally specific in practice, such as race, and reify them for a variety of governmental purposes, including economic extraction, legal subjugation, political representation, and social inclusion or exclusion.[6] States, therefore, do not merely describe and observe; they strive to shape people and practices to fit their techniques of observation.

A central insight of research on state classification is that states rule not just through a monopoly of physical violence but also through the exercise of symbolic violence. As Pierre Bourdieu contends, "Through the framing it imposes upon practices, the state establishes and inculcates common forms and categories of perception and appreciation, social frameworks of perceptions, of understanding or of memory, in short *state forms of classification*."[7] The exercise of symbolic power not only allows the state to naturalize social categories, such as race or age, but it also allows the creation of a collective image of the nation, including who belongs and who does not.[8] However, these "state-centered" approaches have largely overlooked the role of a critical group of social actors for state information-gathering: non-state experts.[9]

EXPERTISE AND THE STATE

Despite scant attention to the role of expertise in political sociological studies of the state, science and technology studies (STS) has produced a vast literature examining interactions between state institutions, state-making, and expert knowledges in a range of areas. STS work demonstrates that scientific experts have played a central role in state-making and the consolidation of state power and political order.[10] In his analysis of science and modern state formation, for instance, sociologist Patrick Carroll argues that the advent of "engine science" transformed the activities of governing by allowing the state to view land, people, and the built environment as objects that could be manipulated and improved.[11] Over time, he suggests, the social, economic, political, and natural orders get engineered together such that they appear more and more inseparable, an insight I develop in relation to sexuality in this book.

Non-state experts have also been centrally involved in technical policy-making, advising state actors on technical issues, and offering opinions in courts.[12] Though expert testimony in courts has a long history, it is increasingly common in legal proceedings as US courts are asked to adjudicate more technical and scientific issues.[13] DNA fingerprinting, causation in toxic torts claims, forensic risk assessment, and other highly technical issues often require non-state experts to provide scientific context in both courts and legislative settings, a topic I return to shortly.[14] But what happens when courts must adjudicate something as multivalent and subjective as someone's sexuality?

As described above, courts are increasingly faced with such questions regarding social categorization and often turn to nonlegal expert knowledges for the answers. While such technocratic practices may increase the legitimacy of these determinations, depending on the social and institutional circumstances, competition between scientific and legal logics may also decrease the legitimacy of state action.

Though Max Weber and decades of subsequent political sociologists have asserted that *legitimacy* is central to modern state power, the cultural aspects of legitimate state authority have traditionally been neglected in favor of focusing on the state's exercise of material domination. However, as sociologist Mara Loveman argues, Weber's definition of the state as an organization that claims the legitimate use of physical force already "yokes cultural and material power together." Indeed, "historical struggles over the exercise of symbolic power were integral to historical struggles over the legitimate exercise of military, political, and economic power."[15] Thus, by focusing on epistemic practices, I highlight the importance of non-state actors and knowledges in supporting the legitimacy of state authority and power. In other words, state institutions must be able to render their own visions and categories of thought natural and self-evident before they can exercise legitimate physical power, such as forcibly detaining a sex offender indefinitely. They accomplish this, in part, by drawing on the social authority of science, in effect conjoining two of the most powerful truth-producing institutions in our culture—science and law.

As this discussion suggests, technocratization can result in hybrid ways of knowing. What does it mean, though, to hybridize legal and scientific logics?

HOW LAW KNOWS/HOW SCIENCE KNOWS

The traditional view of science holds that truth and scientific consensus result from the objective reading of nature, free from social influence. This view reflects a belief in a unitary scientific method wherein scientists evaluate evidence in a disinterested manner leading to one valid conclusion. STS scholars have since shown that science is a deeply social enterprise and that the production of truth and consensus, while bounded by and oriented toward perceived properties of things in the world, are social accomplishments nonetheless.[16] As Bruno Latour argues, the construction of facts is a collective process. Whereas "completed" science assumes that things hold when they are true, "science in action" suggests instead that when things hold they start becoming true. Things become more true, in a sense, the more people are convinced of them. Laboratory ethnographies have shown, for instance, that deriving scientific conclusions is not a direct procedure leading to one endpoint; rather it is a process of interpretation that may have many possible paths and outcomes.

This understanding of knowledge production is as true of law as it is of science. The formalist view of law posits that legal decision-making is a mechanical process of applying legal principles to a set of facts and that normative concerns such as morality and politics are irrelevant. Socio-legal scholarship, however, has shown that, like science, law cannot be extricated from the culture of which it is a part. Law does not operate under one unified, objective logic, but rather "law in action" takes many forms and often does not straightforwardly reflect "law on the books." Scholars analyzing "how law knows" have demonstrated that "law's ways of knowing are as varied as are the institutions and officials who populate any legal system," and that "all of law's ways of knowing are historically specific, evolving in response to developments both internal and external to law itself."[17]

Sorting Sexualities examines not just "how law knows," but conceives of law as a site of social knowledge-making; that is, as a site where truth statements about sexuality (as well as other social phenomena) are created, circulated, and deployed for various ends.[18] Austin Sarat and colleagues note that studying law's knowledge practices allows us to "understand law as an arena in which knowledge is both acquired and produced, in which knowledge is both absorbed from, but also radiated back into, the social and cultural world in which law is embedded."[19] This is particularly important given law's symbolic power. Arguably, the law wields even more classificatory power than science because law comes with the backing of the state.[20]

What happens, then, when these two institutions come together? Both are formal systems of inquiry designed to sift through evidence and derive rational conclusions. But their approaches to fact-finding differ. Law is always time-bound and must arrive at decisions at the end of hearings, whether the evidence is conclusive or not. Science, in many cases, would refuse to make a definitive conclusion. Law's logic is largely retrospective, depending on precedent and past events. Science's mode of inquiry is more prospective. Law, as a general rule, places a premium on continuity. Even when precedent is overturned, jurists must still maintain the integrity of the legal edifice and restore equilibrium. Science, conversely, strives for change and the refinement, and sometimes wholesale overturning, of theories. There is a very big difference, Latour suggests, between a Kuhnian paradigm shift and a change in case law.[21] Revolutionary science may be admirable, but revolutionary law is most often terrifying.

Because of these differences, much of the research on the law-science relationship highlights competition and incompatibility between the two institutions.[22] These inquiries often suggest that law shapes science to its needs, what sociologist Susan Silbey has labeled a "law first" approach.[23] By contrast, co-productionist work on the law-science relationship emphasizes that law and science jointly produce social and epistemological order and shore up each other's authority. Neither law nor science, in this view, are independent, self-regulating producers of truth. Both are social institutions constantly in interaction with other parts of our society.[24]

I draw on the concept of coproduction to theorize how legal and scientific actors, institutions, and discourses mutually constitute sexuality as a regulatory category. The idea of coproduction proposes that the natural and social orders are produced together.[25] STS scholar Sheila Jasanoff suggests that "the ways in which we know and represent the world (both nature and society) are inseparable from the way in which we choose to live in it. Knowledge and its material embodiments are at once products of social work and constitutive of forms of social life; society cannot function without knowledge any more than knowledge can exist without appropriate social supports."[26] This approach suggests that knowledge and social life are mutually sustaining and that knowledge is a vital resource in the management of society, not unlike Michel Foucault's well-known theorization of the power/knowledge nexus.[27] The way we come to know some social object, such as sexuality, is intricately tied to the actions we take in relation to that object. Although coproduction frameworks assert that law and science *both* produce social knowledge, this does not mean that law and science always remain "pure" when they interact. Science may be molded to the needs of law, and law may concede authority to science on certain issues.

Perhaps the most abiding area of concern for scholars interested in the constitutive relationship of law and science has been around questions of expertise and scientific evidence in the courtroom. Law is more than a consumer of science; it also often sets the circumstances under which scientific evidence can be produced and used.[28] As Jasanoff asserts: "'Science,' for the law's purposes, is simply the composite of testimony presented in and around an adjudicatory proceeding, and its quality depends heavily on the skill and intentions of the lawyers who elicit the presentation. The facts that the law constructs (or reconstructs) are thus necessarily different from the facts that scientists construct to persuade their peers in their own rhetorically and procedurally distinctive surroundings."[29] In other words, when science finds its way into court, it is often subsumed within the logic of the legal setting and may not retain its singular status as the primary producer of truth. What obtains, rather, is a picture of science as constructed in that specific legal setting. The result is a hybrid legal-scientific logic, for law is, above all, pragmatic and much less concerned with epistemological "purity" than science.[30]

Indeed, the most "scientific" knowledges are not always the most successful in legal settings. Rather, hybrid knowledge formats consisting of a variety of less reputable sources may be preferred to single-source, "purer" knowledge forms.[31] For example, STS scholar Simon Cole demonstrates how fingerprinting overtook bertillonage (the use of body measures) as the dominant method of identifying criminal suspects even though it was "less scientific."[32] One reason for the success of fingerprinting was its administrative ease: an untrained police officer could take good fingerprints, whereas the bertillonage system was more technically demanding. Lest we think these epistemically "impure" decisions are a thing of the past, I will show that such pragmatic moves remain part of the law-science relationship. As we will see in chapter 7, part of the rationale for selecting items to include on actuarial risk assessments consisted of administrative ease and data availability.

Alongside these concerns with scientific techniques and technologies exist questions of expertise. Who is an expert? How is a court to decide on scientific issues when experts disagree? How much say should experts have? Jasanoff suggests that expert testimony in courts is particularly fraught because each side picks experts who can corroborate their stories, and then experts are exposed to adversarial cross-examination, which "only [brings] home the point that science in legal settings is always bound up with specific constructions of causation, blame, and responsibility."[33] Though experts are supposed to help with fact-finding, what courts often get are two carefully constructed representations of reality influenced by the interests, resources, and ingenuity of the proffering parties.

The law does, however, provide some guidance for adjudicating conflicting expert claims. The *Frye* standard, stemming from a 1923 case considering the admissibility of an early version of the polygraph, established that for expert testimony to be admitted in court, it must have obtained "general acceptance" within the relevant professional field.[34] The 1993 Supreme Court decision in *Daubert v. Merrell Dow Pharmaceuticals* rejected peer review and "general acceptance" (the *Frye* standard) as absolute markers of reliability and reaffirmed judges' power to assess scientific evidence.[35] *Daubert* suggested four criteria for evaluating evidence: (1) Has the theory or technique underlying the testimony been tested and is it falsifiable? (2) Has it been peer-reviewed? (3) What is the technique's error rate, if known? (4) General acceptance (now just one criterion instead of the only one). Though *Daubert* was intended to strengthen the quality of scientific evidence admitted in courts, in reality it appears simply to have had the effect of increasing judicial discretion.[36] Moreover, many states, including Illinois, which I use as a case study, still apply the *Frye* standard, and though the Federal Rules of Evidence serve as a template for evidentiary rules in immigration courts, neither they nor *Frye* or *Daubert* strictly apply because immigration courts are part of the executive branch, not the judiciary.

Given such contestations over science in legal and policy spheres, it is perhaps not surprising that some argue that science legitimates law while others contend it simply politicizes and delegitimates. Notably, Stryker shows that technocratization has limits and legitimates (or delegitimates) law and policy differently for different parties.[37] Her paradigmatic case of the National Labor Relations Act (NLRA), for example, gained legitimacy in the early 1900s among the labor movement because the economic expertise guiding enforcement of the NLRA favored labor. However, this simultaneously delegitimated the NLRA in the eyes of American business, which eventually contributed to the elimination of the economic research unit of the National Labor Relations Board. As this example shows, technocratic decision-making may have different effects for different audiences. Similarly, social science's overall effect on legal decisions seems variable and remains unclear, particularly in the case of courts' choices to use (or ignore) social scientific evidence.[38] Nevertheless, I will show that judges routinely employ social science when adjudicating LGBTQ asylum and sex offender civil commitment cases and that social science carries considerable, though variable, influence in these two legal domains.

In advancing this analysis, this study breaks new empirical ground for sexuality studies, legal studies, and STS. To the extent that any of these fields have addressed the use of social science in legal issues concerning sexuality, attention has been devoted to marriage, adoption, and sometimes discrimination claims.[39] The other significant role that social science, particularly psychology, has played in same-sex legal issues involves the debate about whether (homo)sexuality is immutable and whether sexuality is best considered a status or conduct. While the Supreme Court ultimately endorsed the immutability view in its landmark *Obergefell v. Hodges* decision legalizing same-sex marriage nationwide in 2015, courts still generally avoid defining or explicitly discussing sexuality and sexual orientation and how they can be identified.[40] Notably, this is precisely what adjudicators must do in both asylum claims and sex offender civil commitment determinations.

COPRODUCING RACE, SEXUALITY, AND SOCIAL ORDER

Because legal interpretations of phenomena quickly diffuse beyond the legal sphere to become the basis for universal knowledge, law possesses the power to, at least partially, define social reality. For example, the law shapes racial and ethnic categories and identities, what they mean, and what privileges accrue to them.[41] There has been less attention to the law's influence on sexual identities, but, as with race, the law works to constitute the very sexual subjects it aims to govern.[42] This process delimits certain sexual expressions and experiences that are limited and narrowly constructed, yet appear as social fact. Because the institutional processes are masked, these particular sexual expressions take on the appearance of naturally occurring phenomena that are discovered, not created. Asylum hearings and sex offender assessments provide two illustrations of these reifying and boundary-making practices in action. Indeed, as one of the state's official means of classification, law is a vital force for executing state institutions' visions and categories of thought.

Though sociologists have been slow to theorize sexuality's centrality to state power, recent work has begun to bring this relationship to the fore. Jyoti Puri argues, for example, that in the wake of state liberalization and purported contraction, sexuality provides a particularly fruitful vector for the reassertion of state power and the maintenance of a "state effect."[43]

TABLE 4. Sexuality-based asylum success rates by geographic area

Area	Count	Success Count	Success Rate
Eastern Europe/ Russia	24	8	33%
Latin America	76	22	29%
East Asia	13	3	23%
Middle East and North Africa	14	3	21%
Africa	14	3	21%
Caribbean	10	2	20%
South/Southeast Asia	22	1	5%
Total	173	42	24%

TABLE 5. Racial composition of Illinois SVP program

	White	Black	Hispanic	Mixed/Other
SVP Program	64.3%	26.0%	3.4%	1.3%
Illinois population	77.0%	14.6%	17.3%	8.4%

Similarly, Elizabeth Bernstein demonstrates that the "carceral feminism" that has taken shape around issues of sex work, and especially sex trafficking, simultaneously draws on punitive and welfare logics to guide state policy.[44] Both authors show that punishment and humanitarianism are often two sides of the same coin when it comes to state policies aimed at sexuality, and both logics may operate together to expand the state's reach more broadly over larger swaths of the population and more deeply into individual lives and bodies.

These regulatory practices are inextricably intertwined with race. Though subjects' actual races are important—and racial disparities are evident in both asylum and SVP hearings (see tables 4 and 5)—also important are the processes of racialization in which sexual subjects are embedded. As queer and critical race scholars have argued, the biopolitical management of sexualized bodies and populations depends on processes of racialization that relegate some subjects to exclusion and death while granting others the privileges of inclusion.[45] In reconceptualizing queerness as a process of racialization, queer theorist Jasbir Puar contends that such practices inform "the very distinctions between life and death, wealth and poverty, health and illness, fertility and morbidity, security and insecurity, living and dying."[46] Though racialization often follows traditionally defined racial cleavages, some racial others may be granted conditional acceptance as long as they support heteronormative institutions and nationalism, or what Puar terms "homonationalism." As she further suggests, biopower incorporates many ethnic bodies complicit with an "ascendancy of Whiteness" through the careful management of difference, including the deployment of discourses of sexual repression in other cultures and the creation of new abject subject positions.

These processes are clearly at work in the operation of asylum and sex offender laws. Even when an SVP is White, the legal labeling process discursively and symbolically (and physically, if he is adjudged an SVP) expels him from the realm of (White) citizenship and its accompanying privileges. Conversely, though most asylum seekers are Black or brown, they often profess—or are compelled to profess—devotion to homonationalist values, such as marriage, and to recognize the sexual exceptionalism of the United States vis-à-vis their home countries, which must be thoroughly demonized in order to win asylum. In a similar way that Puar argues that the Muslim terrorist became a foil for the inclusion of (mostly) White queers, the sex offender serves as the abject sexual subject against which the inclusion of other sexual "others" can be justified. These processes—in analogous though opposite ways—legitimate the inclusion of certain racial others deemed fitting by the state and exclusion of certain White subjects whom the state has expelled from the protections of Whiteness. Thus, even though they operate under different state logics—punitive or welfare—they both allow the state to regulate sex, sexuality, and sexed bodies in similar racialized ways.

Such practices have a long history in the United States, where state institutions have been central in granting individuals the identity of citizen along with its concomitant rights and privileges. In determining who does and does not deserve entry into the category of citizen, the state creates and reinforces symbolic boundaries that define "the nation" and who belongs to it. Traditionally, heteronormativity has been a prerequisite for national belonging in the United States, and definitions of the nation have excluded sexual "others," including LGBTQ people.[47] The ideal citizen must be able to reproduce the nation, after all. Queers not only could not fulfill this role, but they were also viewed as degenerates who, if they did reproduce, would produce less-than-ideal citizens.

Immigration policy has historically represented one of the most visible markers of national exclusion for sexual and racial "others," often figured as the same.[48] The Page Act of 1875, for instance, banned Chinese women from immigrating to the United States with the explicit assumption that

TABLE 6. Paraphilia not otherwise specified, nonconsent (PSOSN) primary diagnosis, Illinois SVP program

	White	*Black*
PNOSN diagnosis count	71	61
Total inmate count	245	99
Percent	29%	62%

they were prostitutes. The Immigration Act of 1891 defined broader exclusionary criteria, including provisions barring persons guilty of crimes of moral turpitude. Though moral turpitude was never fully defined, it was understood to encompass (and used to exclude) sexual deviants. Historian Margot Canaday demonstrates that such exclusions were often aimed at southern and eastern Europeans, who were racialized as non-White at the time.[49]

Though less overtly racialized than many immigration statutes, laws aimed at sex offenders connote clear racial messages, and as sociologist Loïc Wacquant notes, "Sex offenders are, along with young Black men from the neighborhoods of relegation in big cities, the privileged target of the penal panopticism that has flourished on the ruins of America's charitable state over the past three decades."[50] Black men are disproportionately represented on public sex offender registries and in state civil commitment programs for sex offenders, and are more likely than White men to be diagnosed with a coercive rape paraphilia as the rationale for civil commitment (see table 6).[51] These findings are, sadly, unsurprising given the criminalization of Blackness in the United States and the long history of representing Black men's sexualities as excessive and dangerous, especially to White women.[52]

The racial politics of sex crimes are further evidenced by the names of recently enacted laws aimed at sex offenders: Megan's Law, the Jessica Lunford Act, the Adam Walsh Act. The list could go on to include many state-level statutes, but their unifying theme is that they are each named after a White child. It is notable, then, that the other primary group addressed by SVP laws is pedophiles, who are often discursively figured as White. In fact, data from the Illinois SVP program show that White men are more likely than Black men to be diagnosed with pedophilia as the basis for civil commitment (see table 7). Despite their race, however, pedophiles are generally considered a special brand of criminal—especially monstrous, incorrigible, and unrehabilitable.[53] Sociologist Jamie Small found that even legal actors tended to believe that pedophiles were lower-class and

TABLE 7. Pedophilia primary diagnosis,
Illinois SVP program

	White	Black
	163	35
Total inmate count	245	99
Percent	67%	35%

that they were physically distinctive and identifiable by sight, findings that harken to the historical interconnections between scientific racism and early sexology.[54] Regardless of the fact that pedophiles as a group may be figured as predominantly White, they are viewed as not deserving the rights of White citizenship. The techno-legal classification processes outlined in this book serve to grant the imprimatur of both law and science to these racialization practices that, in turn, legitimate the granting or curtailment of citizenship rights.

Inclusion in the realm of citizenship is, of course, a central issue in both asylum judgments and sex offender assessments.[55] Both adjudicate the fate of sexual outsiders' possible entry into the national (and often local) community and send larger signals about the boundaries of proper sexual citizenship. Asylum hearings determine whether a foreign sexual other will be able to enter the country as a potential US citizen, whereas sex offender evaluations decide whether an internal sexual other may rejoin the polity as a full citizen, be relegated to the margins of society (via residency restrictions and curtailed civil rights), or be excluded from civil society completely and possibly permanently through indefinite civil commitment. These boundary-making practices are centrally structured around risk determinations, and although risk has received little attention in the literature on the creation of symbolic boundaries, I contend that risk has become a structuring theme in issues of sexual citizenship.

RISK, BOUNDARY-MAKING, AND SEXUAL CITIZENSHIP

Though one might argue that tacit risk calculations have always been part of citizenship determinations (e.g., is this immigrant unlikely to integrate and therefore more likely to commit crimes or depend on state resources?), in the cases analyzed here, risk becomes explicit and highly salient. This might be expected in regard to sexual health, and, indeed, scholars have shown that HIV risk and HIV status do define certain subject positions.[56] But asylum determinations and sex offender evaluations make the relationship between risk calculations and sexual citizenship even more apparent because both processes explicitly invoke risk to justify outcomes. In other words, sexual subjects are defined vis-à-vis their relationship to risk. The development of new knowledges and technologies aimed at determining risk in relation to sexuality has been central to transforming once implicit assessments of dangerousness into formal calculations of risk.

Although risk assessment processes in asylum and sex offender law play out quite differently, both domains create the conditions for knowing sexual subjects primarily through their relationship to risk. The LGBTQ asylum seeker exists only insofar as he faces the risk of persecution from his home country on account of his sexuality. The sex offender, similarly, exists as a sexual subject in the eyes of the state primarily for the risk he poses to the nation because of his sexuality. Risk works as a mechanism for constituting these subject positions, or as one court decision summed up, "The policy is based on the proposition that a person who has committed a sex offense always has the potential to commit a sex offense again in the future."[57]

Furthermore, risk assessment practices in each domain reinforce particular ways of knowing sexuality already present in those legal arenas. On the one hand, until 1990 homosexuals were excludable from the United States based on the notion that they posed a risk to the nation due to their status as "sexual psychopaths." Post-1990, and partially through the mechanism of asylum, homosexuals became potential citizens worthy of national inclusion. Our conception of homosexuals shifted from an exclusionary risk paradigm that viewed them as *a risk to* the nation to an inclusionary one that viewed them as *at risk from* their home countries. A risk assessment process that focuses on whether sexual minorities are recognized as distinct social groups and how asylum seekers' sexual expressions are understood in their local cultures articulates well with a constructionist understanding of sexuality.

Conversely, risk determinations for sex offenders revolve around notions of individualized sexual risk to the nation that position sexuality and sexual risk as an inherent characteristic of an offender, which resonate with essentialist notions of sexuality. As we will see, risk evaluations for sex offenders use actuarial risk assessment tools to predict the likelihood that an offender will engage in future acts of sexual violence. Such techniques are consistent with a turn to actuarialism in crime control and penal practices and with larger shifts in governance away from punishing concrete acts and toward policing risk, or what legal scholars Tom Baker and Jonathan Simon have called "governing through risk."[58]

This "new penology" is primarily concerned with identifying, classifying, and managing groups sorted by dangerousness rather than rehabilitating criminals.[59] Incapacitation is therefore a primary strategy for controlling the distribution of offenders in the population, and the language of probability and risk has replaced earlier discourses of clinical diagnosis and retributive justice. Risk itself is criminalized. Actuarial thinking, as Bernard Harcourt asserts, alleviates our guilt about profiling because we begin to perceive profiled groups as more criminal and thus deserving of punishment and policing.[60] This idea is readily observable in the case of sex offenders, where notions of high recidivism rates and their inability to be controlled through conventional carceral methods legitimizes legal exceptions.

Asylum risk determinations use different risk calculation strategies that are more akin to clinical judgment or what Lorraine Daston and Peter Galison have called "trained judgement."[61] Asylum officers and immigration judges are entrusted as objective fact-finders and risk calculators. Working with far less concrete data than sex offender evaluators, asylum adjudicators must decide the likelihood that an asylum seeker will face persecution on account of his sexuality if returned to his home country. Adjudicators construct a representation of the claimant's home country based on various forms of country conditions evidence, including human rights reports from the US State Department and NGOs and expert affidavits and testimony, and tacitly determine if the asylum seeker's probability of persecution meets the required threshold.

Bringing together the multidisciplinary literatures and theoretical perspectives outlined above allows us to thoroughly interrogate and understand the ways by which knowledge practices shape legal procedures, conceptualizations of sexuality, and the deployment of state power, even as those same practices are contoured by extant social forces. In short, they provide the tool kit for analyzing the mutual constitution of sexuality and social order. Before proceeding to the central analysis of the book, the remainder of this chapter provides some orienting information about asylum and sex offender law.

LGBTQ ASYLUM LAW

The possibility of receiving asylum because of persecution on account of one's sexuality is a quite recent development. The 1951 United Nations Refugee Convention established five categories of asylum protection: race, religion, nationality, political opinion, and membership in a particular social group (PSG). However, the United States maintained policy focused on admitting refugees fleeing communist countries or the Middle East until passage of the 1980 Refugee Act, which brought US asylum policy in line with the UN Convention.[62] Under the new guidelines, petitioners must prove either past persecution or well-founded fear of future persecution on account of one of the protected grounds. The 1990 landmark case of Fidel Toboso-Alfonso, a Cuban man who claimed persecution due to his homosexual identity, established that sexual identity could constitute a PSG. In 1994 Attorney General Janet Reno declared that decision precedential, meaning that sexual minorities no longer had to prove on a case-by-case basis that sexual identity constitutes a PSG. However, LGBTQ people must demonstrate that they *belong* to a protected PSG and that the PSG is persecuted, meaning that in practice they must prove their sexualities. Here it is helpful to look at the asylum process more closely.

The asylum process can begin in one of two ways depending on a petitioner's status. If a migrant is documented, s/he can apply for asylum affirmatively. This means that s/he receives a nonconfrontational hearing with an asylum officer, who may either grant asylum directly or deny the claim and refer it to immigration court. If the applicant is granted asylum, s/he receives residency and the ability to begin the naturalization process a year later. If s/he is not granted asylum, s/he must plead the case to an immigration judge, at which point the process becomes identical to that of a defensive application, which occurs when a petitioner is already in removal proceedings before claiming asylum. In a defensive application, an applicant faces an adversarial hearing before an immigration judge, with a Department of Homeland Security (DHS) lawyer arguing against the claimant. If the immigration judge denies the claim, an applicant may appeal the decision to the Board of Immigration Appeals (BIA). If that also fails, the claimant may appeal to a US Court of Appeals. An asylum seeker can also appeal to the US Supreme Court, but the court has yet to hear a LGBTQ asylum claim.[63]

Given the apparent difficulty of proving one's sexuality and persecution on account of it, some critics have contended that LGBTQ asylum claims are more challenging to win, though others, including some judges and advocates, argue that queer claims require the same level of proof as any other claim and are therefore mostly treated fairly under the law.[64] It is difficult to substantiate either assertion because the DHS does not track the number of asylees granted protection as sexual minorities. However, a 2014 report by the LGBT Freedom and Asylum Network estimated that approximately 5% of all asylum claims in the United States are for sexuality-based persecution. For context, in 2014 approximately 20% of the 23,533 *successful* asylees—about 4,706 individuals—fell under the PSG classification, of which LGBTQ claims are a part. But we cannot know how many were unsuccessful or how many successful claims were for sexual minorities.[65] But the overall grant rate for asylum in the United States averages about 50%, though it varies dramatically by jurisdiction and declined under the Trump administration.[66]

SEX CRIME LAW

With controversies over Title IX and sexual assault on college campuses, an increasingly visible #MeToo movement, and ballooning sex offender registries, sex crimes have gained widespread public attention in recent years. Nearly a million people—disproportionately Black men—are now on public sex offender registries. Several thousand of these individuals are civilly committed in one of the twenty-two jurisdictions that currently allow such indefinite confinement. Though sex offenses have been the subject of moral panics throughout the twentieth century, many of these new laws—including civil commitment, public registries, residency restrictions, and others—have taken a more punitive turn and have become simultaneously more broadly encompassing and personally intrusive than ever before. Sociologist Chrysanthi Leon points out that these developments appear to be part and parcel of the larger punitive turn in American penology that began in the 1980s.[67] However, sex panic has also driven new laws aimed at sex offenders that are even more harsh and restrictive than punishments for other kinds of crime.[68]

In this latest iteration beginning in the late 1980s, a series of highly publicized, though statistically rare, crimes against children engendered public cries for harsher punishment and increased surveillance for sex offenders. The first federal law passed in response to this moral panic was the 1994 Jacob Wetterling Act—named after a boy who was abducted and whose whereabouts remain unknown today—which required states to create sex offender registries. Congress amended this law in 1996 with passage of Megan's Law—again named for a White child victim—requiring community notification of sex offenders living in the area. That same year, Congress also created a national sex offender registry. The latest amendment to this series of laws came in 2006 with the Adam Walsh Act (AWA)—also named after an abducted White child—which requires sex offenders to provide more extensive registration information and increases the minimum required duration of registration for offenders, among other things.[69] In determining registration requirements, some states use a "risk tier" system based on crimes committed, while others conduct individualized risk assessments. Regardless, almost all states currently use risk assessment technologies in some decisions about sex offenders, including determinations ranging from probation requirements to treatment efficacy.

Though the use of actuarial and psychophysiological risk assessment technologies achieved prominence only in the 1990s, risk assessment in some guise has existed since the 1930s with the passage of "sexual psychopath" laws. During this period, ranging roughly from 1930 to 1955, sexual psychopaths were viewed as "deviants with a compulsive sex disorder who were running rampant among us and therefore must be identified, classified, and captured."[70] At the same time, psychiatry was gaining professional legitimacy and used panic over sex crimes to increase its jurisdiction, implicitly promising that psychiatrists could identify, treat, and maybe even cure sexual psychopaths.[71] Psychiatrists were therefore entrusted with the clinical evaluation of sex offenders in order to determine whether they would be amenable to treatment, should be sent to prison, or should be civilly committed in a psychiatric facility. However, civil rights challenges and a crisis of trust in psychiatry's ability to fulfill its promises meant that by the 1970s, psychiatry's role in the identification, treatment, and adjudication of sex offenders diminished considerably, and new professional groups stepped in to fill the void.

Answering the call for more objective and reliable methods by which to predict the riskiness of offenders, a new form of expertise arose in the form of forensic psychology. These professionals rely on actuarial and psychophysiological technologies to predict future sexual conduct. Of the psychophysiological technologies employed, the polygraph is the most common. Indeed, a representative from the Illinois Polygraph Society sits on the Illinois Sex Offender Management Board, and polygraph examinations of sex offenders living in the community are mandated in many states. Penile plethysmography (PPG), or phallometric testing, is still used in many states, as well. Despite criticisms of the accuracy and intrusiveness of these two technologies, they remain in wide use, with at least 37% of adult residential treatment programs reporting use of the PPG and 79% reporting use of the polygraph.[72]

While I address many of these legal developments, the primary focus of this book is the new generation of sex offender civil commitment laws that arose in the 1990s, variously labeled "sexually violent predator," "sexually violent persons," or "sexually dangerous persons" laws, and the assessment practices surrounding these laws. For the sake of brevity, I will refer to these as "SVP laws." These statutes resulted from high-profile sex crimes (though not an actual increase in the number of sex crimes) that induced a moral panic, particularly around child molestation.[73] As of 2018, twenty states and the federal government have enacted SVP laws. Unlike earlier "sexual psychopath" laws, which sought to divert those "too sick" for punishment from criminal sentences into treatment facilities at the front end, new SVP statutes are aimed at the "worst of the worst" and allow the government to seek the indefinite civil commitment of an offender *after* he has served his criminal sentence. As of 2015, there were approximately 5,400 individuals committed under these statutes.[74]

In most jurisdictions, all offenders who have committed "sexually violent" offenses are assessed as they near the end of their criminal sentence.

If this initial evaluator believes an offender may qualify as an SVP, the offender undergoes a more extensive SVP evaluation. If this evaluation also suggests that the offender is an SVP, he receives a probable cause hearing before a judge. Typically, fewer than 5% of sex offenders reach this point. If the judge finds probable cause (and they usually do), the offender is sent to the civil commitment facility to await his SVP trial. The trial itself may be conducted before a judge alone or a jury, depending on the jurisdiction, and the level of proof required to commit offenders also varies by jurisdiction, an issue discussed more in chapter 7. Post-commitment, offenders are periodically reevaluated and may be recommended for conditional release if both the treatment staff and a judge agree that they are no longer a risk to the community.

Though many perceive SVP laws to be punitive, legislatures have been careful to specify that they are for community protection and crime prevention, not punishment, and courts have largely agreed with this rationale. By couching SVP laws within the civil realm, states have been able to fend off constitutional challenges based on ex post facto, double jeopardy, and due process complaints, and ultimately the Supreme Court has deemed the laws constitutional in three high-profile cases.[75] Despite their "civil" appellation, however, commitment hearings look very similar to criminal trials. Defendants are entitled to lawyers, often have a right to a jury, and the required level of proof in many states is "beyond a reasonable doubt."[76] Finally, because criminal law cannot punish a "status" (i.e., a "dangerous person"), making SVP laws civil allows states to work around that obstacle. However, the Supreme Court *has* ruled that SVPs must be distinguishable from the "typical" offender.[77] This sorting and classification process necessitates the cooperation of psychological professionals for the diagnosis of mental disorders and the prediction of future sexual violence.

Equipped with this background, the next chapter offers a closer analysis of these Supreme Court decisions and particularly how they helped firmly ensconce forensic psychology as the state's preferred expertise for managing and classifying sex offenders.

3: FORENSIC PSYCHOLOGY, COMPLICIT EXPERTISE, AND THE LEGITIMATION OF LAW

The previous chapters explained the historical relationship between homosexuality and sex crimes, showing that cultural, scientific, and legal understandings of sexuality are thoroughly intertwined—indeed, that law and science as institutions are embedded in and contoured by extant cultural schemas. Given this insight, the next two chapters demonstrate how particular cultural conceptions of sexuality became further entrenched within state legal institutions through the institutionalization of particular kinds of expertise in each legal complex. As different types of expertise with divergent views of sexuality are institutionalized within legal arenas, they contribute to upholding certain understandings of sexuality—what it is, how it can be measured, which sexual practices and identities are normal and which are not. However, claiming such jurisdictional authority rarely comes without struggle and negotiation, and this axiom certainly holds in the cases of asylum and sex offender law.

Indeed, the epistemic contestations analyzed in this chapter and the next highlight the different ways by which knowledge actors may diffuse legal legitimacy crises. Legitimacy is central to maintaining public acceptance of state governance decisions. When social groups begin to see state decisions as unfair, misguided, or simply bad, they also often begin to see the related state institutions as less legitimate. One way such crises might be remedied is through recourse to techno-scientific reasoning, or technocratization, a process that incorporates techno-science into legal and policy decision-making. Though this process characterizes both the SVP and asylum legal complexes, it plays out rather differently in each.

In the realm of sex offender law, a series of developments in the 1970s and 1980s created an opening for forensic psychology to expand its professional jurisdiction and set the stage for a substantial change in the institutionalized practices of sex offender assessment and management.

Before this time, psychiatry largely managed sex offenders, but doubts over psychiatrists' abilities to accurately assess risk and treat offenders led to their withdrawal from the field. Forensic psychology, in turn, promised to deliver more accurate and objective assessment than clinical psychiatry could and asserted that treatment may even be possible. Consequently, forensic psychology secured for itself professional jurisdiction and authority in the penal management of sex offenders. Forensic psychology offered up its legitimating power to the state without contestation, what I call complicit expertise.

The expert structure in asylum law formed in a very different manner. In 1990, for the first time in the United States, a gay man was granted withholding of removal (a form of relief similar to asylum) due to persecution he had suffered on account of his sexuality. Activists within the gay and lesbian movement quickly realized that there were many issues in the processing of asylum applications for sexual minorities, including a lack of understanding of sexuality and sexual identity among immigration authorities and insufficient documenting of dangerous country conditions for sexual minorities around the world. These activists mobilized to forge networks of lawyers, social scientists, and human rights experts who could educate legal authorities about both of these issues and to create a knowledge database that advocates around the country could draw on to win asylum claims. These activists were eventually successful in not only winning landmark precedential asylum cases but also cowriting government guidelines for evaluating LGBTQ asylum claims and training asylum officers and judges in these procedures. However, they did so by first creating (or bringing wider attention to) the legitimacy crisis to which they themselves then offered the solution. I label this insurgent expertise. And though the process was different, the resolution ultimately helped to shore up the legitimacy and authority of state decision-making.

These contestations over what disciplines and actors would lay claim to expertise regarding sexuality were the first step in the creation of institutionalized ways of knowing sexuality, or what I call "epistemic logics." Although epistemic logics are at least temporarily stable, they can change in response to a variety of political, cultural, and institutional factors. By comparing and holding the logics of the asylum and SVP legal complexes in tension with each other, I show that our understandings of sexuality are not straightforward expressions of an underlying truth of human sexual nature, but that these "truths" are mediated by a host of cultural and social factors that dictate how we know what we know. In essence, actors situated within different contexts enact different sexualities in each legal complex. This is not to say that one epistemic logic materializes sexuality correctly and another does not, but that sexuality itself is a multivalent phenomenon that is constituted differently depending on its institutional, discursive, and material context.

As Sheila Jasanoff says of coproduction, "Solving problems of social order frequently takes the form of producing new languages or modifying old ones.... In the process, scientific language often takes onboard the tacit models of nature, society, culture, or humanity that are current at any time within a given social order," and further, when knowledge changes, "new institutions emerge to provide the web of social and normative understandings within which new characterizations of nature . . . can be recognized and given political effect."[1] In this way, new knowledges about sexuality may give rise to new forms of social control and may provide a backdrop against which new subject positions in need of new state technologies of surveillance, control, and regulation take shape. Coproduction, then, helps us understand how expert knowledges can give rise to new political technologies. Through the enrollment of particular forms of knowledge into its governance practices, the state may import existing cultural grammars of sexuality. By bringing such understandings of sexuality into the state apparatus via expert actors, these cultural views of sexuality are stripped of their subjectivity and presented as objective fact, which in turn helps legitimate the state's actions and policies. Explicating these processes requires a brief detour to consider how I conceptualize expertise.

EXPERTISE AS A NETWORK

Expertise has traditionally been understood as a property of individuals or groups, something that one possesses by virtue of credentials and socialization into a profession.[2] Rather than adopting this "realist view" of expertise, *Sorting Sexualities* advocates a view more in line with that proposed by sociologist Gil Eyal. Eyal suggests shifting the analytical focus from experts to expertise and exploring the "background of practices and the social, material, spatial, organizational, and conceptual arrangements that serve as its [expertise's] conditions of possibility."[3] With this analytical shift comes a reconceptualization of expertise "analyzed as networks that link together objects, actors, techniques, devices, and institutional and spatial arrangements."[4] Such an approach takes up the Latourian task of tracing "expertise in the making" rather than expertise as an already-formed object. This type of analysis emphasizes that expertise is an ongoing accomplishment, not a given fact, and that expert knowledge is "coextensive with the construction of a temporarily stable network."[5]

This move, Eyal points out, also necessitates a rethinking of power. If expert authority is dependent on a network, it behooves network actors to enroll as many allies as possible in the actor-network and to make those links in the chain as secure as possible. Rather than erecting rigid juris-dictional boundaries and seeking an expert monopoly, the most effective actor-networks will be characterized by "generosity." Generosity means that a network of expertise (as distinct from experts) becomes more powerful and influential if it can graft its modes of seeing, doing, and judging onto what others are doing, thus linking them to the network and securing their cooperation.

This approach allows us to follow not only "expertise in the making" but also knowledge in the making as it occurs at the law-science boundary. Alberto Cambrosio and colleagues highlight this possibility when they argue that "facts are not first established by the scientific community and only afterwards mobilized in the political arena. Regulatory facts, i.e. facts which are expected to play a regulatory role, are the result of a hybrid con-struction process integrating heterogeneous elements and, for that very reason, achieve a robust status."[6] This is consistent with the coproduction idea that the way law and science articulate together in the asylum and sex offender domains produces hybrid ways of knowing sexuality—that is, distinct epistemic logics.

I am suggesting, then, that epistemic logics form through the inter-action of networks of expertise and preexisting structures of power. These preexisting structures—such as ruling statutes or institutional norms—influence, though do not determine, the form and properties of expert networks. For instance, sex offender laws that dictate psychological evalua-tion of offenders create an institutional framework in which psychological expertise is given a leg up in relation to, say, anthropology. Asylum law, on the other hand, with its mandate to determine the risk of persecution for subjects in foreign countries, sets up a much more favorable situation for anthropological expertise. Neither one of these structuring factors, how-ever, overdetermines the way a network of expertise will form, what shape it will take, or what functions it will serve. Once formed, and indeed in the process of stabilization, however, networks act back on these preexisting structures to partially shape them, as well. Expert opinions, for example, may become the basis for precedential legal decisions. Thus, these previ-ously crystallized structures and newly formed (or forming) networks act on each other in a dialectical fashion to create at least temporarily stabi-lized frameworks for knowing.[7]

Equipped with this understanding of expertise, I now turn to an exami-nation of the "conditions of possibility" for the creation of a strong forensic psychology network of expertise, beginning with the institutional context that made its formation possible.

FORENSIC PSYCHOLOGY AND
THE OFFER OF OBJECTIVITY

In the late 1930s, states began passing "sexual psychopath" laws engendered by a moral panic around sex crimes. The panic declined somewhat during WWII but then resurged postwar, and by the late 1950s, twenty-seven states and Washington, DC, had some form of sexual psychopath law.[8] These statutes were backed by the authority of psychiatry, which promised to be able to identify, treat, and perhaps even cure sex offenders. The laws took aim at those "too sick to deserve punishment," and therefore diverted those charged under these statutes away from prisons and into psychiatric hospitals. Unlike current SVP laws, sexual psychopath statutes disproportionately targeted low-level offenders, such as homosexuals and exhibitionists, under the "escalation" theory that posited that a "harmless" offense indicated a future propensity to commit heinous sexually motivated crimes.[9] Some psychiatrists voiced concern over such theories and the vagueness of the term "sexual psychopath," which was not, in fact, a proper psychiatric diagnosis at all but a legal creation that provided a veneer of scientific legitimacy.[10] The psychiatric profession never reached a consensus as to the definition of "sexual psychopath," and its legal parameters continued to vary from state to state. In California an offender had to have an "utter lack of power to control his impulses," while in Iowa he had only to have "criminal propensities towards the commission of sex offenses."[11] Treatment and cure—on which sexual psychopath statutes were premised—were therefore impossible since there was no recognized psychiatric diagnosis of sexual psychopathy. As a result, many academic psychiatrists abandoned the field, leaving only those psychiatrists willing to work within the dominant legal framework.[12] However, enough of the psychiatric profession backed the laws to make them workable.

By the 1970s, concerns with the accurate identification of "sexual psychopaths" provoked widespread disapproval, including among the psychiatric profession. In 1977 the Group for the Advancement of Psychiatry issued a report condemning the laws and calling for their repeal.[13] The Presidential Commission on Mental Health and the American Bar Association's Committee on Criminal Justice Mental Health Standards soon joined the call for repeal.[14] Additionally, a string of judicial decisions in the late 1960s and 1970s made it more difficult to involuntarily commit anyone who did not pose an imminent risk, and by the early 1980s most sexual psychopath statutes were either repealed or had fallen into disuse.

The repeal of these laws signaled the end of psychiatry's dominance in sex offender management and the ascension of forensic psychology. Indeed, the 1970s was precisely the time when forensic psychology was coalescing as a field concerned with sex crime. The group that would become the Association for the Treatment of Sexual Abusers (ATSA) began meeting regularly in 1977 and by 1985 had officially formed as a professional organization.[15] The switchover was largely complete by the mid-1990s, as evidenced by amicus briefs submitted in the landmark *Kansas v. Hendricks* Supreme Court case in 1997 upholding the new generation of civil commitment laws for sex offenders. The American Psychiatric Association (APA) submitted a brief against the constitutionality of the laws, while the ATSA submitted a brief (implicitly) supporting them.[16] In a narrow 5-4 vote, the laws were upheld.

The New Generation of SVP Laws

Forces in the late 1980s and early 1990s—including "tough on crime" attitudes and feminist efforts to increase awareness and punishment of sexual violence—gave rise to a new generation of sex offender civil commitment laws. Unlike the earlier laws aimed at those "too sick to deserve punishment," new SVP laws targeted the "worst of the worst." SVP statutes thus contain a three-pronged test for distinguishing this subset of offenders. First, an offender must have committed a "sexually violent crime," which is defined differently in each jurisdiction, but generally requires a contact offense such as sexual assault. The federal government, though, often seeks commitment for those convicted of possessing child pornography, a noncontact offense. Second, an offender must have a mental disorder or abnormality. Jurisdictions vary in the terms they use and the precise definition of mental disorder or abnormality, but Illinois's definition is typical of most states: "'Mental disorder' means a congenital or acquired condition affecting the emotional or volitional capacity that predisposes a person to engage in acts of sexual violence."[17] The broadness of this definition (e.g., the condition can be "congenital" *or* "acquired" and affect "volitional" *or* "emotional" capacity) sets the stage for wide discretion for psychological professionals. The third requirement, as the definition suggests, is that the mental disorder must predispose an offender to future acts of sexual violence. These requirements, aside from the first, which is strictly statutory, necessitate the cooperation of psychological professionals in both the diagnosis of a mental disorder and the prediction of future sexual violence based on that diagnosis. The negotiations around this legal-scientific boundary form the basis of a shared network of expertise that encompasses a wide range of legal and scientific actors and shores up the authority of both law and forensic psychology.

Though I focus on SVP laws because they provide the most obvious site where decisions about individuals' sexualities are rendered, I do not mean to downplay the vast influence that psychological professionals have in many areas of sex offender management. New sex offender laws promulgated since the early 1990s—including registration, treatment, and surveillance requirements—have created a cottage industry tasked with servicing all facets of these statutes, from legal representation to forensic expertise to therapy and treatment. As this suggests, the avalanche of new sex offender laws since the early 1990s has formed an institutional and legal landscape that engenders—indeed, requires—the creation of new networks of expertise to meet the needs of the state.

Where such laws have been passed, states have also generally created Sex Offender Management Boards (SOMBs) tasked with filling in the details of implementation, including what credentials allow someone to become a certified treatment provider for sex offenders and how the state will handle evaluation and treatment of sex offenders in its custody or on supervised release (as most statutes do not specify *how* such things are to be done but merely that they are to be done). These boards provide a prime mechanism for "generosity" and the enrollment of allies in the expertise network. Members of SOMBs typically represent an array of groups, including law enforcement, corrections, probation and parole, prosecutors, public defenders, treatment and evaluation professionals, and victim advocates. The Illinois SOMB also counts two ATSA members among its ranks. With their guidance, the SOMB adopted almost wholesale the ATSA treatment and evaluation guidelines for use in Illinois. This is not an unusual occurrence, as ATSA makes its guidelines available for just this type of use, and many states use them as a template, if not adopting them with minimal alteration, as Illinois has. The Illinois SOMB also provides trainings twice per year on a range of issues related to sex crimes that draw a diverse group of legal and psychological professionals, further strengthening its actor-network. ATSA often supports and provides continuing education credits for these trainings. SOMBs throughout the country also provide spaces for the promulgation of the "containment model," a strategy that explicitly calls for multidisciplinary and collaborative teams in the management of sex offenders.[18] The containment model is now legally mandated in California, though many states use the approach.[19] As the California SOMB website states: "This sex offender management program has three required components: supervising (e.g., probation or parole) officer; sex offender treatment provider; and polygraph examiner, using a victim-centered approach. These three people are the core of the Containment Team, although other team members should participate at times (e.g., the registering law enforcement agency)."[20] This model thus puts supervision, treatment/evaluation, and surveillance in a tripartite relationship based around the premises of risk control. Indeed, the California laws further mandate that the offender's treatment provider conduct static and dynamic risk assessments and share the results with law enforcement.

Having specified the political, legal, and institutional frameworks within which forensic psychology has been able to ascend to its place as the predominant form of expertise in the management of sex offenders, I now want to turn my attention to the actual expert statements (i.e., psychiatric diagnoses and risk predictions) and trace their "conditions of possibility" as well as the way by which the production of such statements has allowed for the extension of the forensic psychology actor-network and the sharing of authority between law and psychology.

CLAIMING DIAGNOSTIC AUTHORITY

The sexual psychopath statutes of the 1930s–1970s required no specific diagnosis. One was deemed a sexual psychopath or not based on the subjective evaluation of a psychiatrist. However, "sexual psychopath" was not a clinical diagnosis, and there was thus no consensus on how to diagnosis a "sexual psychopath" or, indeed, what a sexual psychopath even was. It was, as *Boutilier v. INS* (1967) made clear, a purely legal creation.[21] The advent of the first edition of the *DSM* by the APA in 1952 did not help clarify matters, as it did not include specific diagnostic criteria for mental disorders and took a psychoanalytic approach to diagnosis. The same was true of the *DSM-II*. More explicit diagnostic criteria were finally added in 1980 with the publication of the *DSM-III*. By this time, however, psychiatry had largely exited the realm of sex offender adjudication, and "sexual psychopath" statutes had been repealed or fallen into disuse.

This situation shifted somewhat with the new generation of SVP laws and the entry of forensic psychology. The new statutes required a diagnosis of a "mental abnormality." While still vague, psychologists could work within this framework, and they did so by drawing on a recognized source of psychiatric authority: the *DSM*. Though the *DSM* does not call its diagnoses "mental abnormalities," it *does* provide clear diagnostic criteria, unlike the purely subjective "sexual psychopath" designation of the earlier laws. Notably, no SVP statutes actually require a diagnosis from the *DSM*, only a finding of "mental abnormality," but by drawing on the scientific legitimacy of the *DSM* (and by extension the psychiatric profession despite the APA's opposition to using the *DSM* in this way) and rendering it a boundary object at the law-science nexus, forensic psychology professionals have been able to strengthen their actor-network.[22] Moreover, because the *DSM* provides specific diagnostic criteria, anyone can theoretically trace it backward to the diagnostic details in the *DSM*. Indeed, many defense lawyers in civil commitment proceedings do just this in order to dispute their clients' diagnoses.[23] Being able to defend these diagnoses is a key aspect of being able to construct a strong actor-network and fortify the links in that chain. Forensic professionals must also defend against some within their own ranks and from the psychiatric field, who have asserted that the concept of "mental abnormality" lacks a consistent operational definition. I will return to these controversies shortly, but first I want to consider how forensic psychology has been able to fortify itself against these various attacks at all, let alone establish itself as a trusted form of scientific expertise. The Supreme Court decisions in *Kansas v. Hendricks* and *Kansas v. Crane* together provide a telling illustration of the way that the fuzziness of the term "mental abnormality" has allowed law and forensic psychology to negotiate jurisdictional boundaries and, ultimately, to share authority over the term in a process of coproduction.

The Kansas SVP law, enacted in 1994, was among the earliest of the new generation of civil commitment statutes and quickly faced constitutional challenge. The test case involved Leroy Hendricks, a man with a history of arrests for child sexual assault, including the molestation of two adolescent boys for which he was serving a sentence when Kansas elected to pursue civil commitment. Hendricks admitted that he could not control his "urge" to molest children, especially when he "gets stressed out." He agreed with the state psychologist's diagnosis of pedophilia and further agreed that he was not cured of the condition and also that "treatment is bullshit."[24] The jury unanimously found Hendricks to be a sexually violent predator, and the court found that pedophilia qualified as a "mental abnormality" under the act. Hendricks appealed, claiming that the act violated the Constitution's due process, double jeopardy, and ex post facto clauses. The Kansas Supreme Court did not address his double jeopardy or ex post facto complaints but found that Hendricks's due process rights were in fact violated and, specifically, that the definition of "mental abnormality" used in the SVP Act did not satisfy the constitutional requirement of "mental illness" for the purposes of civil commitment. The state of Kansas appealed, and the US Supreme Court agreed to hear the case.

For its part, Kansas relied on a number of previous Supreme Court decisions upholding similar statutes that coupled "proof of dangerousness with the proof of some additional factor, such as a 'mental illness' or 'mental abnormality,'"[25] including both Illinois's and Minnesota's sexual psychopath-era laws.[26] The state asserted that the SVP Act's requirement of a "mental abnormality" or "personality disorder" was consistent with these other statutes. Kansas was supported by amicus briefs from ATSA and the Menninger Clinic, a forensic psychiatric hospital, which both argued that "mental abnormality" was a workable term. The Menninger Clinic argued, "Neither does the Constitution or prevailing historical practice restrict State civil commitment power to conditions that fit some technical definition of 'mental illness.' Adopting such an approach would inexorably wed the constitutionality of civil commitment statutes to a single phrase—'mental illness'—thereby elevating that term to the status of 'magic words.'" Later the clinic's brief drew on the *DSM-IV*'s cautionary note about diagnosing mental disorders to argue that "psychiatrists themselves concede that they know of no definition that adequately specifies the precise boundaries of the concept of mental illness."[27] ATSA was less strident in its criticism of psychiatry, but it clearly staked out its professional jurisdiction and ability to work within the legal frameworks created by new SVP laws, stating: "The relevant question, though, is not whether clinicians or the legislature created this term [mental abnormality], but whether experts in the treatment and assessment of sex offenders can derive clinical meaning from this term. The answer to this latter question is clearly 'yes.'"[28] In a display of generosity that nicely illustrates the co-production process at work, ATSA proceeded to argue:

> "Mental Abnormality" is governed by its statutory definition, and its clinical meaning is derived when professionals give it specific content. While the term "mental abnormality" does not have a clinical definition, the term has been frequently used in mental health law. As a legal term, its application is governed by its statutory definition, as are other legal terms such as "insane," "incompetent," and "gravely disabled." Like other broad legal classifications of psychiatric or psychological conditions (such as mental illness, mental disorder, mental disease, and mental defect), the term "mental abnormality" becomes clinically meaningful when a psychologist or psychiatrist gives it specific content.[29]

Both the Menninger Clinic and ATSA also critiqued the notion that treatment for sex offenders did not exist, instead offering up their own services (or that of their members in ATSA's case) as evidence of treatment availability. ATSA pointedly concluded, "Sex offender specialists are able to use the term 'mental abnormality' to identify a small subset of sex offenders who have specific paraphiliac disorders and who are at highest risk to reoffend,"[30] a statement that seems rather clearly to say, "We can do it if psychiatrists won't."

Hendricks, conversely, argued that "mental abnormality" was *not* equivalent to "mental illness" because "mental abnormality" was a term coined by the Kansas legislature, not the psychiatric profession. The APA agreed with Hendricks and filed an amicus brief arguing that the SVP Act's "mental abnormality" requirement did not meet the "mental illness" condition for civil commitment, writing, "If 'mental illness' were freely subject to legislative definition (through new terms like 'mental abnormality' or otherwise), or if anyone 'crazy' or 'sick' enough to engage in repeated serious offenses could be civilly confined for that reason, the limits on deprivations of liberty to protect the public safety would quickly disappear."[31] In 1997 the Supreme Court, in a 5–4 decision, sided with Kansas, writing that "the term 'mental illness' is devoid of any talismanic significance."[32] The majority further stated that "we have never required State legislatures to adopt any particular nomenclature in drafting civil commitment statutes. Rather, we have traditionally left to legislators the task of defining terms of a medical nature that have legal significance. . . . Often, those definitions do not fit precisely with the definitions employed by the medical community." The important aspect of these types of laws, the court continued, is that they set forth criteria relating to an individual's inability to control his "dangerousness" and that they are able to distinguish SVPs "from other dangerous persons who are perhaps more properly dealt with exclusively through criminal proceedings."[33] This "volitional control" criterion became the subject of another appeal involving the Kansas SVP law, which I will return to shortly. But first, it is worth considering in more detail how the court upheld the authority of law while simultaneously diminishing psychiatric expertise and shoring up that of forensic psychology.

First, the majority explicitly cited the preface of the APA's *DSM-IV*, where it states that legal definitions, such as "individual responsibility" and "competency," for which psychiatric expertise is often sought by courts, need not mirror those advanced by medicine. It used this statement to assert law's prerogative in defining certain terms, in this case "mental abnormality." In a move that showed some acknowledgment of psychiatry, however, the court further drew on psychiatry's own expert statements to justify its decision, writing that "the mental health professionals who evaluated Hendricks diagnosed him as suffering from pedophilia, a condition the psychiatric profession itself classifies as a serious mental disorder."[34] It cited the APA's 1989 publication "Treatments of Psychiatric Disorders" to back this assertion. Significantly, it also drew on a paper by Gene Abel (a founding member of ATSA) and Joanne Rouleau (a forensic psychology researcher). In a revealing footnote, the court then pointed to debate within the "psychiatric" field (which was, in reality, mostly a debate between organized psychiatry and forensic psychology) to again assert the law's authority to decide between conflicting expert views. This view was upheld even by the dissent, wherein Justice Stephen Breyer wrote: "The Constitution permits a State to follow one reasonable professional view, while rejecting another. . . . The psychiatric debate, therefore, helps to inform the law by setting the bounds of what is reasonable, but it cannot here decide just how States must write their laws within those bounds."[35] Thus, while all of the justices acknowledged that psychiatric expertise (or psychological, as it may be) can help set the parameters of argument, they also clearly maintained law's privilege to adjudicate between competing expert claims. Both the majority and dissent proceeded to do just that, explicitly dismissing the APA's brief, which argued that the "mental illness" requirement was not met by Kansas's SVP Act, and endorsing the amicus brief from the Menninger Clinic, which argued that the "mental illness" requirement *was* met. The court also subsequently invoked ATSA's amicus brief to shore up its assessment of successful possibilities for treating paraphilias in a forensic setting.

Ultimately, then, the court maintained substantial autonomy for the state to define for itself what constitutes a "mental abnormality." Yet it simultaneously drew on the expertise of forensic psychology while disavowing organized psychiatry. This decision crystallizes the debate between psychiatry and forensic psychology over the evaluation and treatment of sex offenders and represents a moment when the expert network cobbled together by ATSA and other forensic organizations displaced that of psychiatry in the penal domain. Perhaps most notable in this episode is the way that the forensic organizations deployed the *DSM* as a malleable boundary object in order to give the term "mental abnormality" meaning in the areas of both law and forensic psychology. Psychiatry refused to do so and instead insisted on maintaining the "pure" psychiatric term "mental illness," signaling a refusal to allow interpretive leeway across social worlds. This debate clearly echoes the controversy over the "sexual psychopath" diagnosis and whether it carried any clinical meaning. Whereas psychiatry seemed quite wary of becoming embroiled in another scandal, forensic psychology evinced clear willingness to fill the absence created by the APA's withdrawal.[36] The epistemic logic dictating how sexuality would be conceptualized in the SVP setting was clearly taking shape.

Less than five years later, in 2002, the Kansas law faced a second constitutional challenge that once again made its way to the US Supreme Court. This case involved Michael Crane, an exhibitionist diagnosed with antisocial personality disorder, and hinged on the level of volitional impairment required by the Constitution in order to civilly commit a sex offender. Kansas sought successfully to commit Crane, but the Kansas Supreme Court reversed the decision, stating that the Constitution, as interpreted in *Hendricks*, requires "a finding that the defendant cannot control his dangerous behavior."[37] The state of Kansas argued, conversely, that the SVP Act and *Hendricks* required no such finding. As in *Hendricks*, ATSA and the APA submitted opposing amicus briefs. ATSA stated that it did not take a position for or against civil commitment of sexual predators, but it again filed a brief for the state of Kansas and took issue with the Kansas Supreme Court's rationale for striking down the law. Specifically, ATSA wrote, "The Kansas court's 'cannot control' substantive due process standard is untenable. Its first incarnation, the 'irresistible impulse' insanity test, has been largely rejected by both the medical and legal professions. Moreover, experts in the field would be unable, as a practical matter, to implement the 'cannot control' standard."[38] For its part, the APA again issued a lengthy critique of civil commitment for sexual predators, this time dedicating three full paragraphs to criticizing ATSA's brief specifically. The APA contended, contrary to ATSA, that

> the very imprecisions of measuring degrees of volitional control do suggest that the idea cannot be fairly used to attach (profound) legal consequences unless the standard is set near the far end of the spectrum. As Kansas now insists, it is in the wide middle range of non-extreme cases that volitional "impairment" would present substantial problems of consistent, workable, objective application.

Finally, it concluded, "Thus, *Hendricks* and *Pearson*, together with the need to avoid the difficulties that (as Kansas recognizes) afflict lesser versions of a 'volitional impairment' standard, support a limiting principle of such severe impairment as to avoid the large gray area: inability to control the conduct, as proved with a high degree of certainty."[39] The dueling positions thus set up a clear jurisdictional skirmish regarding expertise on the topic of sex offender mental health and assessment.

In a 7–2 decision, the US Supreme Court ruled that *Hendricks* did indeed require a diagnosis of a "mental abnormality" or "personality disorder" that made it "*difficult*, if not impossible, for the [dangerous] person to control his dangerous behavior."[40] It was not required, however, that an offender have "complete" lack of volitional or emotional control, as such an "absolutist approach," the court asserted, would be unworkable. Once again, the court invoked ATSA's amicus brief to back this point and, once again, it rejected the APA's brief backing Crane. Thus, the court maintained its prerogative to adjudicate between competing forms of expertise. However, in a move that granted state psychological experts considerable leeway, the majority then wrote:

> We recognize that *Hendricks* as so read provides a less precise constitutional standard than would those more definite rules for which the parties have argued. But the Constitution's safeguards of human liberty in the area of mental illness and the law are not always best enforced through precise bright-line rules. For one thing, the States retain considerable leeway in defining the mental abnormalities and personality disorders that make an individual eligible for commitment.[41]

With this decision, forensic psychologists' pivotal role in diagnosing sexual offenders with a "mental abnormality" that affects their volitional control was solidified. Though the state retained the ultimate authority to decide which "mental abnormalities" would qualify someone for civil commitment, the framework set up by these SVP statutes and Supreme Court decisions granted substantial autonomy to psychological experts in crafting diagnostic categories that fell within the bounds of such laws. Because forensic psychology was willing to relinquish some expert authority by working within the legal framework prescribed by the state to provide diagnostic expertise that psychiatry was unwilling to offer, it was able to secure for itself a considerable domain of expertise within the system. Paradoxically, then, by giving up the exclusive privilege of defining "mental abnormality," forensic psychology actually expanded its epistemic authority and successfully grafted its mode of knowing onto the law. This is further illustrated by an analysis of the development of one of the most commonly used diagnostic categories for SVPs: paraphilia not otherwise specified, or paraphilia NOS.

AUTHORIZING AMBIGUITY: PARAPHILIA NOS

Those considered for civil commitment generally fall into two groups: child molesters and rapists. The *DSM* (since the third edition) provides a clearly defined diagnostic category for the former in the form of "pedophilia" or, in the newest version, the *DSM-5*, "pedophilic disorder."[42] On the other hand, no clear psychiatric diagnosis for rapists exists. Illustrating the considerable diagnostic autonomy afforded to evaluators by the SVP statutes and court decisions, forensic psychology met this challenge with the advent of "paraphilia not otherwise specified, nonconsent" (PNOSN).[43]

Paraphilia is, simply put, sexual attraction or arousal to non-normative stimuli. Paraphilic disorders are the most common diagnoses of mental abnormality in SVP proceedings.[44] Despite significant controversy regarding paraphilia diagnoses in general—and specifically paraphilia NOS, as I will discuss shortly—these diagnostic categories are usually accepted by courts because they are viewed as clinically valid categories that can be accurately and reliably assessed.[45] By definition, however, PNOS diagnoses are idiosyncratic and therefore not generally accepted or agreed upon by psychiatry.[46] Nevertheless, PNOS, along with pedophilia and antisocial personality disorder, constitute the bulk of mental abnormalities represented in civil commitment.

The *DSM-5* provides two primary criteria for diagnosing paraphilias. Criterion A states that paraphilias are "recurrent, intense sexually arousing fantasies, sexual urges, or behaviors, generally involving 1) nonhuman objects, 2) the suffering or humiliation of oneself or one's partner, or 3) children or other nonconsenting persons, that occur over a period of at least

6 months." Criterion B specifies that the person has either acted on those fantasies or urges or that "the behavior, sexual urges, or fantasies cause clinically significant distress or impairment in social, occupational, or other important areas of functioning." It further outlines eight particular paraphilias and gives more specific criteria for them, including pedophilia, masochism, sadism, frotteurism, fetishism, exhibitionism, voyeurism, and transvestism. The residual category "paraphilia not otherwise specified" is meant to capture paraphilic disorders that either are too rare to be included as a specific diagnosis on their own (e.g., necrophilia) or do not quite fit the criteria of one of the other specified paraphilias. Forensic psychologists have used this latter caveat to create the now widely used diagnosis for SVPs of PNOSN, usually for serial rapists. Dennis Doren, former Director of the Wisconsin SVP civil commitment program, is often credited with popularizing the diagnosis with the publication of his *Evaluating Sex Offenders*, which outlines several considerations for making PNOSN diagnoses of sexual offenders and asserts the validity of the category.[47]

However, significant professional controversy surrounds this category, with the split generally occurring between research psychologists and psychiatrists, on the one hand, and practice-oriented forensic psychologists, on the other, where the latter support the diagnosis. Indeed, Allen Frances and Michael First, the chair and editor, respectively, of the *DSM-IV-TR* revisions wrote an article vehemently decrying the use of PNOSN in SVP proceedings.[48] They express deep concern over the reliability of any PNOS diagnosis and particular concern over whether a paraphilia involving "nonconsent" even exists. They point out that there is little research indicating that such a population actually exists and that the diagnosis may simply be medicalizing criminal conduct (i.e., rape). They explicitly state that they never anticipated the residual PNOS category being used in a forensic setting because it lacks an empirical basis and clear diagnostic criteria. They additionally point out that many diagnoses in the forensic setting are occurring erroneously because of a small typo in the *DSM-IV* that was carried over into the *DSM-IV-TR*; namely, that Criterion A for diagnosing paraphilias says that a paraphilia may involve fantasies, urges, *or* behaviors. The editors, on the contrary, state that a paraphilia *must be* a pattern of arousal, not simply behaviors. Overt behaviors are not enough to deduce a paraphilia. In the instance of PNOSN, it is not enough to find a history of rape. Rather, there must be evidence that the offender is primarily aroused by the nonconsenting aspect of the situation to consider a PNOSN diagnosis. In a recent analysis of over one hundred SVP cases where the PNOSN diagnosis was used, however, the majority of court decisions described only behaviors as diagnostic criteria or were unclear as to the criteria used.[49] Finally, they note that "coercive paraphilic disorder" has been proposed as an addition to the *DSM* during every revision since the *DSM-III* and rejected each time due to lack of empirical support.[50]

However, practice-oriented psychologists, and particularly SVP evaluators, generally appear to hold a different view of PNOSN. In direct contrast to Frances and First, for example, Dr. Richard Travis, an evaluator in Illinois, said:

> The legal definition of mental disorder does not equal the *DSM-5* definition of mental disorder, okay? Which is why when the Subcommittee on Paraphilic Disorders for the *DSM-5* . . . oh, they were brilliant in how they worded this in the *DSM*. . . . They said, because the big deal in many courts previous to that was that this particular disorder, especially one they call nonconsenting . . . that was not a disorder that was specified in the *DSM-4*. . . . The *DSM-5* Subcommittee argued a lot about including something called paraphilic coercive disorder, which would've been the same kind of thing. It was not included. . . . So what defense attorneys argued in court is paraphilic coercive disorder or nonconsent was excluded from the *DSM-5*. Not included is not the same thing as excluded. . . . Because the *DSM-5* [is very broad] and it says many dozens of paraphilias have been identified and named, without saying what those dozens are. And it is important for the legal process to be able to diagnose a person with one of those paraphilic disorders. . . . So the *DSM-5* did not want to constrain evaluators who need to diagnose a person with a disorder when there is clearly some kind of disorder.[51]

Though Dr. Travis is referring to the *DSM-5* (not the *DSM-IV* on which First and Frances worked), he gives a completely different impression of what the *DSM* workgroup on paraphilias intended. Where First and Frances insist they *deliberately excluded* any reference to a rape paraphilia and did not support its use in the SVP setting, Travis believes that the reason for the broad wording was precisely to allow evaluators to craft categories usable in court. Many evaluators echoed Travis's sentiments. Dr. Isabel Davis, another Illinois evaluator, said in response to her frequent use of the PNOS category: "The *DSM* says clearly that they've only included about eight of the paraphilias in that section, but that there are hundreds more which they expect will fall under the other specified paraphilic disorder."[52] Similarly, Illinois SVP evaluator Dr. Kim Weitl said of PNOS, "You can ignore it, but that doesn't make the disorder go away. Don't give it a name, but . . . [trails off]."[53] Some expressed bitterness at the APA for making their jobs harder by not including coercive paraphilic disorder in the *DSM-5*, and others suggested it was only a fringe of the discipline that disagreed with the diagnosis, a difficult assertion to support given the prominent psychiatrists who have publicly derided PNOSN. However, PNOSN clearly has considerable support, including among some members of the *DSM-5* paraphilia work-group. Dr. Richard Krueger, a member of that group, said of PNOS, "I think that's a valid sort of diagnostic category. I think the underlying issue is does somebody have a . . . diagnosis which puts them at increased risk for sexual reoffending. . . . I think the civil commitment system is—huge problems with it, obviously . . . but I don't think that's a reason to discard the psychiatric diagnosis. The issue is more societal, basically."[54] Dr. Krueger thus expresses support for the diagnostic category but equivocates somewhat in regard to its use in civil commitment.

Despite a vigorous professional debate and the ultimate exclusion of any sort of coercive paraphilic disorder from the *DSM* (including from the appendix of conditions warranting further research), courts have consistently supported forensic psychology's expert authority to use PNOSN in legal settings. One study of SVP decisions from 2008 to 2011 found that every court that considered the admissibility of a PNOSN diagnosis found it admissible.[55] Often courts even acknowledge the controversy of the PNOSN diagnosis before ruling it admissible, as did the Seventh Circuit in *McGee v. Bartow* (2010).[56] In that case, McGee argued that the explicit consideration and rejection of PNOSN from the *DSM* indicated its invalidity. The court even cited several academic sources backing this assertion before stating: "A frequently cited difficulty in accepting a rape-related paraphilia diagnosis is that the lack of generally accepted standards results in poor diagnostic reliability; that is, different evaluators may be likely to reach different conclusions with respect to the same individual at unacceptably high rates."[57] This is indeed true, as studies show the inter-rate reliability of rape-related paraphilias to be around 0.4, meaning that evaluators agree on that diagnosis for individuals only about 40% of the time.[58] However, the court then acknowledged the other side of the debate suggesting that PNOSN is a valid diagnosis. Notably, the court cited two prominent forensic psychologists to support its ultimate conclusion that PNOSN was admissible: Dr. Dennis Doren (the psychologist often credited with "creating" the PNOSN diagnosis and former Director of the Wisconsin SVP program) and Amy Phenix (a forensic psychologist and oft-called government witness).

In a case just a couple of months later, the Seventh Circuit faced similar issues in *Brown v. Watters* (2010), where Dr. Doren had testified as one of the experts advocating the commitment of the offender under review.[59] Doren's diagnoses in this case included both PNOSN and another controversial diagnosis, antisocial personality disorder.[60] In fact, Doren's testimony evinced many of the concerns voiced by Frances and First regarding the misuse of the PNOSN category, including most notably that Doren's diagnosis seemed to be based largely on behaviors rather than arousal or fantasies. Doren argued that "Mr. Brown's documented sexual arousal during the attacks was . . . indicative of a specific interest in nonconsensual sex."[61] However, by definition a man must be "aroused" in order to commit a penetrative sexual assault, so this observation would seem to apply to any rapist. Doren went on to testify that Brown, in fact, did not exhibit several of Doren's own diagnostic criteria for PNOSN, such as an offense "script," a diversity of victims, and a propensity to offend in circumstances in which he was likely to be caught. Finally, on cross-examination, Doren was asked for a professional organization that endorses his clinical indicators for PNOSN, to which he replied that there "isn't a single one."[62] For his part, Brown called three expert witnesses of his own, two of whom delivered opinions regarding PNOSN. Dr. Lynn Maskel, a forensic psychiatrist, testified that "psychiatrically the disorder [of paraphilia NOS nonconsent] does not exist," and Dr. Stephen Hart, a forensic psychologist, similarly asserted that Dr. Doren had "create[d] [a] fictional mental disorder."[63] The defense then moved for the disqualification of Doren's testimony arguing that it would not meet *Daubert* standards for expert testimony. The court quickly rejected that argument without going into any discussion of the proper evidentiary standards and, in the end, upheld Brown's commitment based on Dr. Doren's testimony, demonstrating considerable deference, not only to the lower court's determinations of expert authority, but also to the expert network supporting PNOSN.

Ultimately, forensic psychology was able to do what psychiatry was not. It accepted a less authoritative role for itself in the diagnosis of sex offenders (i.e., it accepted the fuzzy term of "mental abnormality" while psychiatry rejected it) and worked within the rough legal framework created by the new laws. That is, it effectively rendered the *DSM* a boundary object in order to diffuse jurisdictional struggles and simultaneously advance its own way of thinking. However, by doing so, it gained allies within the legal and penal professions, as well as state and federal government, and thereby extended its chain of allies. Within the broad bounds of "mental abnormality," forensic psychologists were still able to apply their own expert views in making more specific diagnoses, and in some cases, such as that of "paraphilia not otherwise specified, nonconsent," were able to craft diagnostic categories unique to this legal setting. Paraphilia NOS is now commonplace in SVP proceedings and is a prime example of the creation of hybrid knowledge resulting from the "generosity" of the forensic psychological actor-network and the dynamic interplay of law and psychology.

ACTUARIAL ASSESSMENT AND THE EXTENSION OF THE NETWORK

Diagnosis is only one part of the issue that *Hendricks* and *Crane* present for the forensic management of sex offenders. The state must also show that an offender is likely to engage in future acts of sexual violence, and, as with its objection to psychiatric diagnosis for SVPs, the APA similarly opined that "the unreliability of psychiatric predictions of long-term future dangerousness is by now an established fact within the profession."[64] Such insights arose out of the "sexual psychopath" era when one of the primary concerns with the statutes' implementation was the accuracy of dangerousness predictions. Whereas research in the 1970s began to show that subjective clinical prediction was little better than chance (and sometimes worse), forensic psychology offered methods that appeared to be not only more objective but also more accurate. This section details another method by which forensic psychology was able to extend its expert network: the advent of easy-to-use quantitative risk prediction tools.

Actuarial risk assessment technologies have a long history of use in the penal domain, dating back to at least the early twentieth century when the Chicago-school sociologist Ernest Burgess designed a tool for the state of Illinois to predict inmates' likelihoods of success on parole.[65] The use of these tools to determine parole eligibility increased rapidly over the course of the twentieth century, even as the number of states offering parole declined. At the same time, states and parole boards cut the number of items assessed in these tools and focused heavily on prior criminal history. The original Burgess model, for example, contained twenty-one items, but the US Parole Commission eventually trimmed it to only seven, largely for administrative ease.[66] As actuarial thinking gained credence, technologies were developed for use in sentencing, probation/parole, and general violence assessment. However, as Karl Hanson notes, researchers and practitioners noticed that general violence assessment tools did not work well for sex offenders, who often did not resemble more typical violent offenders.[67] Facing this dilemma, in 1997 Hanson developed one of the first actuarial risk assessment designed specifically for sex offenders: the Rapid Risk Assessment for Sexual Offense Recidivism (RRASOR).[68]

The idea behind such tools, whether for general or sexual offenders, is relatively straightforward. They aggregate data on large numbers of offenders and follow them for a specified period of time to ascertain their recidivism rates. Researchers then retrospectively compare those who reoffended with those who did not to determine factors that seem to affect recidivism, and those factors become the basis for actuarial assessment. Offenders to be assessed are then compared to the sample group on the selected factors to predict one's likelihood of recidivism. In the case of the Static-99—created by Hanson and David Thornton and now the most widely used risk assessment tool for sex offenders in the United States—both a relative and absolute risk level is predicted.[69] That is, an individual receives a numerical score ranging from –3 to 12 that places him in a relative position to other similar offenders so that an evaluator may say, for instance, that John Doe received a score of 5 and therefore falls into the group that is 2.7 times more likely to recidivate than the typical offender. The score also comes with a point estimate and confidence interval of that group's predicted recidivism. A score of 5 might predict a 27.3% chance of reoffense over the next five years. I will discuss the development of these instruments in more depth in chapter 7, but this brief sketch should provide a general idea of how these technologies work.

As this brief description might suggest, actuarial tools facilitated the expansion of forensic psychological expertise in a number of ways. First, the tools were designed for easy use by administration. The RRASOR contained only four items that were easily obtainable from an offender's administrative file and, indeed, was originally created explicitly for administrative use by the Canadian penal system for which Hanson worked.[70] Specifically, the RRASOR was meant to identify sex offenders' risk in order to match them to the proper rehabilitative program. The RRASOR was soon expanded into the Static-99, which incorporated the four items from the RRASOR and added another six. But like the RRASOR, the ten Static-99 items were ascertainable mostly from an offender's administrative record, making the tool easily usable by administrative workers, parole/probation officers, and social workers with minimal training. Thus, these technologies crystallized forensic psychological expertise regarding risk assessment and made it transportable across domains.

Second, the advent of actuarial risk prediction for sex offenders granted increased scientific legitimacy to forensic psychology. All of my interviewees cited the development of actuarial risk prediction as the most significant advance in the field. As former ATSA president Dr. Michael Miner commented, "The best research that has happened in this field since I've been in it has been around the area of assessment, the development of these actuarial assessment tools."[71] Similarly, Dr. Krueger believed that "Karl [Hanson] has really revolutionized the whole notion [of actuarial assessment]."[72] It is hard to argue with these beliefs. Empirical studies consistently show that actuarial risk prediction is significantly better than clinical prediction.[73] However, the most positive assessments still place the predictive power of these technologies at around 70%. This led many interviewees who viewed actuarial assessment as a great accomplishment to simultaneously acknowledge its limitations, particularly in regard to civil commitment, as Dr. Miner did:

> Karl Hanson and all of his students . . . have done a really great job of this kind of stuff, but it has major limitations, most of which I feel are glossed over and not considered. I mean . . . I am very glad that whenever a major decision in my life was done based on a test that had an [area under the

curve] of .70, number one, I could study for that test, and number two, there were other factors taken into consideration. . . . I think our practice, whether we're talking assessment or treatment, is ahead of our knowledge base.[74]

Despite many opinions that actuarial assessments are still not accurate enough to make such significant life decisions, courts have readily taken them up as scientifically sound, and, in a show of "generosity," the inventors of these instruments mostly support this use. Hanson opined that he is "an advocate for . . . empirical risk assessment," but cautioned, like Dr. Miner, that it should only be "one piece of information" in SVP considerations.[75] Despite these caveats from researchers, practitioners and courts generally accept actuarial assessments without much questioning.

Over 90% of jurisdictions now allow actuarial risk assessment tools in SVP proceedings.[76] In Illinois, state prosecutors have successfully pursued *Frye* hearings in every county in order to ensure the admissibility of such technologies.[77] Several state supreme courts have likewise considered the admissibility of actuarial risk prediction and found it acceptable.[78] The Illinois Supreme Court case *People v. Simons* (2004) is illustrative.[79] In a bench trial, Simons was found to be a sexually violent person subject to civil commitment based on the testimony of two psychologists who both used actuarial tools—including the Static-99—to conclude that Simons was "substantially probable" (the legally mandated standard in Illinois) to commit future acts of sexual violence. Simons appealed on the grounds that the psychological testimony based on the actuarial prediction of his sexual risk should not be admitted because the actuarial technologies were not first subjected to a *Frye* hearing. The appeals court agreed. The Illinois Supreme Court, however, found that actuarial risk assessment (ARA) was not a new or novel technology, that at least nineteen other states relied on some form of actuarial prediction to form opinions of sex offenders' recidivism risk, and that it enjoyed wide acceptance in the professional literature. In addition to extensively citing other courts to have considered the issue (all of which found ARA admissible), the Illinois court also cited many prominent forensic psychologists, including Hanson and Thornton, the creators of the Static-99. Quoting an article by two well-known forensic psychology scholars, the Illinois decision stated:

The principle of actuarial superiority is not novel. It has been tested extensively, and has broad acceptance in the literature, both in general, and in the specific literature concerning sexual offending. Similarly, the science underlying ARA is not new. Statistical decision theory and its application to human judgment have been around for fifty years. The same methodology has been applied in numerous, diverse contexts, including weather forecasting, law school admissions, disability determinations, predicting the quality of the vintage for red Bordeaux wines, and predicting the quality of sound in opera houses.[80]

The decision goes on to cite another forensic psychologist who refers to ARA as a "quantum leap forward" in the "science of violence risk analysis."[81] Taken together, the Illinois court cited no fewer than ten forensic psychologists in its defense of ARA and ultimately found that the technology satisfied the *Frye* standard.

Like cases involving diagnosis and "mental abnormality," then, courts have also generally come down on the side of actuarial risk assessment. Unlike decisions about diagnostic issues, however, courts do not routinely consider the controversies or shortcomings of ARA. The quantitative nature of these risk technologies likely lends them an aura of objectivity that puts judges more at ease in comparison to the more subjective nature of diagnosing mental illness. However, as I will discuss in more depth in chapter 7, processes of quantification, like those involved in the design of ARA instruments, always involve political decisions that are typically erased in the final product.

In sum, as this section has shown, the epistemic logic found in the domain of sex offender law was created through the iterative interactions of legal-institutional structures and the expert network of forensic psychology. The institutional context of the 1970s and 1980s created an opening for forensic psychology to offer a better way of solving the problem of the penal management of sex offenders. Discontent among legal actors, civil rights advocates, and even the "psych" professions with psychiatry's questionable track record of handling sex offenders allowed forensic psychologists to step in. Whereas psychiatrists often relied on psychoanalytic techniques that seemed subjective, forensic psychologists employed diagnostic criteria from the revamped *DSM-III* that lent more transparency to their diagnoses. Forensic psychologists' ability to point to specific "objective" criteria for determining sexual deviance, coupled with their willingness to allow interpretative flexibility in the term "mental abnormality," made the *DSM* a powerful boundary object capable of bridging the law-science divide. Similarly, confronted with psychiatry's inability to accurately predict future sexual violence, forensic psychologists developed quantitative actuarial technologies that were both technically superior to clinical judgment in terms of accuracy and offer clearly delineated steps that anyone could seemingly follow.[82] These instruments had the added bonus of working mostly from administrative records, which meant they were usable not only by psychological professionals, but also by less-skilled treatment providers and even parole and probation officers. While these technologies ceded some authority from psychology, they strengthened its actor-network and simultaneously brought added legitimacy to state decision-making regarding sex offenders.

The next chapter examines a rather different way by which epistemic actors helped stem a legal legitimacy crisis and how a network of lawyers, activists, and academics capitalized on legal developments in asylum law to advance their preferred way of knowing sexuality in the newly created domain of sexual orientation–based asylum.

4: INSURGENT EXPERTISE AND THE HYBRID NETWORK OF LGBTQ ASYLUM

Unlike the domain of sex offender law, there was no preexisting or entrenched form of expertise on LGBTQ asylum to displace. Rather, LGBTQ asylum advocates largely had to forge their own path. The challenge for would-be asylum experts was not displacing a preexisting knowledge way but rather *creating* an entirely new form of expertise that simply did not exist before the political, institutional, and legal developments of the late 1980s and early 1990s. Documentation of country conditions for LGBTQ people, a requirement for proving persecution in asylum claims, did not exist in any consistent or consolidated form at the time. Similarly, awareness and knowledge of global sexual expressions and how to judge sexual identity narratives was lacking among government and immigration officials. "Common sense" was the accepted logic in 1990. Moreover, few immigration lawyers even knew about the possibility of someone claiming asylum based on their sexual orientation, which necessitated a consciousness-raising strategy, not just for adjudicators, but also for practitioners. Yet while the institutional setting is quite different in asylum compared to that in sex offender law, the broad strategy of constructing expertise is rather similar. Following a legal-institutional reconfiguration, epistemic entrepreneurs mobilized to create a network of actors oriented around a socially informed, global perspective on sexuality and sexual identity. Rather than erecting rigid jurisdictional boundaries, these early actors used a strategy of generosity to enroll as many allies as possible, both inside and outside the official immigration authority structure. Though particular individuals are central to the expert network, their expert authority stems less from any particular credentials and more from the chains of allies subscribing to their way of knowing.

The first significant institutional opening came in 1985 when Fidel Toboso-Alfonso, a gay Cuban man, appeared before an immigration judge in Houston, Texas, for deportation proceedings and sought asylum based on his sexual orientation. Toboso-Alfonso claimed fear of returning to Cuba because he had been persecuted for being gay. He alleged that he was forced to register with the government as a homosexual, submit to periodic medical examinations and detentions, and on one occasion was sent to a forced labor camp for sixty days because of his sexuality. Key to Toboso-Alfonso's case was his assertion that these punishments were due to his *status* as a homosexual, not because of any particular *conduct*. This was an important distinction in 1985, for many US jurisdictions still outlawed sodomy (and the US Supreme Court would uphold those sodomy statutes the following year). Ironically, Toboso-Alfonso's lawyer drew on laws like these that specifically targeted homosexuals in the United States as evidence that homosexuals constituted a recognized "particular social group" (PSG). Ultimately, the immigration judge determined that homosexual identity could serve as the basis for a PSG and deemed Toboso-Alfonso's story credible and plausible, but because of a drug possession charge found him ineligible for asylum. The judge did, however, grant Toboso-Alfonso withholding of removal, a ruling that was subsequently appealed by the Immigration and Naturalization Service (INS). Indeed, the INS was compelled to appeal the decision because at that time the 1952 McCarran-Walter Act designating homosexuals as "psychopathic personalities" unsuitable for entry into the country remained in effect. It was not until immigration reform in 1990 that this restriction would be repealed.

In its appeal to the Board of Immigration Appeals (BIA), the INS argued that "socially deviated behavior, i.e. homosexual activity, is not a basis for finding a social group within the contemplation of the Act" and that such a conclusion "would be tantamount to awarding discretionary relief to those involved in behavior that is not only socially deviant in nature, but in violation of the laws or regulations of the country as well."[1] The BIA rejected this reasoning and denied the appeal, finding instead that Toboso-Alfonso was persecuted because of his "status of being a homosexual." This 1990 BIA decision was the first to declare that "homosexuals" could constitute a PSG and thus be eligible for asylum because of their sexual orientation.

In 1993 an immigration judge directly granted asylum to Marcelo Tenorio, a gay man from Brazil, helping to solidify this area of law. Then in 1994, Attorney General Janet Reno declared *Toboso-Alfonso* precedent, meaning gay people would no longer have to prove on a case-by-case basis that they constituted a PSG in their home countries. These developments, along with the repeal in 1990 of the ban on homosexuals entering the country, set the legal and institutional stage for LGBTQ asylum advocates to begin agitating for further change.

However, it is also important to consider the political context for developments in asylum law. Unlike sex offender law, because immigration courts are part of the executive branch, changes in asylum policy can be affected by presidential administrations. Notably, for instance, it was under Bill Clinton that *Toboso-Alfonso* was declared precedent, and as will be discussed below, it was under Barack Obama that Immigration Equality, the largest LGBTQ immigrant rights organization in the United States, was able to begin training asylum officers. On the opposing side, during George W. Bush's administration, Attorney General John Ashcroft pursued what is widely viewed as a purge of liberal judges from the BIA. Thus, the executive branch plays a more important role in the legal landscape of asylum than of sex offender law. But the executive branch is not the sole determining force. Toboso-Alfonso's case was granted under Reagan and affirmed by the BIA under George H. W. Bush. Moreover, asylum policy is not solely determined by the executive branch. While some policies can be changed, and immigration judges can be dismissed to make room for those more ideologically similar to the current administration, much of the story is about precedential decisions and establishing institutionalized epistemic practices that cannot be easily changed with the whims of a particular administration. While Trump could appoint judges who would be less friendly to LGBTQ asylum claims, he could not undo the documented paper trail produced by the State Department on LGBTQ rights or the routine practice of using anthropologists and human rights experts as witnesses in asylum hearings. Nor could he reverse BIA or circuit court precedent.

Given these political variables, it is perhaps not surprising that the early 1990s (mostly after Clinton's election) witnessed the proliferation of organizations focused on queer immigration issues, including groups like the Lesbian and Gay Immigration Rights Task Force (which would become Immigration Equality), the International Gay and Lesbian Human Rights Commission (IGLHRC), and the Midwest Human Rights Partnership for Sexual Orientation (MHRPSO, which would become Midwest Immigrant Rights Advocates, or MIRA). These groups, among others, engaged in an extensive project of building networks of lawyers, academics, human rights workers, and other advocates with the explicit goal of influencing immigration policies for LGBTQ people. In regard to asylum, this network had three primary goals: (1) raise awareness of LGBTQ asylum in general, including educating lawyers and would-be asylum seekers; (2) build a knowledge base of human rights information regarding sexual minorities; and (3) improve the problematic processing of LGBTQ asylum applications. These groups have been extremely successful in their endeavors, in part by first creating a small-scale legitimacy crisis around the adjudication of LGBTQ claims that their hybrid expertise network was poised to resolve. The next two sections will consider how they have done so.

BUILDING HUMAN RIGHTS EXPERTISE

A statutory requirement for any successful asylum claim is proof of persecution. One part of this is a claimant's subjective fear, which is demonstrated through a petitioner's credible testimony and is discussed in the next chapter. The other requisite entails providing "objective" evidence of dangerous conditions for the claimant's PSG in the country in question. The problem for LGBTQ asylum seekers in the 1990s—and even into the 2000s—was that few sources of "objective" country conditions evidence covered LGBTQ issues. This included the US State Department Country Reports on Human Rights Practices (the Reports), which immigration courts generally prefer to use as an indicator of country conditions around the world. These reports almost invariably come into evidence in any asylum hearing, and case law allows these reports to be given significant weight. For instance, *Reyes-Sanchez v. U.S. Attorney General* (2004) dictates that judges may rely "heavily" on State Department Reports.[2] The Fifth Circuit in *Rojas v. INS* (1991) characterizes the Reports as "relatively impeccable sources" and states that they are "the most appropriate and perhaps the best resource the [BIA] could look to in order to obtain information on political situations in foreign countries."[3] The Ninth Circuit has said in reference to State Department Reports that "it is well-accepted that country conditions alone can play a decisive role in granting relief."[4] The First Circuit has gone so far as to say that "in certain circumstances" adjudicators may "give the contents of such reports appreciable—even determinative—weight."[5]

Given the weight State Department Reports carry, when they are silent on LGBTQ issues, several possible challenges arise. One possibility is an adjudicator assuming that no mention of sexual or gender minorities in the report means there are no human rights abuses of such groups. For instance, a judge denied a gay HIV-positive Venezuelan man's asylum claim based in part on the fact that "the country report made no mention of human rights violations against homosexuals or individuals with HIV or AIDS."[6] In this case, the judge privileged the silence in the country report over the testimony of the director of AID for AIDS, an organization that worked closely with the gay and HIV-positive community in Venezuela, who testified that the government of the country condones the denial of treatment of gay men with HIV by both public and private healthcare providers and refuses to prosecute employers who require HIV testing (and a negative result) as a condition of employment.

A second closely related issue arises when country reports include some information on LGBTQ issues but not enough to establish persecution. This is especially problematic for claimants who are detained and/or without legal representation and who may not have the resources to ascertain other sources of information on country conditions. As Neil Grungras, Director of Organization for Refuge, Asylum and Migration (ORAM), said, "Most country reports, if it does have LGBT, it usually has a very, very small section, and it is very inadequate.... It usually lumps all the Ls, the Gs, the Bs, the Ts, the Is together, and it's not very illuminating if you're trying to find out what's really happening in that country."[7] Nielan Barnes, a sociologist who serves as an expert witness in asylum claims, further expounded on this issue:

> The government attorneys often will submit nothing to support their argument that country conditions are fine and if they do . . . they provide copies of tourist magazine advertisements and articles about how great Mexico, South America is if you want to come visit. Or they'll provide some of the US State Department Reports, which are very problematic in that they have a lot of contradictory information, and often they will leave out major human rights violations that have occurred in those years. I've done a comparative analysis looking at all the US State Department Reports from 1999 to present and comparing what they say is happening in Mexico around gay rights and transgender human rights to what's really happening looking at various data points trying to triangulate the hell out of it to say, okay, well these murders actually occurred in these few years, and here's the US State Department Report saying nothing about that.[8]

A veteran immigration judge echoed this sentiment, saying that "a lot of the country conditions reports are a little bit vague," before continuing on to assert:

> There are things within those State Department Reports that are very helpful to judges in making decisions. But they are also limited in a sense that they say, so there have been no reports of political disappearances, however . . . this group reports X or that group reports Y, and then if you go back to those groups and see what are they actually reporting—wait a minute, there's a big problem there.[9]

Therefore, if the State Department Reports are privileged above other evidence or serve as the only form of evidence in a claim, LGBTQ petitioners may not be able to provide sufficient objective evidence to meet the legal requirement of proving persecutory conditions.

Third, country reports may present only a bird's-eye view that does not well reflect conditions on the ground. Attorney Peter Perkowski commented on this issue saying, "Just because you can get married in Mexico

City doesn't mean you don't any longer have roving hordes of gangs and/or police officers and governmental agents still harassing, beating, torturing, and murdering LGBT people."[10] But government lawyers will often use this argument against Mexican and many South American asylum seekers. Former BIA and immigration court judge Paul Schmidt likewise asserted that it can be difficult to counteract a State Department Report claiming that conditions are improving if the claimant doesn't have an expert witness: "You usually need an expert who can comment, 'Yeah, I've read the State Department Report. Yes, there are efforts being made, but here's why those haven't really been sufficient to date. They're more aspirational than real. I'm going to give you ten examples of recent incidents where people were harmed and the police were unable to assist them, or several of them [where] the police actually participated.'"[11] Experienced immigration lawyers now often feel the need to recruit experts anytime they have cases from such countries. Midwest Immigrant Rights Advocates (MIRA), for instance, almost always tries to have an expert who can provide more detailed testimony about country conditions when they have Mexican claimants. Indeed, this view among advocates is supported by judicial decisions, such as that of Alejandro Gutierrez, a gay claimant from Mexico who was denied relief in part because "the State Department reports state that conditions are improving for gay and lesbian persons."[12]

To combat these issues, asylum advocates began building a network of lawyers, activists, and academics who shared information on country conditions and legal strategies. One of the earliest and most important organizations to address human rights violations of LGBTQ people was the International Gay and Lesbian Human Rights Commission (IGLHRC, now OutRight Action International), founded by Julie Dorf in 1990 in San Francisco. Fresh out of college and inspired by her time living and studying abroad in the Soviet Union, where she encountered people who had been imprisoned for being gay, Dorf decided to create an organization dedicated to fighting for LGBTQ rights internationally. One major project for her organization involved aggregating country condition information regarding LGBTQ human rights. As she explains, she drew on the activist atmosphere around HIV/AIDS in San Francisco at the time to bring together like-minded people:

> Being based in San Francisco in that period of a lot of activism primarily because of the AIDS epidemic . . . it was very easy to find other people like myself who had a deep connection and knowledge of communities in other parts of the world. And so through just personal networking and activism we pulled together a whole bunch of people like myself who had their own personal files documenting persecution in other countries, pri-

marily Eastern Europe and Latin America. Those were the first regions of the world . . . where we had kind of depth of knowledge and a lot of immigrants . . . who lived in San Francisco or had come to San Francisco. So very, very early on we realized that documentation of our persecution was the name of the game in the human rights space.[13]

In these early days of creating a knowledge base, volunteers would gather every Monday night to scan newspapers and clip articles to begin building case files on various countries. These volunteers—and eventually a paid staff—would also call human rights workers in nations around the globe to get further information. IGLHRC then provided these files to lawyers who were willing to take on LGBTQ asylum claims, as Dorf further explains:

> Primarily what we did as a service was in the small network of attorneys who were taking cases like this primarily . . . in New York and L.A. . . . Attorneys would know to get in touch with us . . . and we would basically copy our country files and send them these packets of documentation to attorneys all over the US and Canada and elsewhere in the world, you know, to help them in their claims. And sometimes we would provide expert testimony or find them the right expert testimony, that kind of stuff.[14]

Over the years, IGLHRC aggregated information on many countries and began digitizing their documentation to provide easier access to lawyers. Shortly after Dorf departed from IGLHRC in 2000, the asylum project was wound down, and the documenting and dissemination project moved to MIRA, where it remains today.

Other organizations soon followed IGLHRC into the asylum arena. The Lesbian and Gay Immigration Rights Task Force (LGIRTF) was founded by lawyers in Los Angeles in 1994 and quickly formed working groups in other major cities. LGIRTF would eventually become Immigration Equality, the largest legal advocacy organization dedicated to queer immigration issues. Following IGLHRC's lead on documenting country conditions, Heather McClure, an anthropologist, formed the Midwest Human Rights Partnership for Sexual Orientation in Chicago in 1996, which eventually became part of the National Immigrant Justice Center under the auspices of the Heartland Alliance. McClure conducted her dissertation research in Guatemala and with Guatemalan asylum seekers in the United States and became one of the first experts to write an affidavit that she made available to any lawyers or experts seeking a model for how to prepare such a document for immigration hearings. These LGBTQ-focused groups further allied with NGOs such as Amnesty International and Human Rights Watch to better document human rights violations against LGBTQ people around the globe and to advocate domestically for improvements in the processing of LGBTQ asylum claims.

With this alliance between activists, lawyers, and social scientists, this network began lobbying the State Department to include information on LGBTQ people in its annual country reports. As McClure explains:

> One of the things that we did after I got back from Guatemala was to [get] in touch with everybody who I knew had country condition information. And believe me, it was like an afternoon of calls; there were so few people. . . . And so I got in touch with as many people as I could and we formed a very informal group where we pooled our documentation, and I called the State Department and got in touch with the two people who really are the editors of the State Department's Human Rights Reports, and I asked them to take a look at our documentation. And they didn't promise anything, but it was such a clear gap, you know? And so I forwarded them all of our documentation. IGLHRC forwarded them all of their documentation. And we just started this campaign to try to convince the authors and editors of those Human Rights Reports to be more inclusive.[15]

The State Department was responsive and by the mid-1990s slowly began to incorporate LGBTQ information into the Reports. However, many advocates still view the information included in these Reports as inadequate and sometimes even misleading, and several groups continue to push for further improvements.

Nevertheless, this process of network creation resulted in change in the area of asylum policy and established a network of expertise on LGBTQ asylum issues. Activists such as Julie Dorf of IGLHRC became recognized experts in the field of LGBTQ asylum not necessarily because of her credentials (she holds only a bachelor's degree), but because of the way she fashioned herself into a "lay expert" at the center of what became a large and influential network. Indeed, Dorf, through her connections with former congressman Barney Frank, was instrumental in getting Janet Reno to issue the directive to the INS to recognize gays and lesbians as a "particular social group" under asylum policy in 1994.[16] This is not to say that asylum advocates shunned credentialed expertise. McClure held a PhD from a prestigious university, as did many of the academic social scientists who became part of the advocacy network. But lawyers and human rights workers not trained in social science research also became well-versed lay experts in issues of sexuality and sexual cultures around the globe. This becomes even clearer when we look to two of the other major goals of the early movement: education and consciousness-raising.

EXPERT EDUCATORS

A major issue with processing LGBTQ asylum claims in the 1990s involved adjudicators' interpretations of sexuality. Most immigration officials lacked a sophisticated understanding of sexuality and sexual identity, and when it came to determining whether an asylum claimant had sufficiently proven his or her sexuality, many adjudicators simply fell back onto "commonsense" judgments.[17] Because this was a new area of law in the early 1990s, many adjudicators simply did not understand how to process sexuality claims, what questions to ask, or what would count as persecution on account of one's sexuality. Furthermore, many immigration lawyers knew very little about this area of law if they knew anything at all. The expert network that formed around asylum in the early 1990s formulated strategies to combat these obstacles and, eventually, to institutionalize its epistemic authority.

One strategy was to conduct presentations and trainings with immigration officials, including asylum officers and immigration judges. These trainings began through local lobbying, particularly in San Francisco, where the asylum office was receptive early on to advocates' efforts. Heather McClure, through her joint project with Michael Heflin at Amnesty International, responded to a request from that office for training on human rights conditions for LGBTQ and HIV-positive people in Mexico and Central America. Julie Dorf and Lavi Soloway likewise responded to the San Francisco asylum office's openness and conducted trainings there. MIRA has also started conducting trainings for asylum officers in Chicago. After moving to New York, Immigration Equality began conducting trainings with asylum officers and immigration judges there. This eventually became a formalized arrangement when the DHS Office for Civil Rights and Civil Liberties held a "listening session" on LGBT issues, where Immigration Equality representatives suggested that asylum officers needed training on LGBT issues. DHS agreed, and in 2010 Victoria Neilson, then Legal Director of Immigration Equality, began training asylum office supervisors. Beginning in 2011, an LGBTI segment taught by Immigration Equality was added to the six-week training course that all new asylum and refugee officers must complete. These trainings provide one setting for asylum advocates to expand their actor-network through teaching not only content but also their preferred technique for evaluating LGBTQ asylum claims.

Additionally, this training is crystallized in the form of a manual jointly produced by Immigration Equality and the US Citizenship and Immigration Services (USCIS). As a technology that bridges the divide between the social scientifically informed asylum advocates and asylum adjudicators, the Immigration Equality–USCIS training manual is a key boundary object. For instance, the reading resources included in the module comprise both legal decisions and social scientifically informed law review articles on LGBTQ asylum issues. The manual also guides readers to other key players in the asylum advocacy network, such as IGLHRC. It further details information on what kinds of questions are appropriate to ask in order to determine a claimant's sexuality, explains what kinds of persecution sexual and gender minorities often face that are unique to those groups, and even includes explicitly constructionist definitions of gender and gender identity. In the "LGBTI Terminology" glossary, gender is defined as "the social construction of what society values as the roles and identities of being male or female; assigned at birth to every person; does not always align with gender identity," and gender identity is defined as "a person's inner sense of being male or female, both, or neither, resulting from a combination of genetic and environmental influences."[18] The manual similarly implies that sexuality is at least partially socially constructed by addressing the ways that sexual expressions, behaviors, and identities vary from culture to culture. For example, it states that "the way that applicants express themselves may be different from what an interviewer would expect from an LGBTI person in the United States."[19] The manual also invokes the APA's statement against attempts to change people's sexual orientation. In these rather subtle ways, asylum advocates impart LGBTQ-inclusive techniques and social scientifically informed knowledge about gender and sexuality in ways that can be easily incorporated into asylum adjudicators' usual routines.

Speaking about one of the early trainings he conducted with asylum officers, Lavi Soloway commented:

> I remember one officer putting up her hand and asking me—and this is worth mentioning because there were many times in my career in courtrooms and asylum offices, particularly courtrooms—she put up her hand and asked us, "If a male officer raped an individual who is now an asylum applicant and the asylum applicant claims or asserts that that violent act against him was because he was gay, how do we understand that because wouldn't that sexual act by the police officer mean that police officer was gay?"[20]

Sexual assaults like this are common in LGBTQ asylum claims, but without understanding the cultural context in which the penetrating man is not viewed as gay, an adjudicator could easily find no nexus between the claimant's persecution and sexuality. Advocates, however, have established an epistemic scaffolding in this area of law that implores adjudicators to account for cultural context and the cultural variability of sexuality.

In a similar vein, advocates have also worked to create ways of knowing sexuality that do not depend on explicit discussions of sex acts or stereotypes. Explaining the progress made in this area, Aaron Morris said:

> One of our pro bono attorneys had a debrief with me after an asylum interview, and one officer did ask something pretty crazy, which was, "Are you a top or a bottom?" with the expectation that the person would know what that was and have an answer. And before she had a chance to object, the client just said, "Oh, I'm a bottom," and it wasn't that big of a deal to him. But, like, that's a [really] inappropriate question. None of that's really happened . . . since [Victoria Neilson] trained all the asylum officers. So they're pretty sensitive to LGBT issues and what is appropriate and is not appropriate.[21]

Indeed, guidance on the appropriate questions to ask has been institutionalized in the training manual created by USCIS and Immigration Equality: "The applicant's specific sexual practices are not relevant to the claim for asylum or refugee status. Therefore, asking questions about 'what he or she does in bed' is never appropriate."[22] This background work by advocates has established the basis for narrative accounts of sexual identity as the primary way of knowing sexuality in asylum policy, as I will discuss further in the next chapter.

Another strategy for educating adjudicators was simply to make LGBTQ asylum claims and use them as opportunities to teach asylum officers and immigration judges about these issues firsthand. Soloway explains:

> Part of the training happens when attorneys are doing very good work and bringing very strong cases. And giving officers a chance in their actual role as adjudicators to learn all of this, to see it for themselves and to experience it as somebody asking probing questions and follow-up questions. That's really the most important way to teach the officers about the context, the breadth, the nuance of these cases.[23]

Heather McClure similarly described how she used asylum claims to advance a more constructionist view of sexual identity that didn't posit identity as something one is born with and knows immediately but rather as something that develops over time and is culturally specific:

> So one of the things that I was struck by is that there are these unexamined assumptions that gay and lesbian people have been knowingly gay and lesbian their entire lives. And that comes with a very privileged perspective. . . . [O]ur public discourse in this country is now assuming that gay and

lesbian people are *here*. . . . But that notion in the majority of the world was completely foreign and completely odd. . . . [W]e wound up arguing [that] based on the realities of these men's lives that a sexual identity—the self-identification of being gay or lesbian—was so impossible to imagine that there wasn't language for it. There was no social space to explore it, to say nothing of personal space to explore it. So it just was beyond the realm of what was possible in the countries that most of these men [were from]. . . . And we just argued, well, *desire is different from identity*. And, you know, these gay men have loved men from time immemorial in their lives, but they didn't necessarily have the language or the support to claim that desire and transform it into an identity [emphasis added].[24]

As these quotes illustrate, asylum advocates became very well-versed in sociological and anthropological views of sexuality and sexual identity and brought those ideas into court with them, not only to educate adjudicators but also because it was sometimes necessary to be armed with such knowledge to win claims.

When lawyers aren't doing the educating themselves, however, they often turn to experts to provide written affidavits and testimony, and use these as opportunities to educate, as well. As Shannon Minter, Legal Director of the National Center for Lesbian Rights (NCLR), explained, sometimes experts can be used to disabuse adjudicators of misleading stereotypes:

Sometimes issues come up, like this used to come up a lot with—and it still does—with gay men and with lesbians. . . . How do you prove you're gay? . . . That can be a problem if the officer has certain preconceptions of what a gay person looks like or acts like or what kind of history they have, and the person doesn't correspond to some stereotype or template that the person has. So it could be helpful to have an expert there to be, like, "Hey, there's different kinds of gay people" or "There's different kinds of transgender people, and a lot of people have a similar history to this person, and just because a person has this particular history doesn't mean that they're not gay or not transgender."[25]

Experts may also provide added cultural context around gender and/or sexuality in order for an adjudicator to understand why a claimant may face a threat. Suyapa Portillo, an assistant professor of Latino/a and Chicano/a studies who serves as an expert witness in asylum claims, discussed a case where she had to explain Honduran gender norms to the court:

I had a woman—a butch woman now who in Honduras was like a feminine model but has transitioned into sort of a gender-nonconforming butch. So oftentimes I have to explain what that means if she were to return to this part of Honduras where she was a reigning queen model looking like a man. . . . Femininity and being thin and ultra-feminine is considered really important in Honduras and a sign of being a woman . . . what it would mean for her to go back to that hometown, and not only would she experience discrimination from family members and friends but then also from society in general. Newspapers would just really rip her apart.[26]

Thus, while lawyers representing asylum seekers often fashion themselves into "lay experts" on topics of gender and sexuality, courts sometimes want the added authority of a credentialed expert declaration.

Sometimes lawyers will draw on this type of social science expertise without calling an expert witness. Attorney Peter Perkowski explained that he will often use academic articles when he doesn't have access to an expert:

I'm not going to say it's easy, but you can establish this whole macho culture through social science research, for example, without needing to have an expert. It's not as neatly encapsulated as in an expert report but there are publications where you can point to that describe the macho culture and its effect on attitudes and things of that nature.[27]

As the experts I interviewed discussed, though, they do not often directly cite much social science research in their affidavits for asylum claims. They may explain social science concepts, as Portillo did above regarding gender, but most often when drafting statements for courts, they primarily cite human rights reports and other sources in that vein.

Nevertheless, social science research does sometimes find its way into asylum proceedings and can make a substantial impact. Perhaps the most significant example is the precedent-setting *Hernandez-Montiel* (2000) case.[28] In its decision, the Ninth Circuit drew on a bevy of social science research in explaining its determination to grant asylum to a "gay man with a female sexual identity." Most of the court's use of social science scholarship appears in the section where it considers sexual identity as the basis for a "particular social group" under asylum law. Though this broad question had already been decided in *Toboso-Alfonso* and a handful of other cases throughout the 1990s, the Ninth Circuit saw fit to lay out its reasoning in some detail, presumably because "gay men with female sexual identities" was a new formulation of the broader category of "homosexuals" named in *Toboso-Alfonso*. It drew heavily on social science and legal scholarship with a sociological slant to support this move. For instance, in asserting that "sexual orientation is set in place at an early age,"[29] the court cited legal scholar Suzanne Goldberg's article "Give Me Liberty or Give Me Death:

Political Asylum and the Global Persecution of Lesbians and Gay Men," in which she draws on sexuality studies scholarship to explain what sexual orientation is and, in particular, that it is more than simply a behavior that one can easily change. The court proceeded to invoke the authority of both the American Psychological Association and the American Psychiatric Association to support this point. The decision also deployed early sexology researcher Alfred Kinsey (albeit somewhat erroneously), anthropologist Gilbert Herdt, and other constructivist legal scholars to assert that "sexual identity is inherent to one's very identity as a person" and, importantly for this case, that sexual identity may manifest itself outwardly in dress or appearance.[30] Where the BIA had deemed Hernandez-Montiel's PSG as "homosexual males who dress as females," and thus suggested that he could simply stop dressing as a woman so as to not be identified as gay, the Ninth Circuit repositioned his outward appearance as part of his sexual identity and therefore something he should not be compelled to change.[31] Finally, the court buttressed its decision with the expert testimony of Latin American studies professor Thomas Davies.

Admittedly, *Hernandez-Montiel* is atypical in its extensive use of social science. Asylum decisions are more likely to cite human rights reports, and when they do reference social science, it is generally through expert witnesses. Notably, however, *Hernandez-Montiel* is frequently cited in asylum decisions as the basis for recognizing sexual minorities as a PSG. Indeed, it has been cited at least 134 times. So while social science research is not often directly cited, the very framework for recognizing sexual minorities as eligible for asylum came about in part due to the judicious deployment of social science. Moreover, as I have shown, immigration lawyers who routinely represent LGBTQ asylum seekers have cultivated a sophisticated understanding of gender and sexuality that they routinely present in courts and asylum offices. As sociologist Nielan Barnes, who frequently serves as an expert witness, said:

> Typically, the public defenders or public law centers that I'm working with and the pro bono lawyers, they're very sophisticated. Most of them are extremely—they get it. Either they already know what I've just talked about in terms of identity development and the process and the context, or they understand it very quickly if it's a new case for them.[32]

Thus, even when it is not in the form of academic articles and books, social science still finds its way into asylum proceedings. By translating social science concepts into legally cognizable arguments, asylum advocates transform these very concepts into boundary objects transposable across both legal and social scientific domains.

Raising (Legal) Consciousness

Early in the development of this area of asylum law, however, advocates faced the challenge of spreading this type of knowledge—or, indeed, the knowledge that sexual minorities were even eligible for asylum—to other immigration lawyers. In response, several advocacy groups began holding workshops and clinics to teach lawyers the basics of LGBTQ asylum law. Beginning in the early 1990s, IGLHRC held clinics for lawyers the first Saturday of every month. Immigration Equality and MIRA soon followed suit, and these clinics continue today. Organizations such as Immigration Equality, MIRA, and NCLR also maintain networks of pro bono attorneys that they work with on an ongoing basis and to whom they frequently refer clients. But perhaps the single most important action taken to spread knowledge about the nuts and bolts of the asylum process for queer people was the creation of a manual entitled *Preparing Sexual Orientation-Based Asylum Claims: A Handbook for Advocates and Asylum Seekers*. Heather McClure, Lavi Soloway, and Christopher Nugent created the first edition of this manual in 1997 and made it freely available to anyone interested in learning about sexual orientation-based asylum. They were particularly interested in distributing it to lawyers, but they consciously wrote it in accessible language so that asylum seekers themselves could understand the process, as most asylum seekers do not have legal representation. The manual contains information on topics ranging from the basics of immigration law to details of how to complete an I-589 (the asylum application) and what kinds of evidence claimants should prepare. The handbook is now in its third edition and continues to be freely available on Immigration Equality's website.

Though it is not unified into a single discipline as is forensic psychology in the case of sex offender law, the hybrid expert network created by asylum advocates has been extremely successful in drawing on sociological and anthropological knowledge in combination with sophisticated lay expertise of gender and sexuality to shape the way asylum adjudicators understand sexuality. In fact, these experts have arguably been *more* influential in their efforts than has forensic psychology. To be sure, forensic psychologists command considerable authority in the management of sex offenders and have carved out significant professional discretion in diagnosis and risk assessment, and oftentimes their opinions in SVP hearings are determinative. Asylum experts, by contrast, more often wield less authority in the actual court setting. But they have, to a significant extent, contoured the epistemic background for knowing sexuality in asylum claims. From *Toboso-Alfonso* to *Hernandez-Montiel*, asylum advocates used legal decisions not only to win victories for queer claimants, but also to educate adjudicators about human rights and sexual identity issues and set standards for how courts should determine PSG status, persecution, and beyond. These efforts have led to a decline in the use of stereotypes to determine claimants' sexualities and the consistent striking down by appellate courts of such decisions when they do occur.[33] Beyond precedent-setting case law, the expert network of asylum advocates has institutionalized its epistemic authority in USCIS training of asylum officers and the inclusion of LGBTQ human rights issues in the State Department Country Reports on Human Rights Reports. Furthermore, organizations such as the NCLR and Immigration Equality now have rather easy and consistent access to the federal agencies that oversee the asylum process as a way of voicing concerns directly to immigration officials. Some early advocates now have positions whose sole duties involve liaising with the government. Julie Dorf, for instance, went on to co-found the Council for Global Equality, through which she works with the State Department and other governmental agencies on inclusive US foreign policy.

CONCLUSION

This and the preceding chapter have explicated how different networks of expertise came together in the arenas of asylum and sex offender law to shape the epistemic logics of these legal domains. Though the precise processes that allowed each network to influence these state knowledge practices differ in the details, the overall picture is rather similar across domains. In both instances, state institutions expressed a new need for methods of rendering sexual subjects legible for state action, and institutional, legal, and political changes created an opening for epistemic entrepreneurs to insert themselves into the organizational "machineries of knowing."[34] This might be understood as a shift in the "intellectual opportunity structure," or what Tom Waidzunas defines as "those aspects of a multi-institutional field of knowledge production that render it more or less vulnerable to the activity of social movements and [scientific and intellectual movements]."[35] In the cases of sex offender and asylum law, the intellectual opportunity structure is closely intertwined with, and perhaps nearly indistinguishable from, both the political opportunity structure and legal opportunity structure.[36] For forensic psychology, the most relevant changes included the relative withdrawal of psychiatry from the field of sex offender management and the passage of an array of new laws targeting sex crimes in the early 1990s that induced a need within state institutions for new methods of measuring and classifying sexual subjects. For asylum experts, developments included the 1990 BIA decision granting withholding of removal to a gay man and the recognition among advocates and government officials alike that relatively little was known about how to process sexuality-based asylum claims.

However, neither forensic psychologists nor asylum advocates attempted to claim exclusive epistemic authority over their respective issues. Rather, both proceeded through a process of "generosity" that attempted to enroll as many allies into their networks of knowing as possible through careful negotiations and the use of strategic boundary objects, such as the *DSM* and the USCIS training manual. Thus, forensic psychologists were unable to wholly control the definition of "mental abnormality," but by ceding some authority for themselves and cooperating with the existing legal structures, they were able to strengthen their expert network, bring legal actors on board, and institutionalize their epistemic authority more easily, while also re-legitimating the civil commitment of sex offenders in the public's eye.

Similarly, though asylum experts could not rewrite existing asylum laws to include sexual or gender minorities, they *could* use the elasticity of the law to create new "particular social groups" that included queer people and then teach as many people as possible how to make those same claims. Just as forensic psychologists used the *DSM* as a boundary object that could bridge the science-law divide, asylum experts drew on social scientific knowledge of sexuality that they strategically translated into legally cognizable arguments and even government training manuals to enroll adjudicators and immigration authorities into their network of knowing. Unlike the case of SVP determinations and forensic psychology, though, asylum advocates had to actively push their expertise onto the state, which, in most cases, was not simply welcomed as forensic psychological expertise was in SVP adjudications. Rather, asylum advocates had to first bring attention to what they viewed as improper—and illegitimate—means of adjudicating LGBTQ claims, including what they believed were incorrect means of determining individuals' sexualities and inadequate documentation of LGBTQ human rights abuses by the State Department.

Non-state expertise may therefore legitimate state power and decision-making in quite different ways. Where forensic psychology responded to a largely external legitimacy crisis by straightforwardly offering its expertise to bolster state power, asylum experts contributed to creating the very crisis to which they then offered a solution. I have called these complicit and insurgent expertise, respectively, but both modes of intervention ultimately shored up state authority and legitimacy. The insurgent expertise of asylum advocates, however, has not been fully absorbed into the state apparatus like the forensic psychologists who derive their livelihoods from state contracts for the evaluation and treatment of sex offenders. Thus, asylum advocates maintain more room to criticize state policies (and continue to vocally do so), even as they are partially institutionalized within the state apparatus (through official DHS trainings, for instance). Thus, even as they continue to challenge state policies and legal decisions, their presence at the table, so to speak, may still work to increase the legitimacy of the asylum process for external actors.

At a very general level, then, we can note some similarities in how each expert network formed. Both formed in the wake of institutional recon-figurations that called for new forms of knowledge as new processes of classification and social control centered around sexuality took shape. But why, despite forming contemporaneously and addressing the same general phenomenon of "sexuality," did such divergent epistemic logics result? What conditions gave rise to one way of knowing the sexualities of sex offenders and another for queer people?

As I suggested in the introductory chapters, a host of political and insti-tutional factors contributed to this divergence, including the increasing separation of LGBTQ people and sex criminals in the cultural imaginary (a separation that was reinforced and bolstered by these new techno-legal classification practices), different levels of political and cultural salience, and divergent laws and legal precedent. Yet I also want to suggest that two other factors played distinctive roles.

First, the social movement activism and cause lawyering specifically aimed at improving the adjudication of LGBTQ asylum claims has been largely absent for sex offenders. Sex offenders are, of course, not particu-larly sympathetic subjects and have not drawn significant public support, and there has therefore been considerably less pressure on the state to treat them humanely. This is changing somewhat as small groups of activists have drawn more attention to the negative effects of policies such as life-time public registration and indefinite civil confinement, especially for juveniles. But organized activism against the use of certain technologies, such as the penile plethysmograph (discussed more in the next chapter), has meant that the most invasive techniques for discerning sexuality have not been used on LGBTQ asylum seekers.

This affects a second major factor that shapes epistemic logics: data availability. Legal anthropologist Sally Engle Merry describes the ten-dency to build measures around the kind of data available and to continue to rely on those sources of data as "data inertia."[37] Her idea helps explain, in part, why particular strategies for determining persecution, risk, and even subjects' sexualities have formed the way they have. For example, the availability of large-scale studies of sex offender recidivism have allowed the creation of actuarial risk assessments for sex criminals, but no analo-gous body of data exists for determining the risk that asylum seekers may face. Notably, the UN, in conjunction with several NGOs, is developing an

LGBTI Inclusion Index with the goal of quantitatively rating every country in the world according to its treatment of LGBTI people.[38] Should their efforts come to fruition, it would not be surprising if the LGBTI Inclusion Index became a major, and perhaps determinative, force for deciding persecution risk in LGBTQ asylum claims, displacing the current more "subjective" methods. Likewise, if a less invasive and more scientifically sound method than phallometric testing were developed for ascertaining one's sexuality, it would likely eventually be deployed in asylum determinations.

With these thoughts in mind, in the next two chapters, I turn to an analysis of how sexuality is determined and what counts as empirical evidence of sexuality in each legal complex. Specifically, I ask more directly how the epistemic logics I have begun to describe here influence how state institutions classify sexual subjects and examine the circumstances that have given rise to drastically different approaches to determining subjects' sexualities.

5: ASYLUM SEEKERS AND SIGNS OF QUEERNESS

In 2009 an Iranian gay man arrived in Germany to seek asylum from persecution based on his sexual identity. Under the requirements of the Dublin Regulation, because the man had passed through the Czech Republic first, he was required to return and lodge his complaint there. Germany, therefore, initiated proceedings to send the man back until it was revealed during those proceedings that the Czech Republic sometimes used something called phallometric testing to verify asylum seekers' sexual orientations. Phallometric testing uses an instrument called a penile plethysmograph, or PPG, to measure the tumescence of a man's penis in response to various visual and auditory stimuli. The most commonly used PPG consists of a silicone ring filled with mercury that is placed around a man's penis. As the penis grows, changes in the mercury send electrical signals to a machine that provides an output tracking size variation. Advocates of the technology assert that it provides an objective measure of one's sexual arousal and therefore one's sexual orientation.

The revelation that this technique was being used on asylum seekers in the Czech Republic caused outcries across the European Union and at the United Nations. The German administrative court reviewing the Iranian man's application refused to send him back to the Czech Republic, where he might face such a procedure and criticized use of the PPG as degrading and a gross violation of privacy. Soon thereafter, the EU Agency for Fundamental Rights issued a report also condemning phallometric testing.[1] The Organization for Refuge, Asylum and Migration devoted an entire report to attacking the scientific validity, legality, and ethics of PPG use with asylum seekers.[2] In May 2011, then–EU Home Affairs Commissioner Cecilia Malmström also criticized the procedure, saying, "The practice of phallometric tests constitutes a strong interference with the person's private life and human dignity. This kind of degrading treatment should not be accepted in the European Union, nor elsewhere."[3] The UN High Commissioner for Refugees similarly denounced phallometry for asylum seekers and concluded that the practice was, in fact, illegal under European law.[4] All of these criticisms and the eventual legal pronouncement rested, at least in part, on the rejection of the notion that sexual orientation, or even sexual arousal, could be accurately assessed by measuring penile tumescence. Determinations of individuals' sexualities, the court declared, must instead be based on claimants' testimonies.

In the Philippe-Pinel Institute in Montreal, the situation looks very different. Here, I entered a room aptly called "the cave," where researchers and psychiatric staff conduct PPG testing on convicted sex offenders. In the center of the large black-walled room stands a platform surrounded on three sides by 3D projection screens through which the staff can create virtually any situation they wish, populated with avatars that are custom designed to appeal to the sexual tastes of whomever is participating. These avatars are particularly useful for gauging the arousal of pedophiles, for they allow practitioners to get around the ethically dubious practice of using child pornography to assess their sexual arousal. This sophisticated system, which cost around $1.5 million to create, allows programmers to manipulate every aspect of a virtual avatar, from facial features and body size down to nearly a dozen features of the avatar's genitals. I ascended the platform to enter the virtual reality simulator and donned the 3D projection goggles, at which point a seductively posed, though clothed, woman appeared before me. As I sat in the chair and gazed around the room, the researchers leading the tour informed me that they could see where I was looking. The goggles not only allow the operators to create elaborate three-dimensional scenes but also to track the participant's eye movements. This allows them to know if the subject is attempting to avoid looking at the scene in order to control his arousal. I removed the goggles, and just as suddenly as she appeared, the virtual woman was gone, and I was back in a dimly lit room surrounded by white screens.

Unlike the outcry that ensued over the Czech Republic's use of phallometric testing of asylum seekers, such objections are generally dismissed when they involve sex offenders. Though the Philippe-Pinel Institute is the only place with such a sophisticated setup, PPG testing similar to that done at the institute is a routine aspect of legally mandated sex offender treatment and supervision in the United States, Canada, and parts of western Europe. In regard to use of the PPG on sex offenders, US courts have heard the very same challenges levied by asylum advocates: that it violates the right to privacy, freedom from intrusive medical procedures, freedom from unnecessary searches, freedom of religion, and, uniquely to sex offenders, freedom from self-incrimination. With the exception of some circumscribed privacy protections, courts have dismissed these complaints, ruling instead that the state's interest in determining a sex offender's sexual desires outweighs the rights of the offender. Nestled within these judicial decisions is the tacit assumption that phallometric testing accurately assesses one's sexual desires through the physical measurement of the erect—or as is usually the case with the PPG, the barely erect—penis.

Why do these two areas of the law come to such drastically different conclusions about the proper way to determine someone's sexuality? Part of the explanation, as we can begin to surmise from the above vignettes, certainly involves the more successful advocacy efforts of those representing asylum seekers in comparison to those (few) defending the rights of sex offenders. But a significant part of the story also revolves around the distinct epistemic logics guiding state decision-making. As the previous chapters illustrated, the epistemic machinery of these two legal complexes varies significantly, affecting how state officials determine what knowledges count as expert in each setting. This chapter and the next take another step to analyze how, given their respective forms of expertise, both legal domains attempt to measure subjects' sexualities. That is, what counts as empirical evidence of sexuality? Just as the divergent epistemic logics dictate different forms of expertise, they also differently define the empirical. Though the types of expertise that inform legal decision-making in each domain do not directly determine what counts as evidence of sexuality, they significantly influence it. For instance, sociology and anthropology generally subscribe to a social constructionist view of sexuality, resulting in an understanding of sexuality as inextricably bound up with social forces. Forensic psychology gives significantly less consideration to social factors and instead focuses on the individual, allowing for a much more facile and direct connection between the body and sexuality.

One result of these competing foci is a greater emphasis on the individual and the body in sex offender assessments and, conversely, a larger role for social context in asylum claims. However, experts do not wield the only or ultimate authority in defining sexuality. The types of evidence and expertise that influence decision-making are highly structured by the legal institutions themselves and the norms that configure their environments. Rules of evidence, required levels of proof, governing statutes, and the definition of subjects under scrutiny (e.g., mentally ill criminal or deserving refugee) all partially dictate what forms of evidence "count" and how much weight they are granted.[5]

Despite many differences, in both domains a jumble of messy facts and opinions enter at one end, and neatly packaged objective legal determinations come out the other. Though both areas of law depend on a combination of narrative and bodily evidence to prove one's sexuality, the exact type of evidence and its interpretation vary considerably. This is the result of the extent to which actors believe the proffered evidence to be *direct measures* or *indirect indicators* of sexuality. Although both areas depend on both types of evidence to some extent, those in asylum adjudications tend to approach the measurement of sexuality through indicators, or signs, of a rather inaccessible subjective state, whereas experts and decision-makers in sex offender evaluations tend more often to believe their data to be direct measures of one's sexuality.

In her comparative study of high energy physics (HEP) and molecular biology, Karin Knorr Cetina shows that the two disciplines approach the empirical in quite distinct ways.[6] The objects of knowledge for HEP are too small to ever be seen except indirectly by detectors, too fast to be captured and contained in a lab, and too dangerous to be handled directly. The existence of these particles can only be indirectly established by the footprints they leave when passing through specialized measurement devices. This is what Knorr Cetina calls "negative knowledge." It is not non-knowledge, but rather a type of knowledge based on the interpretation of signs. Whereas proper measurements in most fields count as evidence, measurements in HEP are virtually meaningless until placed in the context of a particular theory. HEP experiments thus operate in a space of liminal phenomena working with "things which are neither empirical objects of positive knowledge nor effects in the formless regions of the unknowable, but something in between."[7] Molecular biology, on the other hand, is strongly oriented toward positive knowledge and relies on maximizing contact with the empirical world. Biological experiments depend on the ability of the researcher to manipulate physical objects. In this epistemic culture, measurements *are* data. The sign processes relied upon in HEP are constantly turned away from in molecular biology. "The signs in this case," as Knorr Cetina explains, "are not used as a window upon an underlying phenomenal reality that one seeks out as a clue to understanding. Rather, they are data in their own right."[8]

Knorr Cetina's comparison is rather similar to what we find when comparing asylum and sex offender adjudications, with asylum law often relying more on "negative knowledge" and sex offender law tending toward what is understood to be "positive knowledge." Each domain's position vis-à-vis the PPG as illustrated in the opening anecdotes may help clarify this distinction. Where the PPG is accepted as a direct and objective measure (positive knowledge) of sexual arousal and orientation for sex offender assessments, it is rejected in favor of claimants' narratives (negative knowledge, as I explain below) for asylum decisions. As chapter 1 showed, these two approaches—narrative analysis and bodily examination—have historically competed as the preferred methods of ascertaining someone's sexuality.

On the one hand, as Foucault has suggested, the confession has acted as one of the West's most highly valued techniques for the production of truth, especially in regard to sexuality. Though Foucault focused on the religious tradition of confession and its later adaptation for psychiatry, it is particularly apropos for legal settings, as well. Foucault suggests that the confession is a ritual "that unfolds within a power relationship, for one does not confess without the presence (or virtual presence) of a partner who is not simply the interlocutor but the authority who requires the confession, prescribes and appreciates it, and intervenes in order to judge, punish, forgive, console, and reconcile."[9] His statement captures well the dynamics of both asylum hearings and sex offender evaluations, where individuals are compelled to reveal the most intimate details of their lives for judgment by an authority figure who possesses the power to determine the credibility of the applicant's claims. As this description suggests, the confession depends on a process of interpretation by an interlocutor. In other words, it is, like high energy physics, a science of signs. Moving back into the realm of psychiatry, Knorr Cetina asserts:

> Analysis is the progression from outward signs (the patient's symptoms) to the motivating forces that are the elements of psychic activity. Unlike the previous type of science, psychoanalysis does not process material objects but rather processes *signs*. The office ritual of the couch and the way inquiry is conducted produces these signs. When they elicit and interpret these signs, psychoanalysts are *reconstructing the meaning and origin of representations.*[10]

Thus, eliciting a sexual narrative is a process of producing signs that must be placed in the context of a particular theory to gain much meaning. In other words, narrative is a form of negative knowledge.

On the other hand, early medicine and sexology relied heavily on the body and physical signs of difference to identify sexual "deviants," often understanding homosexuals to be a "third sex" or degenerates. Therefore, many sexologists sought physical signs of difference on or in queer bodies by measuring body parts and positing that homosexuals had different voices, hair growth patterns, musculature, and skin than heterosexuals. This approach located sexual difference on and in the body and, like scientific racism, depended on biological determinism to position sexually "deviant" bodies as evolutionary "throwbacks" that were less developed than "normal" men and women.[11]

Despite the commonalities with scientific racism, most sexologists were sympathetic to homosexuals and believed that homosexuality should not be criminalized because it was an inborn abnormality, or if it was acquired that it was nearly impossible to change. To this end, they also pursued lines of inquiry that look more familiar to us today, including attempts to trace the heredity of homosexuality and to analyze hormones, which they hoped would prove the inborn nature of homosexuality. Given this historical trajectory, it is perhaps no surprise that we still strongly associate the body with explanations of sexuality. Indeed, the more sophisticated techniques of modern science that have given rise to pronouncements of a "gay brain" or a "gay gene" reinforce this view. Similarly, psychological studies attempting to identify how gay men's faces, voices, or walks differ from straight men's rest easily with notions of the embodied nature of (homo)sexuality.

Though these studies often garner sensational headlines announcing the discovery of the "gay gene" and the like and are held up as proof of the immutability of homosexuality by the LGBT movement, the scientific consensus is far less settled. The landmark "gay brain" and "gay gene" studies, for instance, have never been replicated, and some researchers have even found results contradicting the original studies. Research examining the same phenomena often come to conflicting conclusions, and average effect sizes are generally quite small.[12] The best research today suggests that sexuality is most likely a product of nature and nurture, though researchers in different disciplines seldom even agree on what counts as nature and what as nurture. Maternal hormonal fluctuations, for example, may count as an environmental factor for a behavioral geneticist but a biological factor for a sociologist. However, these controversies are mostly hindrances to the legal process, which must arrive at a decision at the end of a hearing, regardless of the settled or unsettled status of the science. It must, in the face of uncertainty and given the evidence available, make a pronouncement regarding someone's sexuality, and it must do so in a way that maintains the legitimacy of law—that is, it must appear objective. Given such uncertainty, how does this happen?

The remainder of this chapter and the next will be devoted to explicating precisely what kinds of evidence each area of law draws on, how those pieces of evidence are put together to make determinations of individuals' sexualities, and what consequences these divergent epistemological practices have for understandings of sexuality in each legal complex. Despite their differences, sexual determinations in both arenas are the dual product of (1) how someone talks about their sexuality and (2) how their body and bodily acts become performatively implicated as evidence in that narrative. However, institutionally specific epistemic logics position these two types of evidence—narrative and bodily—differently such that narrative predominates in asylum hearings while bodily evidence and quantified indicators reign in SVP proceedings. Sexuality is therefore materialized quite differently in each domain with consequences for how sexuality is understood ontologically. That is, is it intrinsically identifiable in or through the body, or does knowing sexuality depend on social context?

NARRATING TRAUMA, NARRATING IDENTITY

The hearing began with Aneesha questioning Maria. Maria testified that she had a hard time growing up in Mexico. She had four brothers, and all of her friends were boys. She preferred to play with boys, and the other kids teased her because, in her words, she was "different." They called her "marimacha," which is a derogatory slang term for lesbians in Mexico.

At the age of fourteen she met Alejandro, who would become the father of her son. Alejandro told Maria that he was eighteen, but she later found out that he was in his twenties. His parents insisted that she come live with them when they caught her and Alejandro alone in the house one day and thought they were having sex. Maria's parents agreed, and at fourteen she was sent to live with Alejandro and his parents. After a few months, Alejandro started drinking heavily and raping her. If she refused to sleep with him, he would beat her. At one point Alejandro tried to get Maria to have sex with a friend of his, too. She remained there for about thirteen months, but after the incident with the friend, she decided to run away to the US, where her sister already lived.

Her first entry to the US was in June 1993 when she was already pregnant with her son, though she did not know it when she fled. Her son was born in March 1994 in the US and is a citizen. Maria testified that she dated one man when she first came to the US but used being pregnant as an excuse not to have sex with him. When she was seventeen she realized that she was a lesbian. A friend of her sister teased her, saying things like "I think you like women," to which Maria replied that she did not. But at one point the woman told Maria that she was going to kiss her. Maria said nothing but let the woman kiss her. That's when she knew she liked women.

EXCERPT FROM FIELD NOTES,
CHICAGO IMMIGRATION COURT, DECEMBER 2013

Maria went on to tell the court about later meeting Emilia, who also had a young son. They became partners, raising their sons and sharing a life together for twelve years before the relationship ended. Mourning their breakup, Maria returned to Mexico to be with her mother, only to again encounter the misogynistic violence that forced her to flee initially. After enduring threats and physical violence that were ignored by the police, Maria soon returned to the United States. But this time she was apprehended at the border and charged with illegal reentry, rendering her ineligible for asylum. Her testimony, however, along with that of her son eventually secured Maria withholding of removal. But what is it about Maria's story that made it sufficient for this immigration judge to grant her relief?

Maria's narrative is typical in many ways. She begins by describing

feeling "different" at a young age, especially because of her gendered behavior and preference for playing with boys, a trope that draws on stereotypes of gender nonconformity among queer people. She then narrates an
internal process of coming to terms with her sexuality that is complicated
by her abusive relationship with Alejandro, her parents' conservative beliefs, and the social pressure she feels to continue dating men. Maria's
lawyer skillfully led her through these events to bring her to the key moment: she kissed a girl, and she liked it. That feeling of difference is finally
realized in Maria's revelation that she is, in fact, gay.

We might note that, while not belaboring it, Maria's story does draw on
some forms of bodily evidence: gendered stereotypes and, later at the be-
hest of the government lawyer, testimony that she had sexual relationships
with women. Yet these are relatively minor aspects of Maria's narrative,
and in her oral decision, the judge appears to consider them little, instead
determining that Maria's overall narrative was "candid and credible," despite lacking significant corroborating evidence. Indeed, the law allows
for an asylum seeker's credible testimony to sustain her burden of proof
without further corroboration.[13] In practice, many adjudicators still want
corroboration, and, in practice, many things aside from a claimant's narrative—including stereotypes and bodily demeanor—may play an evidentiary
role. However, as Maria's case illustrates, narrative evidence tends to carry
the day in asylum proceedings, and attempts to rely on purported bodily
indicators of sexuality have been rebuffed by courts. But why?

Aside from the social movement and political factors discussed in
earlier chapters, asylum claims also suffer from limited data availability.
Adjudicators must accept that there is perhaps no way to definitively prove
one's sexuality and that asylum seekers are unlikely to have a large social
network of people who know about their sexuality and can corroborate it.
Moreover, whereas adjudicators believe that membership in some other
categories of asylum, such as race or religion, can be more "objectively"
proven through physical appearance or otherwise, the equivalent criterion
for queer people (i.e., gendered stereotypes) is legally prohibited.

But I also want to argue that the politicized deployment of expertise
within particular legal complexes is key for deciding what will count as
credible empirical evidence of sexuality. As sociologist Tom Waidzunas has
shown, skirmishes between the ex-gay movement and psychiatry pushed
the APA to adopt physiological measures—namely, the PPG—as the gold
standard for measuring sexual orientation.[14] In the face of testimonies
from "ex-gay" people that they had changed sexual orientations, the APA
deemed such narratives a less reliable form of evidence than physiological
measures. Yet the asylum complex—with its hybrid legal activist/social scientific approach to knowing sexuality that draws heavily on the expertise of
sociology and anthropology—elevates narrative as its preferred evidence.

The Sexual Identity Narrative

For asylum seekers, the key aspect of a credibly constructed sexual narrative revolves around identity and its development.[15] The overall structure of the stories offered in asylum claims often follows the Western "coming out" narrative, similar to Maria's claim above. As Laurie Berg and Jenni Millbank concluded from their study of Australian and Canadian LGB asylum claimants, those most likely to be successful are those who conform to Western notions of linear identity development and a fixed sexual identity.[16] This is echoed in my own fieldwork, where lawyers typically guided their clients through a series of questions meant to elicit just such a trajectory of identity development. Interviewees consistently reiterated the importance of this narrative. Victoria Neilson, former Legal Director for Immigration Equality, offers an illustrative response:

> The most important thing is, with any kind of asylum case, the person's own testimony. The more you can get the applicant to talk about their own internal coming-out experience, how he or she first began to realize they were gay, what their first romantic encounter was, how that came about, how that made them feel. If they had a more significant relationship, how that came about, what made that feel special for them, what lengths they had to go to keep that hidden if they were in a country where that would have put them in jeopardy. I think the more you can get someone to talk about those details, the more credible they sound.[17]

The importance of a petitioner's narrative is similarly echoed in judicial decisions. The 2005 case of William Kimumwe demonstrates this point:

> The IJ's [immigration judge's] conclusion that Kimumwe has not established eligibility for asylum is simply not supported by the record. At the outset, I take issue with the IJ's statement that Kimumwe presented no objective evidence to confirm his homosexuality. It is unclear what type of evidence would satisfy the IJ. Kimumwe testified he was openly gay. He stated he realized he was gay when he was seven years old. He presented a letter from a Kenyan orphanage administrator, Kemba Andrew Waakl, indicating that Kimumwe was gay. After carefully perusing the record, I have found no evidence whatsoever that would contradict Kimumwe's claimed sexual orientation and accept that he is openly gay.[18]

Here, the court emphasizes the importance of Kimumwe's testimony that he was openly gay and, furthermore, that the court accepts that testimony as a piece of *objective* evidence.

Also often part of these narratives is the movement from closeted in one's home country to "out" in the United States. This movement "coincides with unidirectional spatial migration towards the nation of refuge, culminating in the liberating moment of the refugee hearing where the claimant can officially 'come out' to the state who will protect her and allow her the freedom to be openly 'gay' 'lesbian' 'bisexual' or 'transgender.'"[19] Savvy lawyers know this trope and will often conclude their questioning with queries designed to get at both the claimant's arrival at her "final" sexual identity and the sense that only the US context can allow such liberatory sexual expression.[20] For instance, Maria, discussed above, said in response to being asked why she wanted to stay in the United States, "I want you to give me the opportunity to be me," and Liu, a gay Malaysian asylee, said that being in the closet would be "going against who I am."[21] In order to further draw out this idea, the final question from many lawyers will be: "If you are allowed to stay in the United States, what do you hope to do?" or "What will happen if you are not allowed to stay?" Kwame, a gay Togolese asylum seeker, offers an illustrative reply to the latter question: "I would have a miserable life. I would have to watch my back constantly, and I would probably end up in jail or killed. I want to have a family with another man someday, and I could not do that in Togo."[22] Petitioner's responses almost always include hopes of finding a partner, living openly as gay, and often having a family.

Implicit in this line of questioning is the assumption of a teleological development of sexual identity resulting in one final endpoint. However, this is not always how sexual identity develops, even in the United States.[23] People may identify as heterosexual but have same-sex sexual contact. Others may come to a queer identity without having same-sex sex. Still others may shift identities over time, even moving around from straight to gay to unlabeled and beyond. While more typically "Western" narratives are common, a variety of narratives can achieve credibility when framed properly.

In 2005 the Ninth Circuit ruled on the case of Miguel Pozos, a (possibly) gay man from Mexico. Pozos admitted homosexual conduct while living in Mexico (part of his persecution claim included being forced to work as a prostitute) but insisted that he had not engaged in any homosexual sex since coming to the United States. He testified that he continued to have sexual fantasies about both men *and* women and disavowed a homosexual identity. The decision states that "both Pozos and the social worker who examined him testified that they did not know what Pozos's sexual orientation was," and later that Pozos "was diagnosed with sexual aversion disorder, and has eschewed sexual relations with either gender."[24] The court ultimately granted Pozos asylum based on imputed homosexual identity without ever settling on what his sexual orientation was. This case is unique but suggests that rigid sexual identity categories viewed as immutable are not always necessary for successful asylum claims, nor are linear sexual identity development narratives.

Though many critics have denounced the asylum process for requiring an "immutable" identity, in setting the standard for what constitutes a "particular social group," the BIA stated in *Matter of Acosta* (1985) that "whatever the common characteristic that defines the group, it must be one that the members of the group either cannot change or should not be required to change because it is fundamental to their individual identities or consciences."[25] This definition is more flexible than many critics assume. One could include religion, a category explicitly protected by the 1980 Refugee Act, in this definition of immutable. Even though one can change religions, it is protected as a trait that one should not be compelled to change. Sexual orientation is similar in this respect. In fact, the USCIS-Immigration Equality training module for asylum officers adjudicating LGBTQ asylum claims makes this clear in its definition of a "particular social group": "the group is comprised of individuals who share a common, innate characteristic—such as sex, color, kinship ties, or past experience—that members cannot change or . . . the group is comprised of individuals who share a characteristic that is so fundamental to the members' identity or conscience that they should not be required to change it."[26] The manual goes on to state that asylum officers can choose whether to classify sexual orientation, gender identity, or intersexuality as either innate or fundamental but that both characterizations are protected.

Bisexual claimants frequently disrupt preconceived notions of sexuality as either heterosexual or homosexual and fixed. As the Immigration Equality *Asylum Manual* states of bisexual petitioners, "Asylum adjudicators often want the issues in cases to be black and white. It is not hard to imagine an asylum adjudicator taking the position that if the applicant is attracted to both sexes, she should simply 'choose' to be with members of the opposite sex to avoid future persecution."[27] While questioning José Lopez, a bisexual Guatemalan man whose hearing I observed, the DHS attorney asked, "So being with a man is something you can control or not?" to which José, slightly confused by the question, answered yes. During re-direct, however, his lawyer corrected the confusion:

LAWYER: The government attorney asked you earlier if you can control who you're with, and you said yes. But you can't control how you feel, right?

JOSÉ: No.

LAWYER: And how do you feel?

JOSÉ: I notice pretty girls, but I am more attracted to men.[28]

José's lawyer here shifted the focus from a concrete act (being with a man) to the more subjective frame of feelings and attraction and was successful in getting her client recognized as bisexual by the court. When I asked Victoria Neilson if she had ever had a client who had past heterosexual relationships and how she went about showing that the client could still be queer, she offered a response that I quote at length for its edifying power:

> Sure, that comes up with some frequency. I think . . . some people are bi-sexual, and . . . I think that identity is probably more misunderstood than L, G, or T. I think there's sort of a different narrative if somebody had a, say, heterosexual marriage in the past. One is like, "Well, I didn't come out until later in life," which seems pretty easy to comprehend. Or it could be like "I kind of always knew I was gay, but I tried to marry to see if that could make me 'normal,'" or "I tried to marry to please my family." I think that narrative works. I think a true narrative that's a little harder for an adjudicator to understand is "Yes, I loved my husband, and that could've worked. But it didn't just because of our personalities. And now I'm in love with a woman, and that's who I want to be with the rest of my life." I think that is also true in some instances, but I think that can be harder for an adjudicator to understand, how like your sexual orientation is immutable and fundamental to identity if it's mutable.[29]

Though Neilson admits that bisexual claims are often more difficult, they are by no means impossible. Indeed, all of my interviewees had successfully represented bisexuals or claimants with past heterosexual experiences—sometimes even spouses and children. These cases depend heavily on claimants' credibility and how they will be perceived in their home country. As immigration attorney Michael Jarecki stated: "There's just a heteronormative understanding of lifestyle in a lot of these countries and then there's 'other.'"[30] Thus, if one can show that a bisexual will be perceived as "other" in his/her home country, claims are winnable.

However, bisexual claimants may still find it difficult to offer credible narratives in a culture that continues to be pervaded by bi-erasure, especially when they lack quality legal representation. This was a central issue in the 2016 case of Ray Fuller, a purportedly bisexual man from Jamaica, whose claim was denied by the Seventh Circuit. Fuller was unrepresented, and the immigration judge found his overall claim to be not credible. But she took particular issue with his claim of bisexuality. In a heated dissent, Judge Posner wrote in response:

> The weakest part of the immigration judge's opinion is its conclusion that Fuller is not bisexual, a conclusion premised on the fact that he's had

sexual relations with women (including a marriage). Apparently the immigration judge does not know the meaning of *bi*sexual. The fact that she refused even to believe there is hostility to bisexuals in Jamaica suggests a closed mind and gravely undermines her critical finding that Fuller is not bisexual.[31]

Though there were other flaws with Fuller's case, as Posner's dissent suggests, bisexual people may continue to face considerable difficulty convincing adjudicators of their queerness, particularly without a lawyer familiar with the legal terrain.[32]

Nevertheless, as several of these examples suggest, claimants are increasingly able to challenge entrenched understandings of sexual identity by enlisting the help of specialized lawyers and experts, who know how to shape unfamiliar narratives for American adjudicators and can testify to the diversity of sexual identities and experiences around the world. Francesca Polletta asserts that we understand stories in relation to familiar plotlines we have heard before, what she calls canonicity.[33] New stories are therefore heard against a backdrop of familiar ones, and people try to fit new narratives into familiar plots. Familiar storylines thus create a commonsense belief system that can act as a barrier to those trying to effect social change. However, we also expect multiple meanings in narratives, which leaves room for individual interpretation, and this interpretability goes against the force of canonicity. Because of these characteristics, storytelling has the potential both to reinforce and challenge the normative order depending on the structural and cultural context.

An asylum applicant's story must do at least two things: convince an adjudicator that one is truly queer and demonstrate past persecution or legitimate fear of future persecution on account of that queer identity. As Jeffrey Alexander suggests, any successful cultural performance requires that speaker and audience share a common set of cultural codes, yet by simple virtue of being an immigrant, an asylum seeker is unlikely to share the same cultural codes as an immigration judge or asylum officer.[34] Without this knowledge, or a lawyer with this knowledge, an asylum applicant's chances of success fall precipitously.[35] Polletta and colleagues get at this issue at a more general level when they write: "Institutional personnel need a certain kind of story but need it be the client's story. The story must be at once conventional and authentic. For that reason, institutional personnel often coach clients on how to tell their stories properly."[36] Susan Berger highlights this dynamic in her study of sexual orientation asylum claims, where she argues that lawyers and other advocates sometimes help petitioners craft credible narratives for presentation to immigration officials.[37] Shannon Minter, Legal Director for the National Center for Lesbian Rights, described the importance of having familiarity with the US immigration system:

> It's not that people are fabricating or forcing their history into a particular narrative. It's helping them pick out from all the stuff that's happened to them and all the different, you know, infinite variety of detail and circumstance. They don't know necessarily what's relevant to an asylum officer, and . . . it's super helpful if they can have someone who knows what the process is and what an asylum officer is going to be interested in help them be prepared with that information.[38]

As Minter suggests, then, it may require assistance from someone familiar with US cultural codes to translate some narratives into something recognizable to a US audience. Returning to a consideration of the case of Geovanni Hernandez-Montiel introduced in chapter 4 is helpful.

Hernandez-Montiel was a Mexican man who sought asylum in 1995 in the United States after being abused by his family and schoolmates and being raped and assaulted by the police. During his hearing, Professor Thomas Davies testified that different groups of homosexuals in Mexico face varying levels of abuse. Gay men who take the stereotypical "female" role, he stated, are subject to greater abuse and discrimination, and thus, "gay men with female sexual identities" constitute a distinct group in Mexico. The judge, however, found Hernandez-Montiel's social group to be "homosexual males who wish to dress as a woman [sic]" and concluded that his abuse was due to his choice to dress in women's clothing, not because he was gay. On appeal, the BIA agreed with the judge, classifying Hernandez-Montiel's social group as "homosexual males who dress as females" and further that "he was mistreated because of the way he dressed (as a male prostitute) and not because he is a homosexual."[39] The Ninth Circuit issued a decision in 2000 that roundly criticized both the judge and the BIA. Drawing on Professor Davies's expert testimony and a bevy of other social science research, the court ruled that "gay men with female sexual identities" constitute a particular social group in Mexico: "Their female sexual identities unite this group of gay men, and their sexual identities are so fundamental to their human identities that they should not be required to change them."[40] The court further noted that "gay men with female sexual identities outwardly manifest their identities through characteristics traditionally associated with women, such as feminine dress, long hair and fingernails."[41] Hernandez-Montiel was rescripted from a cross-dressing prostitute to someone with a fundamental sexual identity manifested through his physical appearance.

Some criticized this decision, claiming that the court conflated gender and sexuality. Sexualities scholars have argued for a distinction between gender and sexuality for some time, so to suggest that sexuality manifests through gender presentation seems only to reinscribe stereotypes of feminine gay men and masculine lesbians. Critics subscribing to this view seem to prefer to classify Hernandez-Montiel as a transsexual.[42] This construction is overly narrow. First, Hernandez-Montiel self-identified as a "gay man with a female sexual identity."[43] Second, queer communities in Mexico use a variety of classificatory schemas to construct sexual identities, some based on gender role, others based on object choice, and still others, like Hernandez-Montiel's, that are a hybrid of the two, and none of these necessarily map squarely onto institutionalized US identity categories.[44] Rather than conflating gender and sexuality, then, the decision sets a precedent for accepting sexual identities that are unfamiliar to Americans and pushes adjudicators to carefully consider cultural context.[45] Notably, Hernandez-Montiel's identity *did* require corroboration in the form of an expert witness, which is not unusual for an out-of-the-ordinary claim. Indeed, it is consistent with the notion of claimant's narratives as elicited *signs* that must be placed in a particular context to make sense. While the signs generated through the narratives of claimants with more recognizably Western identities may be easily interpreted by American adjudicators, it often takes an expert to provide the cultural context necessary to make "foreign" sexual identities legible for state classification efforts.

Cultural Context and the Interpretation of Narratives

Consistent with the notion of narratives as elicited *signs* that must be placed in a particular context to make sense, asylum claims always include information on conditions in the petitioner's native country. While some claims only use this information to corroborate assertions of persecution, many also provide cultural context for understanding sexuality cross-culturally. As one US immigration judge stated:

> When you look at categories, and if a person identifies as queer or as bi or this or as that, what does that actually mean? . . . What you have to always do is really look very carefully at the information that exists about the culture and the country and the politics of the place the person's going to. And sexuality has very different nuances in these different countries.[46]

Similarly, sociologist Nielan Barnes, who serves as an expert witness in asylum claims, explained that she provides testimony "about identity development in a context where it's been repressed and contested, and so obviously it takes time and it's context specific."[47] She continued on to explain that non-US queers may not offer consistently linear narratives that US audiences are most familiar with and may refer to themselves at various points as a gay male, a cross-dresser, or transgender, and may use those terms interchangeably. Her job is to explain that "no, actually, this is part of the development of identity, and also for people who don't live in, say, White middle-class USA or Europe that the coming-out process looks entirely different and it means something entirely different."[48] Barnes thus emphasizes the importance that anthropological and sociological exper- tise may play in providing the necessary interpretive context for sexuality- based asylum claims.

The Ninth Circuit's decision in *Hassani v. Mukasey* (2008) lends support to Barnes's declaration. Hassani, a gay man from Iran, was denied asylum by an immigration judge based in part on the judge's assumptions about how a gay man would act. The judge found Hassani not credible based on those assumptions and refused to allow his expert witness to testify to contextualize his testimony. The Ninth Circuit found this denial to violate Hassani's due process rights and granted him a new hearing, writing that "the record is peppered with the IJ's expressions of doubt where expert tes- timony might have bolstered Hassani's claims."[49]

Critics of the use of phallometry on asylum seekers also asserted the importance of cultural context in assessing individuals' sexualities. In its report criticizing this practice, the Organization for Refuge, Asylum and Migration wrote:

> Human sexual response is highly subjective and varied, and differences in
> that response are magnified cross-culturally and among different sexual
> orientations and gender identities. It is therefore impossible to develop a
> single, standardized set of images to accurately and objectively measure
> sexual response, particularly during plethysmographic testing.[50]

The worldwide rejection of plethysmographic testing on asylum seekers highlights both the belief that sexuality, including arousal, depends on cultural context and the rejection of bodily evidence as the primary way of evaluating sexuality in asylum proceedings.

In sum, the above section demonstrates the importance of narrative and its interpretation for discerning sexuality in asylum claims. There is no assumption that sexuality is directly measurable by or accessible to adjudi- cators. Rather, carefully constructed stories about a claimant's attractions, feelings, and subjective identities contextualized within the petitioner's native culture act as signs or indicators of an underlying sexuality. As the next section shows, when judges have attempted to use bodily indicators, such as gender presentation or sex acts, as direct measures of sexuality, they have been largely rebuffed by appellate courts.

Bodily Acts and Gender Presentations

If interpreting narratives represents the indirect method of measuring sexuality, then appeals to the body represent the direct approach. The previous section argued that narratives are the primary means of generating evidence to classify sexuality in asylum claims; this section will reiterate that point by showing how alternative forms of evidence are routinely rejected or circumscribed. However, I first must briefly address the ways by which the body *does* come into play for asylum seekers. Although precedent and agency guidelines prohibit using stereotypes or sex acts as direct indicators of a claimant's sexuality, petitioners and their lawyers still sometimes draw on these "commonsense" conceptions of sexuality when making arguments.

Perhaps the most prominent way by which the body becomes important for asylum claims is through the use of gendered stereotypes to demonstrate queerness. Attorneys often describe their clients as gender nonconforming when it is true, and they do so for a reason. As Aaron Morris states, "Stereotypes are my best friend and my worst enemy. If you walk in and you are like a male dancer hairstylist who is especially effeminate and meets the expectation of what a gay guy might look like, probably they're not going to be that concerned about your sexual orientation." On the other hand, he continues, "If you are more of a linebacker . . . who has either naturally developed almost no stereotyped sexual orientation aspect or attribute or has tried very hard not to do those things, then it's harder."[51] Claimants may even use such stereotypes when their culture subscribes to them. Kwame Twumasi, a gay Togolese asylum seeker, did just this during his testimony: "I was like a girl. Only difference is I have a penis."[52] Moreover, gender nonconformity often plays into persecution claims for queer claimants, as the 2013 case of Dennis Vitug demonstrates:

> From the age of three, Vitug knew he was "different." He was effeminate and played with Barbie dolls and other toys meant for girls, which his family resented. Throughout his childhood, Vitug was teased and bullied by his classmates for "being a sissy." . . . In high school, Vitug continued to be teased and bullied by his classmates because of his perceived effeminate behavior and homosexuality. The principal called Vitug into his office numerous times, threatening to expel him if he did not change and "act accordingly."[53]

Indeed, all of the hearings for gay male claimants that I observed during my fieldwork included testimony of some kind of gender nonconformity at some point in their lives, whether they currently presented effeminately, claimed to favor cooking over sports, or said their childhood friends were all girls. Even so, being an effeminate man does not guarantee a successful claim, and being masculine does not guarantee an unsuccessful one. As all of my interviewees proclaimed, and my observations corroborated, being "feminine" may help, but regardless of a claimant's gender expression, it is the overall narrative and evidence that make or break a claim. As Keren Zwick, Director of the National Immigrant Justice Center's LGBT practice, said, "It's consistency of behavior with a story."[54] Immigration attorney Daniel Tenreiro echoed this sentiment:

> I know there's been some controversy, and I totally disagree with some of the—like a *New York Times* article that was out there a few years ago that basically said you have to femme it up. I think, [if] you're a drag queen, then by all means be a drag queen and be who you are. But if you're not, I think that can actually really backfire because it's not going to be believable.[55]

As Tenreiro's quote suggests, *if* the body comes into play in asylum claims, it must fit within the overall narrative presented. Reiterating the importance of contextualizing all evidence of sexuality and gender, Heather McClure, an early advocate for LGBTQ asylum and an anthropologist who served as an expert witness for many years, explained that during the formative years of LGBTQ asylum law, judges would say things like "you don't look gay. You look like a manly man to me." She therefore often explained that "codes of masculinity are different in different countries,"[56] and that basing decisions on US-centric gendered stereotypes was inappropriate. Appellate courts now routinely strike down decisions using such logic.[57]

In the particularly illustrative and highly cited *Razkane v. Holder* (2009), the Tenth Circuit vacated a judge's asylum denial based on inappropriate use of stereotypes to discredit the claimant. The unanimous decision included a strongly worded admonishment of such arbitrariness in the law:

> To condone this style of judging, unhinged from the prerequisite of substantial evidence, would inevitably lead to unpredictable, inconsistent, and unreviewable results. The fair adjudication of a claim for restriction on removal is dependent on a system grounded in the requirement of substantial evidence and free from vagaries flowing from notions of the assigned [immigration judge]. Such stereotyping would not be tolerated in other contexts, such as race or religion.[58]

In that same case, the government lawyer in immigration court asked Razkane's country conditions expert what would happen to someone who "looked gay" in Morocco, to which he responded, "Ma'am, I'm sorry, I can't help you with that. I just don't know what it means to look like a gay."[59] Such statements work to debunk gender-based stereotypes and have moved evidentiary standards in asylum proceedings away from a focus on the body as a source of knowledge about sexual orientation.

Nonetheless, the issue has continued to come up since a pair of BIA decisions in 2008 suggested that particular social groups must be "socially visible" in the claimant's home country to be recognized for asylum protection in the United States.[60] In their co-created training module for asylum officers, however, Immigration Equality and USCIS sought to correct the interpretation of this requirement among some judges who believed it meant that claimants must be identifiably queer in some immediate, visible way. The manual states, "Some adjudicators mistakenly believe that social visibility or distinction requires that the applicant 'look gay or act gay.' In this context, social visibility or distinction does not mean visible to the eye. Rather, this means that the society in question distinguishes individuals who share this trait from individuals who do not."[61] The manual goes on to explain that applicants may express themselves differently than LGBTQ people in the United States and may claim to be visible as a sexual minority in his or her home country even though s/he does not seem stereotypically gay by US standards. It further elaborates that cultural cues regarding sexuality vary from culture to culture and that some applicants may not even identify with labels such as "gay" and "lesbian." Addressing this issue during our interview, Victoria Neilson said, "Somebody might not come in and say, 'I'm a transgender woman from Ecuador.' She might just come in and say, 'I'm a woman' or 'I'm an effeminate gay man,' even though they look like a woman. . . . [T]hey don't have to adopt the . . . politically correct New York/San Francisco language to have an identity that should be protected."[62] As this suggests, it is not necessary to adopt a Western identity or enact a stereotypical gender performance to make an asylum claim, and adjudicators are increasingly aware that they cannot base universal notions of what it means to be gay on Western stereotypes.

The body often also comes into play for asylum seekers when actual sex acts are considered. However, as the following section shows, it is really a *narration* of the body and sex acts that is considered by courts, and is therefore less a form of direct knowledge than another type of narrative evidence consistent with the identity narratives described above. Like stereotypes, sex acts are more likely to be deemed relevant when they are part of a larger narrative of discovering and expressing one's sexual identity, as we saw in Kofi's asylum hearing discussed in the introduction.

In other situations, adjudicators explicitly reject any reliance on sex acts as a requirement for proving sexual orientation. After an immigration judge deemed Ingrida Mockeviciene "at best . . . a non-practicing lesbian" and rejected her asylum petition, the Eleventh Circuit expressed its skepticism with such reasoning, asserting, "The fact that Mockeviciene had not been in a recent relationship with a woman is not probative of her sexual orientation."[63] In another case before the Second Circuit, the court rejected the immigration judge's rationale that "no one would perceive Ali as a homosexual unless he had 'a partner or cooperating person,'"[64] a statement that suggests people can only identify gay people if they are having same-sex sexual relations. Once again emphasizing the importance of placing indicators of sexuality in context, the court went on to write that the judge's comment "appears to derive from stereotypes about homosexuality and how it is made identifiable to others. It is certainly not grounded in the record, which, as IJ Vomacka noted in another part of the decision, suggests that 'an unmarried adult man with no children would be suspected of being a contemptible homosexual in Guyana.'"[65] It is also notable how questions about sexual acts may reinforce gender inequalities in asylum determinations by favoring men who are more likely to have greater access to the public sphere to find sexual partners, both in their home countries and in the United States. To the extent that adjudicators ask such questions, men may therefore be able to offer more "typical" coming-out narratives familiar to US judges, as well.

However, government attorneys and asylum officers do sometimes continue to ask questions about or base arguments on sex acts, despite consistent refusals by judges, and especially appellate courts, to accept such evidence as probative. For instance, I witnessed a government attorney argue that an asylum seeker had provided no evidence of his sexuality except his own "self-serving testimony" and that he had failed to obtain corroborating letters from the "only two people in the world who could unequivocally prove that he is gay."[66] In the attorney's argument, the only two people who could prove the claimant's sexual orientation were those with whom he had sex. The judge rejected this argument.

Recent guidance to asylum adjudicators now explicitly directs them to avoid asking probing and inappropriate questions about sex acts. United Nations guidance instructs officials, "Enquiries as to the applicant's realization and experience of sexual identity rather than a detailed questioning of sexual acts may more accurately assist in assessing the applicant's credibility."[67] Likewise, USCIS training states: "The applicant's specific sexual practices are not relevant to the claim for asylum or refugee status. Therefore, asking questions about 'what he or she does in bed' is never appropriate."[68]

Overall, these findings suggest that the body has become less important in asylum law over time.[69] Stereotypes and "common sense" cannot serve as the basis for a judge's decision, and though sex acts may be taken to signal queer identities at times, it is also clear that sex acts are not *required* to make a valid asylum claim and may not be enough to sustain a claim on their own. Indeed, guidance to adjudicators instructs them to avoid overly intrusive questions about sex acts in favor of questions about one's felt identity. Moreover, when sexual acts become part of a claim, they are not necessarily taken as *direct* evidence of one's underlying sexuality. Rather, like issues of gender nonconformity, sex acts are contextualized within larger narratives and thus become further signs to be interpreted. For instance, Kofi's attempted intercourse with a woman, described in the introduction, was not dispositive of heterosexuality. Rather, it was placed in a larger narrative trajectory before conclusions about Kofi's sexuality were drawn. This is consistent with the overall finding that narrative evidence is the most determinative for asylum claims. As we will see in the following chapter, however, the process of measuring and classifying the sexualities of sex offenders looks quite different.

6: SEX OFFENDERS AND THE DETECTION OF DEVIANCE

After returning from the lunch break, the assistant attorney general continues her questioning of Dr. Leavitt, one of the state's expert witnesses. They go into extensive detail about Hill's past offenses, sexual and otherwise, and then they turn to his time in prison. Hill participated in sex offender treatment with the Department of Corrections (DOC) for nearly four years while incarcerated, but he did not complete the full course of treatment. Dr. Leavitt reports to the court that one way to reduce risk is to complete a comprehensive sex offender treatment program, but he has serious concerns about the treatment offered by the DOC. Specifically, it only relies on self-report. It does not include psychosexual assessments that gauge "what turns him on," that is, whether violence and suffering arouse him.

CIVIL COMMITMENT TRIAL OF RANDALL HILL,
COOK COUNTY CRIMINAL COURT, MARCH 2017

The final paper of the session compared arousal measured via PPG with self-reported arousal among rapists and child molesters (CMs). Though both rapists and CMs reported greater arousal to adult women, CMs showed greater arousal to children on the PPG. This paper generated an interesting discussion. The presenter said she was surprised that CMs showed different arousal than what they reported even after she assured them that she wasn't with law enforcement and that their results were completely anonymous. Her conclusion was that they were either lying (though she was baffled as to why they would lie) or that they weren't aware of their arousal to children (as measured by minute changes in their penile tumescence). One therapist in the audience chimed in that "they [sex offenders] don't even know what we mean when we say 'deviant.' They ask, 'Is sleeping with someone other than my wife deviant'?" This actually seemed like a valid clarifying question to me given the high prevalence of infidelity in our society, but it was clearly a black-and-white issue in her mind and one that marked sex offenders as willfully uncooperative. Another audience member offered the explanation that some people "just like to lie." They seemed completely unaware

of the extensive research on social desirability of interview responses. I did hear
one audience member say "socially acceptable," but unlike the other comments,
this one wasn't taken up for discussion.

ATSA ANNUAL MEETING, MONTREAL, QC, NOVEMBER 2015

Just as with asylum seekers, narrative and bodily evidence come together
to support legal claims about sex offenders' sexualities, but as the above
episodes from my fieldwork suggest, they cohere in quite different ways.
Whereas asylum law heavily weighs a claimant's identity narrative as a
sign of an unobservable inner sexual self, sex offender narratives are more
likely to be channeled through more "objective" technologies or deployed
to support and contextualize more objective assessments of one's sexuality. Partially underlying this evidentiary stance is the assumption that sex
offenders will never be fully forthcoming about their sexual desires and
behaviors, which may be true in many cases since disclosure of continued
paraphilic interests may form the basis for indefinite civil confinement
rather than access to treatment. The researcher in the second vignette,
with her confusion about the mismatch between the PPG and self-report
findings, evinces a telling faith in the power of technology to get to the
truth of sexuality by bypassing the subject. She appeared not to consider
the consequences of the laboratory context, the social desirability of particular responses, or, indeed, the distinct possibility that the test subjects
were telling her their own self-perceived truth. As a participant in another
session commented, "Most arousal is between the ears." So why is there so
much continued effort to find arousal only between the legs?

Such efforts depend on the assumption that if only we can perfect the
technology, we can directly measure something called "sexuality." Under
this epistemic logic, signs themselves become data. An erect penis during
a PPG examination *is* sexual attraction. Sexuality itself is materialized
through the technology of the PPG. Similarly, sexual danger is given concrete form and quantified by actuarial risk assessments. While these assessments are not straightforward materializations of sexuality in precisely
the same way as PPGs, they nevertheless purport to consider a bundle of
indicators related to sexual violence and return an objective measure of
an offender's future sexual risk. Overall, there is a greater effort in sex offender evaluations to distill or transform signs of one's sexuality into direct
technical measures of that person's sexuality. In other words, the process
of interpreting indicators is not seen as interpretation so much as direct
reading. This statement applies with different weight to the various types
of evidence produced for evaluations, and I will consider each in turn in this
chapter, beginning with the sexual narrative.

NARRATING DEVIANCE

Abundant narrative evidence undergirds SVP determinations. But unlike the personalized and self-presented stories of asylum seekers, those of sex offenders are routed through technical instruments, such as the *DSM* or polygraph, to create rationalized narrative trajectories. That is, while evaluators' reports run dozens, if not over a hundred, pages, and they may offer hours of testimony in civil commitment proceedings, these detailed narratives are ultimately in service of proffering a technical diagnosis from the *DSM* and legitimating recidivism predictions. As socio-legal scholar Mona Lynch asserts of sentencing guidelines, the quantitative criminal history metric is imbricated in a "debate about the moral makeup of the juridical subject to be punished" that simply becomes a "post-hoc label to legitimate a priori moral judgment of the defendant."[1]

A similar pattern holds for the narratives presented in regard to SVPs. Legal scholar Kathleen Kendall notes, for instance, that women offenders are more often subsumed within psychiatric discourses.[2] Because female offenders violate norms of femininity, their stories are often rationalized through such diagnoses; otherwise we cannot make sense of their actions. Sex offenders' stories are similarly subjected to a formally rational logic that reduces complex narratives into technical language that rationalizes their actions (if only by declaring them irrational and incomprehensible outside such technocratized language). Thus, although SVP narratives are filtered through a more formal rational logic than are those of asylum seekers, narratives remain important in this legal complex, as well.

The Sexual Narrative

In civil commitment hearings for SVPs, the sexual narrative consists of two key elements: the master file, as it is referred to in Illinois, and the clinical interview, both of which are presented via expert witnesses.[3] The master file includes all of the offender's records in the state's possession, which generally encompasses criminal, disciplinary, and medical records, and, importantly, mental health and sex offender–specific treatment records. Anything an offender says in treatment becomes subject to court review, which can often incentivize offenders to avoid sex offender–specific treatment for as long as possible so as not to provide details that may be used against them in SVP hearings. Finally, though polygraphs and PPGs are not generally admissible in US courts, they may partially undergird an expert's testimony, in effect becoming part of the record without ever being formally acknowledged. Indeed, many jurisdictions have declared that PPG evidence can be used in civil commitment cases because of the exception to hearsay evidence in such proceedings.[4] Even if they do not influence the initial commitment hearing, polygraphs and PPGs will ultimately become important in determining an offender's progression through treatment, risk level, and potential for release.

The aptly named "master file" is perhaps the perfect illustration of what sociologist Dorothy Smith calls "textually mediated forms of ruling."[5] It consists of a set of texts that allow details of an offender's biography to be crystallized, removed from their local context, and transported across time and distance. This file is the most important piece of any evaluation, for it forms the basis of the actuarial risk assessment and often of the psychiatric diagnosis, as well. In many ways, the master file allows the creation of "objectified forms of consciousness and organization."[6] A psychologist tasked with evaluating a potential SVP may never actually interact with that person. It is not unusual for an evaluator to complete a risk assessment and give an offender a psychiatric diagnosis without ever talking to him because many offenders' lawyers instruct them not to speak with the state-appointed experts. Because of the offender's right to refuse to speak with the state psychologist, and thanks to the design of the actuarial instruments, the evaluation procedure is *designed* to make human interaction unnecessary for the legal process.

For example, in the SVP proceedings that I observed for Jordan Lowe, the state called two psychologists, one of whom, Dr. Brucker, had used the master file and conducted a clinical interview to arrive at his final assessment, and another, Dr. Wood, who had based his conclusions only on the master file. Both produced the same actuarial risk scores, and both gave the same *DSM* diagnoses.[7] Dr. Brucker, who had conducted a clinical interview with Mr. Lowe, even testified that he first produced his report before speaking with Mr. Lowe (who had refused the initial interview on lawyer's advice), and that his final report completed after the clinical interview reflected only "slight" modifications: the interview did not change his ultimate conclusions. Furthermore, Dr. Brucker's responses to questions from both the state and defense drew almost exclusively on information from Mr. Lowe's master file. Both Dr. Brucker's and Dr. Wood's diagnoses of "paraphilic disorder otherwise specified: nonconsent" depended only on master file information. During his deposition, Dr. Wood also mentioned that Mr. Lowe's PPG results figured into his conclusion.[8] Although PPG test are not generally admissible in Illinois, courts have determined that experts in SVP trials may partially base their opinions on the results of such testing.

Actuarial risk instruments provide an even clearer picture of how human interaction is rendered redundant in sex offender evaluations. As discussed previously, actuarial risk assessments work by comparing an individual to aggregate data collected on a large sample of offenders along an array of factors determined by researchers to correlate with recidivism rates. Most actuarial tools are designed to use only information available from official documents. The Static-99R—the most widely used actuarial risk tool in the United States—is a ten-item assessment that requires information about the offender's demographics, criminal history, and victim information. An evaluator simply plugs in the answers to these questions, and a risk score ranging from –3 to 12 is produced along with a corresponding group re-cidivism rate. To obtain a recidivism prediction, an evaluator must choose the correct reference group for the offender, of which there are four for the Static-99R: routine, non-routine, preselected for treatment need, and high risk/high need. For instance, the predicted sexual recidivism rate for an offender who scored a 6 and was placed in the high-risk/high-need category (as most offenders being considered for SVP status are) would be 31.2% over five years and 41.9% over ten years. Through this process, an offender's biography is distilled into a set of numbers. This represents the process of creating ordered psycho-legal knowledge from a vast set of ob-servations that may have several possible interpretations.[9] In essence, the Static-99R acts as an inscription device, and as science studies scholars Bruno Latour and Steve Woolgar point out, "Inscriptions are regarded as having a direct relationship to the original substance."[10] In this case, the risk score, label, and predicted recidivism rate are taken to be directly re-lated to the offender, and particularly to his sexuality and sexual risk.

Although it is often not completed in time for civil commitment pro-ceedings, sex offenders must also provide a "sexual history" narrative. As the previous discussion illustrated, asylum seekers do something similar, but the questions they address typically inquire about their first recollec-tions of same-sex attractions and perhaps sexual encounters. The interro-gations sex offenders face delve much deeper into their intimate thoughts and behaviors, including the types of sexual fantasies they have and what they think about when masturbating. Significantly, sexual histories of sex offenders often employ the polygraph, as well, which seeks to "objectively" measure via the body one's subjective testimony.

The polygraph works off the assumption that lying causes emotional changes that result in physiological responses in the body and, further, that we can mechanically read and interpret those bodily responses. It assumes that lying causes unique emotional, and hence physiological, changes that truth-telling does not—in other words, that deception is emo-tionally more difficult than honesty. In the 1923 *Frye* decision ruling that an early version of the polygraph was inadmissible in court proceedings, the DC Circuit Court skeptically wrote that "the theory seems to be that truth is spontaneous, and comes without conscious effort, while the utterance of a falsehood requires a conscious effort, which is reflected in the blood pressure."[11] Polygraphs remain inadmissible in most legal proceedings today. Nevertheless, polygraphs have a long history of use with sexual "deviants." Perhaps most notoriously, the polygraph was used during the "Lavender Scare" to ferret out suspected homosexuals working for the US government.[12] Beginning in the late 1980s, Oregon became the first state to routinely use the polygraph in the treatment and management of sex offenders, and by 2009, 79% of community-based programs and 56% of residential programs in the United States reported using polygraphs.[13] Thus, despite scientific controversy and its inadmissibility in court, the polygraph enjoys widespread use in the management of sexual offenders in the United States, and courts routinely uphold its use for this population.

Though estimates of the polygraph's accuracy range from just better than chance to upward of 90%, as historian of science Ken Alder points out, the polygraph works less because of its scientific accuracy and more because people *believe* it works.[14] It is thus less of a scientific test of truth than a tool for facilitating disclosure. Sidestepping questions of scientific validity, then, many professionals who work with sex offenders subscribe to a view similar to that of Sean Ahlmeyer and colleagues: "The polygraph is not a test, but a treatment tool designed to elicit a client's admissions to past behaviors and monitor current behaviors. Many therapeutic interventions that do not meet the standards requiring adequate documentation of practice standardization, reliability, and validity, are nonetheless effectively utilized in the field."[15] This opinion was echoed in a session devoted to polygraph use at the 2015 annual meeting of the Association for the Treatment of Sexual Abusers (ATSA), where the presenters delivered the take-home message that polygraphs can help obtain information—about number of victims, sexual acts performed, continuing fantasies, and so on—that you might not otherwise get. In fact, they suggested that offenders are fourteen times more likely to report data useful to assessment, treatment, and supervision when given a polygraph examination. Some in the audience voiced their reservations about using polygraphs and felt instead that they could get the same information by building a trusting therapeutic relationship with the offender, which is a real concern for many treatment providers given that, to the extent a polygraph is seen as necessary, it tends to send the message that the offender is seen as inherently deceptive. However, in the context of rapid legal decision-making, there is generally little time to develop a trusting relationship between a therapist and an offender.[16] Rather, adjudicators and evaluators often want a quick snapshot of an offender's sexual behavior or his compliance with treatment and/or probation conditions.

One common use of the polygraph involves the "sexual history interview," which an offender may complete at one or more various points on his journey through the legal system. ATSA provides guidelines for conducting sexual history clinical interviews that many states adopt either fully or partially.[17] It suggests that a sexual history cover at least the following: history of sexual experiences, nature and frequency of sexual practices (including masturbation and risky sexual activities), paraphilic interests and behaviors (both abusive and non-abusive), history of sexually abusive behaviors, information about victims, context of abusive behaviors, and more.[18]

Although treatment, including polygraph examination, is ostensibly voluntary while incarcerated or committed, an offender's refusal to submit to a polygraph may result in adverse repercussions. In a series of cases from Kansas, prisoners brought suit against the state for "withholding privileges" after their refusal to cooperate with treatment, including completing polygraph and PPG testing.[19] In all three cases, the courts sided with the state, determining that the prison's interest in rehabilitation outweighed the prisoners' privacy rights and, furthermore, that the prison was within its right to "withhold privileges" for refusal to participate in a voluntary program, even when "withholding privileges" included actions that seemed punitive, such as being sent to a higher security facility. Similarly, SVPs in Illinois generally will not be considered for conditional release until progressing to at least stage 4 of treatment.[20] To move from stage 2 to stage 3, however, an offender typically must pass a sexual history polygraph.

Once offenders are released into the community, completion of sexual history polygraph examinations usually becomes mandatory as part of treatment. Dr. Donya Adkerson, a treatment provider and risk evaluator in Illinois, elaborated on what concerns her when conducting a sexual history:

> So what our program looks for in a sexual history test is clarifying information that's going to impact safety planning. . . . So what we're looking at—is there a history of sex beyond what we already know? Is there a more extensive history of sexual offending against children that's going to suggest that pedophilic orientation? Have they offended against males as well as females because that increases the risk level? Have they offended against strangers? Another factor that increases risks. Have they done other kinds of offending that we don't know about? So we're trying to get those parameters together that are going to help us do the best safety planning with the client to have a better understanding of their risk level.[21]

Like testimonies from asylum seekers that seek to construct a developmental narrative, sexual history interviews with sex offenders attempt to create a fuller picture of an offender's path to sexually deviant behavior. Unlike asylees' stories that concentrate on *identity*, however, sexual history interviews are concerned primarily with *behavior* and *desire*. Although sexual offenders are asked about sexual behaviors and desires, they are in effect supplied an identity. Just as the sodomite ceased being a temporary aberration and became the "homosexual" through his inscription in medical discourse, so today do "psych" professionals generally consider many paraphilias, like pedophilia or sadism, to be lasting orientations. In fact, the *DSM* does not allow "pedophilic disorder" to be classified as "in full remission" as it does for other paraphilias.[22] When I asked Dr. Richard Travis why this was the case, he responded as follows:

> Because that is one paraphilic disorder that is all about attraction to a particular . . . The thing about pedophilia is, it's not a desire to do a certain act or like something where your stress builds up and then you have to relieve it by showing yourself or, you know, get the excitement of looking in somebody's secret life when they don't know you're there. . . . It would be like me having heterophilic disorder in full remission at some point, you know? . . . I'm terminally straight. And people who [are] aroused mainly by children, they're terminally that: aroused by children.[23]

Because these sexual subjectivities are highly medicalized and criminalized, sex offenders can rarely prevent their narratives from being subsumed into these dominant discourses in the way that asylum seekers can sometimes successfully push against canonical understandings of sexuality. Through the sexual history confessional, sex offenders supply the details that allow state and medical officials to classify them as both criminal and mentally abnormal. Whereas asylum seekers may narrate and enact a particular performance of identity, the polygraph engenders—and even forces—the performative enactment of a deviant identity for the sex offender.

Another frequent use of polygraphs is the "maintenance test"—that is, a polygraph examination to ensure that an offender is abiding by the terms of his probation or supervised release and is not engaging in any behaviors that might lead to reoffense. Maintenance tests are often legally mandated as a condition of an offender's release from prison, and in Illinois they typically take place every six months (generally at the offender's expense). Though offenders have challenged this condition in courts around the country, judges routinely uphold it, generally giving the rationale that it is reasonably related to the treatment and rehabilitation of the offender. Many courts further add that polygraph examinations are reasonably related to deterrence and public safety, as well. Thus, the polygraph acts at different stages—first the sexual history and later the maintenance exam—as both a confessional and surveillance technology that simultaneously constructs and verifies a sex offender's narrative.

In sum, sexual narratives by both asylum seekers and sex offenders often suggest an inherency to sexuality, though in different ways, and, importantly, that inherency seems much more ingrained in sex offender risk assessments than in asylum hearings. For instance, though asylum seekers frequently insist that being openly gay is being "who I am," there is much less explicit discussion of sexual fantasies, desires, and behaviors than in the case of sex offenders. Asylum seekers also do not have to contend with a medicalizing discourse that views their sexualities as abnormal, leaving considerably more room for resistance and flexibility in the sexual identities they construct before the state. As chapter 5 demonstrated, immigration officials have begun to accept narratives that evince an inchoate social constructionist view of sexuality. Even when asylum seekers make essentialist statements that might suggest a fixed internal state of sexuality, either in the mind or body, their narratives are not channeled through the actual physical body in the way that sex offenders' stories are—that is, through the technology of the polygraph. This is imperative, for, as Andrew Balmer and Ralph Sandland suggest:

> These confessional apparatuses are performative in that they serve to enact a deviant, criminal desire and thus function to constitute the offender as a [pedophile] there and then, thereby avoiding his deception or denial of his crimes and making him more amendable to risk-management strategies. . . . An important consequence of the use of the polygraph and plethysmograph is that it constitutes the sex offender's abnormality as bodily and as fundamental.[24]

This bodily abnormality articulates nicely with the medicalization of sexual deviance, rendering it nearly impossible for sex offenders to resist an "abnormal" label. This theme will become even more apparent in the following section, where I consider how the body becomes implicated as direct evidence of deviant sexuality.

MATERIALIZING SEXUALITY THROUGH THE BODY

A widely used technology for determining a sex offender's sexual preferences is the penile plethysmograph (PPG). More than a third of residential treatment facilities for sex offenders and approximately 28% of community-based treatment programs in the United States report using it.[25] Like the polygraph, which aspires to ascertain the truth of an offender's sexual narrative via the body, the PPG seeks to know a subject's sexual desires via bodily measures. As sociologists Tom Waidzunas and Steven Epstein argue, "Phallometric testing 'materializes' male desire through a particular conjoining of bodies, knowledge, and technology that renders that desire perceptible and measureable."[26] It further depends on what they call "technosexual scripts." Building on the idea of sexual scripts by pointing to the ways that technology mediates our understanding of sexuality, Waidzunas and Epstein argue that the PPG only works given the presumption of a "normal" man who responds mechanically to visual stimuli. Moreover, the PPG assumes that a flaccid penis cannot be indicative of any arousal state, that male arousal is completely centered on the erect penis, and that male sexuality is unemotionally task driven. Such assumptions often go unremarked in risk adjudications for sex offenders where the erect penis indicates arousal, which in turn indicates orientation and presumably action.

In the commitment hearing of Jacob Sandry in Illinois, for instance, the court sought to determine whether the PPG was admissible as part of an expert's testimony. Its reasoning is unusually blunt but illustrates well the tacit assumptions adopted by most courts when considering PPG evidence:

> The contours of our inquiry are limited to whether there is some reasonable connection between the methodology and what it seeks to measure. . . . The reasonableness inquiry is fairly straightforward in this case. Quite simply, penile engorgement is a plausible measure of sexual arousal. This observation ends the reasonableness portion of the inquiry.[27]

In its final determination, the court continued:

> To conclude, since there is a logical, plausible, common-sense connection between sexual arousal and penile engorgement, experts who rely upon the PPG test, which purports to measure this connection, are being reasonable within the meaning of *Frye*. Moreover, since the test is widely used, it is apparent that it is accepted by a substantial number of those who work with sex offenders, though it is far from clear that this group constitutes a majority. Some of these experts consider it the best tool for assessing recidivism. These two factors satisfy the *Frye* test as articulated by the Illinois Supreme Court.[28]

With this decision, the court simultaneously upheld the validity of the PPG as a measure of sexuality and the authority of forensic psychology to assess that validity. Perhaps more importantly, with its appeal to "common sense," the court also upheld its own authority to dictate what counts as authoritative knowledge. Thus, the law and forensic psychology mutually constitute and reinforce each other's authority.

In another Illinois commitment case, the state prosecutor attempted to make the connection between arousal and penile response very clear to the jury:

[Pedophilia] is also told by tests that check your physiological responses to certain stimuli . . . and that is the plethysmograph thing you heard about. Spend 30 seconds thinking about a plethysmograph. This is a test that determines or measures sexual arousal, basically involuntary reaction. Picture it. You are going in some sterile, the most unerotic setting you can ever imagine with several people all around you. There are people in the room in his case at least Dr. Wasyliw with all his machinery in what can never be described in a sensual kind of way and they show dirty pictures of little kids and they do it with this wire wrapped around the man's penis. A man who in Mr. Grant's word has a cloud of a sexually dangerous person hanging over his head. A man who has to be thinking in his head I am going to try to be as unaroused as possible. I don't know if a person would be thinking about Mickey Mantle's baseball scores or whatever but anything but arousal. And in that context they show him pictures of prepubescent girls and while trying to put himself into a mental cold shower he still has a 35 percent increase.[29]

Here, the prosecutor uses several rhetorical strategies to position the PPG as an objective and accurate assessment of sexual arousal, and even more pointedly (and performatively), to suggest that it reveals pedophiles: "[pedophilia] is *told* by tests that check your physiological responses." He goes on to assert that the PPG measures involuntary response, which suggests that the defendant cannot control his sexual urges and helps to establish the desire/action nexus. Finally, he sets the scene of the PPG test as a sterile laboratory setting devoid of any erotic elements partially to overcome one of the shortcomings of the PPG and this particular defendant's results: a 35% increase in penile tumescence. It is typical of phallometric testing to have a quite small change in penile tumescence. Subjects rarely become "fully" aroused. Yet these rather small responses are taken as objective indicators of sexual arousal.

This also raises questions regarding the laboratory setting of PPG testing. Where asylum seekers' claims are embedded in particular cultural contexts, there is considerable effort to remove this context in assessing sex offenders' sexualities. Indeed, this was a major objection to PPG use on asylum seekers. If we accept the proposition that attraction depends significantly on cultural codes of beauty and, as research is beginning to show, that sexual attraction can often be context-dependent and vary depending on one's relationship with the person, then the lab setting seems to present a challenge.[30] Commenting on why some of his patients reported not showing arousal during PPG testing, a forensic psychiatrist who routinely depends on such tests told me, "The pictures they were shown were not appealing to them, were not attractive. . . . [T]hey used to use a slide deck from the 1970s with those big hairdos and bell bottom pants. Now they have kind of moved to a newer version of it, but earlier that was going on, so the people didn't find that attractive."[31] Assumptions of a universal and mechanical male sexual response gloss over the possibility that attraction likely varies along many cultural dimensions, such as race, age, and one's sexual socialization.

Sometimes courts turn to scholarship to back up their assumptions about and reliance on the PPG. Perhaps the most commonly cited article is Jason Odeshoo's "Of Penology and Perversity: The Use of Penile Plethysmography on Convicted Child Sex Offenders," a non-peer-reviewed law review piece.[32] The Ninth Circuit cited this piece in its highly influential *United States v. Weber* (2006) decision, quoting the passage that defines PPG testing as a procedure that "involves placing a pressure-sensitive device around a man's penis, presenting him with an array of sexually stimulating images, and determining his level of sexual attraction by measuring minute changes in his erectile responses."[33] This sentence makes a direct connection between sexual attraction and erectile response, allowing courts to make that connection, as well. Like the asylum legal complex, however, most decisions do not rely extensively on scholarship. Rather, a small handful of cases draw extensively on extant scholarship, and then most other decisions simply cite those cases as shorthand, as we saw with *Hernandez-Montiel* in asylum jurisprudence. Indeed, the reason that Odeshoo's article is more highly cited than other articles is due in large part to its place in the influential *U.S. v. Weber* (2006) decision.

Nevertheless, other scholarship explicitly lays bare the plethysmograph's assumed connection between desire, arousal, and action. In *United States v. Rhodes* (2009), the Seventh Circuit cited psychologist Dean Tong's article in which he wrote:

> The PPG, when administered properly, represents a direct and objective measurement of a man's level of sexual arousal to normal versus sexualized stimuli. Since there is a strong relationship between an individual's pattern of sexual arousal and the probability that he may or will act upon that arousal, an important first step in gauging one's propensity to sexual deviancy is to obtain an accurate assessment of that person's sexual arousal patterns, which is precisely what the PPG does.[34]

All but one decision (and a couple of dissents) concerning the PPG in my archive either explicitly or implicitly accept these assumptions about the PPG, maintaining a belief in the test's ability to directly measure sexual arousal and therefore attraction, oftentimes even as they simultaneously acknowledge the controversy surrounding the technology. This simultaneously upholds the authority of forensic psychologists who administer the tests and courts to impose such testing.

Occasionally, courts do question the PPG. For example, in *U.S. v. Mc-Laurin* (2013), the court first explicitly laid out the assumptions of the PPG that are normally left tacit before using those logical leaps to strike a requirement that an offender undergo PPG testing as part of his supervised release:

> This examination involves the use of a device known as a plethysmograph which is attached to the subject's penis. In some situations, the subject apparently may be required, prior to the start of the test, to masturbate so that the machine can be "properly" calibrated. The subject is then required to view pornographic images or videos while the device monitors blood flow to the penis and measures the extent of any erection that the subject has. The size of the erection is, we are told, of interest to government officials because it ostensibly correlates with the extent to which the subject continues to be aroused by the pornographic images.[35]

Rather than simply assuming that erectile response equals sexual arousal, this court makes that assumption explicit, in part to illustrate the invasive nature of the test. In the case of *Billips v. Virginia* (2007), a dissenting opinion makes the assumption very clear and goes further by highlighting the intellectual uncertainty surrounding the PPG and likening it to the polygraph:

> In sum, the available data about plethysmographs reveals a scientific community dramatically divided over their reliability and accuracy. The studies of plethysmographs vary drastically in their conclusions. Some reports show an extremely fallible method, susceptible to manipulation from the subject and often misidentifying the subject as a sex-offender or as a non-offender, while other studies report high accuracy rates. In this respect, plethysmographs and polygraphs, both of which measure physiological responses, are similar. Both require an *assumption* that the physiological response measured directly reflects the emotion and behavior purportedly being measured.[36]

My interviewees, too, acknowledged the shortcomings of the PPG despite using it in their own assessments of sex offenders. In discussing the PPG, Shan Jumper, Clinical Director of Illinois's SVP program, said:

> It's not a perfect test. Probably the most common thing that we see is, we get, as far as we can tell, a valid test that the guy shows no arousal at all.

. . . So he's not showing any arousal to healthy or deviant stimuli. And it's unlikely that that would be the case. And if that were true in the case, the person would be asexual, which isn't very likely. So a lot of times, it doesn't capture somebody's arousal.[37]

Here Jumper maintains faith in the test's ability to measure arousal *when it is present*. He places blame on the test itself rather than the assumptions about sexuality underlying the test. Thus, if the test does not show a man's arousal, it is not because the PPG is measuring something that does not actually capture arousal, but because that particular testing situation was an anomaly.

CONCLUSION

I have suggested that the dominant epistemological approaches to understanding and classifying sexuality in asylum and sex offender law differ with respect to what each domain considers empirical evidence of sexuality. Where asylum adjudicators tend to take an indirect knowledge approach to determining someone's sexuality through the interpretation and contextualization of signs generated through narrative accounts, decision-makers in sex offender evaluations more often employ inscription devices meant to objectively materialize sexuality or directly represent particular characteristics of the offender. This is not to say that indirect knowledge never informs sex offender assessments nor that direct knowledge never informs asylum determinations. Indeed, many forms of narrative evidence, including clinical interviews and the "master file" inform SVP decisions, and some forms of physical evidence may be considered in asylum proceedings. But narrative evidence in the SVP legal complex is more likely to be subjected to a formal rational logic to produce technical diagnoses or routed through inscription devices, like actuarial risk tools. Conversely, physical evidence, such as sex acts and gendered stereotypes, in the asylum complex are narrativized. Thus, bodily acts are circumscribed within an overall epistemic logic that weighs a claimant's identity development narrative more heavily and rejects reliance on bodily indicators alone.

Ultimately, then, these two legal complexes differ in the underlying epistemological assumption of whether sexuality is directly discernible through technological interventions or must be surmised from indirect indicators. A possible objection to this assertion is that something like the PPG *is*, in fact, an indirect indicator. What I have tried to show in this chapter, though, is that this is not how the PPG and accompanying technologies are understood within this particular legal complex. Rather, it *reveals* one's true sexual arousal (and therefore orientation). If one shows arousal to prepubescent children during a PPG examination, the evaluator is likely to, at least provisionally, consider that person a pedophile. Similarly, one might object that actuarial risk instruments are likewise simply indicators. Once again, however, these instruments are taken to offer direct measures of one's sexual risk.

Additionally, a critic might simply say that all of these differences can be boiled down to the fact that asylum law is concerned with identity and therefore is trying to measure that, while sex offender law seeks to punish criminal sexual behavior and thus concentrates on that. My analysis, however, should have already made it clear that these lines are not nearly so crisp in practice. Asylum law *does* protect groups bound together by identity, but as the previous chapter showed, courts have granted protections based on forms of conduct associated with queerness and even to those who reject queer identities but may have such identities imputed to them. Moreover, there is significant slippage in how sexual identity is understood in asylum law. Does it require sex acts? Explicit adoption of a certain identity? Sexual desire for particular bodies? Any and all of these may be taken as evidence of queerness depending on the context of the overall narrative.

Conversely, sex offender laws ostensibly control sexual behaviors, but as the label "sex offender" makes obvious, the state assigns a sexual identity to those convicted of illegal sexual behaviors. Furthermore, though civil commitment statutes are careful to avoid overtly stating that they punish a type of person, it is quite clear that the "sexually violent person" label is a legal and social identity. And SVP proceedings, like those for asylum, vacillate between taking desires, behaviors, and identities as indicators of sexuality. A particular behavior may be the basis for an offender's arrest, but his evaluation could reveal desires (e.g., arousal to children) that suggest an underlying identity (e.g., pedophile) not (yet) revealed through action. Thus, my analysis, while attempting to untie this Gordian knot of significations, reflects the ambiguity of the polysemous term "sexuality" as it is used in these arenas and, indeed, in society writ large.

I have attempted to demonstrate that because state actors are charged with ascertaining individuals' sexualities, but "sexuality" is not defined, courts draw on preexisting institutional logics and cultural schemas to create divergent ways of knowing sexuality in each legal realm. State knowledge is thus already socially and culturally structured before final decisions are rendered. Sexualities scholars have shown how cultural assumptions about sexuality influence scientific examinations of sexuality, producing knowledge about it that is already contoured by social forces.[38] Similarly, I have shown that social forces shape how sexuality is constituted in state institutions by creating conditions under which divergent epistemic logics become institutionalized in different state institutions.

Despite all of this ambiguity, we can still draw some conclusions about how these different epistemic logics affect conceptualizations of sexuality in each legal arena. Assumptions about how sexuality is best measured simultaneously suggest beliefs about where sexuality is located. For forensic psychology and the legal culture of sex offender evaluation, the primary belief is that sexuality flows from the individual and can therefore be gauged through measuring the individual body, monitoring his behavior, and ascertaining his desires. Sexuality in this paradigm is largely essential. The legal environment of asylum law and its contributory experts, on the other hand, provides space for social context. Though asylum seekers generally claim that their queer identity is "who I am," suggesting an essentialness to sexuality, there is also substantial recognition of the constructedness of sexuality. Asylum law has recognized that sexual identity categories vary around the globe, that a capacity for sexual fluidity exists, and that sexual acts carry different meanings in different cultures. By approaching the classification of sexual subjects in different ways, state institutions, in conjunction with non-state expert actors, powerfully contribute to the naturalization of differences along the lines of sexuality. In other words, divergent epistemic logics governing how state institutions know LGBTQ asylees or sex offenders help to reify the historically recent cultural shift distinguishing homosexuality and sexual criminality.

Certainly, the specific settings under consideration here are significantly different. One concerns the admission of a foreign subject; the other concerns the release or confinement of a convicted felon. Clearly, the stakes are different, as are the subjects under scrutiny. There is presumably a stronger presumption of dishonesty for a felon facing a possible lifetime of civil commitment compared to a civilian seeking refuge, though it should be noted that asylum seekers may also have an incentive to lie in order to remain in the country, and this alleged concern for fraud has led to stricter requirements in asylum applications.[39] I am suggesting, however, that epistemic logics already reflect these political and institutional concerns. Forensic psychology was chosen in part because of the perceived objectivity of its evaluative and classificatory methods and its ability to categorize reticent subjects. Likewise, anthropological, sociological, and human rights experts are brought to bear on asylum adjudications because of their ability to evaluate and contextualize sexual identities and behaviors that may be illegible to US state administrators.

These differences point to two additional factors that are important for creating the conditions under which indirect narrative or direct bodily evidence become the predominant forms of evidence in each setting. These are expertise inertia and data inertia. Both describe the tendency for organizations to replicate previous approaches to measurement rather than to create new ones. Creating new forms of measurement requires considerable infrastructural investment and generally depends on actors with expertise in the phenomenon to be measured. Given the state's previous use of psychiatrists in the penal management of sex offenders, it took only minimal effort to shift to the use of forensic psychologists, who largely claimed the same domain of expertise. Expertise inertia explains less in the asylum legal complex because there was no clear existing expertise for adjudicating LGBTQ claims. However, it was easier for the immigration apparatus to accept the insurgent expertise of asylum advocates and fit them into existing informational infrastructures (e.g., adding an LGBT section to State Department Country Reports on Human Rights Practices) than to create that expertise in-house.

Similarly, data inertia occurs because organizations tend to depend on already-existing data or data that is easily collectible and commensurable. It requires significant cultural and analytical work to create new categories and collect new kinds of data. This is, in part, why the State Department often relies on NGOs and organizations in other countries to report human rights information to them, which is then compiled into specific country conditions reports. The lack of available data for adjudicating asylum claims in general, and LGBTQ claims in particular, also helps explain why adjudicators elevate narrative evidence. In the face of data scarcity and more "objective" forms of evidence, narrative becomes the most reliable and available form of information. Adjudicators would surely prefer more concrete data, though, and it would not be surprising to see the adoption in the near future of the LGBT Equality Index (currently being developed by the UN) as an objective indicator of country conditions for LGBTQ people. Conversely, reams of data are often available for adjudicating SVP cases, and given a long history of relying on technologies like the PPG and polygraph—and more recently actuarial assessment—and no exogenous pressures to change, data inertia prevails.

Social pressure has, however, affected the asylum complex. Social movements advocating for LGBTQ people have increased the social acceptance of gender and sexual minorities and therefore the resistance to using techniques seen as inhumane or degrading on queer people. But it is important to note that this acceptance has come at the price of erasing queer people of color and portraying the LGBTQ community as predominantly White. The face of the gay and lesbian movement has often been White, middle-class, and male. This is reflected in the fact that "coming out" narratives have become the default trope in US culture for comprehending queer existence. Yet this trope has been criticized by queers of color for being characteristic of White middle-class male experience, and therefore one that does not necessarily capture their own journey of self-discovery or self-identification. Even the seemingly more generous epistemic logic of the asylum complex, then, may risk erasing and failing to recognize some kinds of queer experience.

In the end, however, classification practices that differ for LGBTQ people and sex offenders further cements the historically recent social distinction between these two groups. The effects of these competing epistemic logics can also be seen in the risk assessment practices of each state domain. While asylum adjudications depend on assessing the risk a petitioner would face *from* his home country, SVP determinations revolve around calculating the risk the offender would pose *to* his community. The next two chapters explain how these risk calculations play out and constitute sexual subjects as potential citizens or social pariahs.

7: QUEER SUBJECTS AND THE CONSTRUCTION OF RISKY COUNTRIES

FRAMED BY DANGER: CONSTITUTING SEXUAL SUBJECTS THROUGH RISK

Risk assessment has become a central tool of modern governance. This, I contend, is as true for evaluating sexual subjects as it is for discerning the risks of toxins, environmental pollutants, and a host of other fixtures of modern society. Assessing risk is fundamental to both asylum and sex offender adjudications, although the processes proceed quite differently in each legal complex. Whereas asylum determinations depend on a qualitative and largely tacit calculation of the probability that a claimant will face persecution if returned to his home country, sex offender decisions employ actuarial risk assessment tools in an explicit, quantitative process of assessing the probability that an offender will commit future acts of sexual violence. Though their purposes and processes are different, risk assessments in both areas of law make risk a central element of sexual governance and in the definition of sexual subjects. In short, risk mediates sexual citizenship.

This chapter and the next illustrate how risk has become central to the governance and classification of sexual subjects. I first show how risk calculations are performed in each setting and then how those risk assessment techniques undergird different forms of recognition for sexual subjects vis-à-vis risk. I ask: How is "sexual risk" rendered cognizable for legal decision-making? What is seen as a "risk object" in these legal calculations? Risk assessment, perhaps more than any other technology of knowing, determines how state institutions manage sexual others, but at the same time it resonates with other ways of knowing sexuality. In asylum, risk is determined through a process that involves assessing the risk of a cultural setting for an individual or group of individuals (a "particular social group," or PSG). That is, risk is a structural and cultural characteristic of a particular country, and adjudicators must attempt to discern a claimant's individualized risk in that setting through careful contextualization. This approach clearly resonates with the asylum complex's ways of understanding sexuality presented in chapter 5, which revolve around contextualizing sexual narratives within a specific cultural setting.

In sex offender adjudications, risk is determined through a process of individualized assessment using tools that are universal, or understood to be anyway—actuarial tools, polygraphs, PPGs, mental health diagnoses, and psychological testing. In other words, the individual himself is seen as the source of risk. Structural or cultural factors are not considered, even though, for instance, more than 90% of sex offenders are men, suggesting a strong gender socialization component. Culture seems to be a factor only when it is *other* cultures.[1] Once again, these risk assessment practices are clearly in line with the more essentialist and individualized conceptualization of sexuality found in the sex offender legal complex. Although actuarial tools are presented as objective technologies that remove human judgment and bias from risk adjudications, subjectivity continues to find its way into these decisions. As research in other settings has shown, actuarial assessments often "black box" evaluators' discretion and present risk estimates as objective indicators, rather than acknowledging the subjective decisions that necessarily go into such determinations.[2] Other work similarly shows that actuarial assessments often have racial and gender biases built in to their design.[3] For example, some actuarial tools, including some for sex offenders, produce higher risk estimates for individuals who live in areas with low employment prospects or have family members with criminal histories, factors more likely to negatively impact people of color.

Despite one assessment approach being highly qualitative and "clinical" and the other being quantitative and actuarial, both are seen as objective assessments. The judge in an asylum claim is, in essence, positioned as an objective risk calculator in a similar way as actuarial risk assessment technologies are in sex offender hearings.

One goal of this section, then, is to demonstrate that risk is a culturally structured way of dealing with social problems. It is not a preexisting, inherent reality. Because risks often remain invisible and are based on causal interpretations, Ulrich Beck explains, they "initially only exist in terms of the (scientific or anti-scientific) *knowledge* about them. They can thus be changed, magnified, dramatized, or minimized within knowledge, and to that extent they are particularly *open to social definition and construction.* Hence the mass media and the scientific and legal professions in charge of defining risks become key social and political positions."[4] More generally, risks are open to cultural definition. In their statement of this cultural conception of risk, Mary Douglas and Aaron Wildavsky argue that public concern with environmentalism shifted from a focus on national security to environmental risk not because the objective risks at issue changed but because cultural actors (namely, social movements) reframed the debate.[5] In other words, "whatever objective dangers may exist in the world, social organizations will emphasize those that reinforce the moral, political or religious order that holds the group together."[6] In short, risk perceptions are central to the social construction of reality, and sexual risk definitions therefore evolve with cultural views. Risk assessment processes, I suggest, are thus also boundary-making processes that help to reify symbolic divisions between "good" and "bad" sexual subjects, between citizens and noncitizens. We can begin to see this if we look at the historical relationship between sexuality and risk.

SEXUALITY AND RISK: A BRIEF HISTORY OF DANGEROUS SUBJECTS

Often when we think of sexuality and risk, it is in the context of sexual health, especially in relation to disease transmission and prevention.[7] Feminist work of the last several decades has also brought the issue of sexual assault to the forefront of thinking about the relationship between sexuality and risk.[8] Scholars have given less consideration to how risk has become a dominant lens through which to construct and regulate sexual subjects before the state. This has been a long-term strategy by the US state, but it is crystallized in certain settings today more clearly and explicitly than it has been in the past.

Sexual others have long been portrayed as diseased or otherwise threatening to the nation. Narratives of contagion have been used to demonize queers by purporting that they would spread their "vice," contaminate the community or nation, and even bring death (most recognizably via HIV/ AIDS).[9] These ideas were codified into law in many arenas, including immigration, military, and welfare policy.[10] However, while the idea of risk or danger certainly structured thinking around these policies and views, it is only recently that risk has crystallized as an explicit state strategy of managing sexual subjects. Even the "dangerousness" prediction called for under sexual psychopath statutes differed in quality from that which is performed today. Dangerousness for sex psychopaths was wholly tied to their diagnosis as a psychopath from which danger was deduced. Today, an explicit risk assessment process makes such determinations, and as Robert Prentky and colleagues assert, "Though the constitutional underpinnings of [SVP] laws appear to put the 'mental disorder' and 'dangerousness' prongs on equal footing, in reality it is fair to say that most of the focus in the implementation of these laws falls on dangerousness. The mental disorder prong has little or no role in determining who is committed and who is not."[11]

This emphasis on risk comes with a larger shift toward a precautionary logic that is refiguring the institutions of law and science in the management of sexual and violent offenders. This preventative logic can be seen in its strongest form in sex offender management, where there is an attempt, as Nikolas Rose puts it, to "bring the future into the present."[12] This is accomplished through the "'naturalization' of risk itself within the body of the dangerous person."[13] Naturalizing risk within the body of the sex offender legitimates the idea that exceptional legal measures, or what legal scholar Richard Ericson calls "counter-law," are needed to deal with these "anti-citizens." One form "counter-laws" take is "laws against law": "New laws are enacted and new uses of existing laws are invented to erode or eliminate traditional principles, standards, and procedures of criminal law that get in the way of preempting imagined sources of harm."[14] In the case of sex offenders, courts have carved out exceptions to the ex post facto, commerce, and confrontation clauses, as well as circumscribing double jeopardy and due process protections.[15]

In an illuminating comparison of the *Lawrence v. Texas* (2003) and two Supreme Court decisions regarding sex offender registration and community notification rendered the same year (*Smith v. Doe* and *Connecticut v. Doe*), sexualities scholar Joseph Fischel shows that the humanity and careful consideration granted to the "homosexual" in *Lawrence* is denied the "sex offender" in *Smith* and *Connecticut*.[16] Where Justice Anthony Kennedy, writing for the majority in *Lawrence*, carefully deployed social science and history to rebut the arguments of *Bowers*, just three months earlier in *Smith*, he refused to do so (as did Justice William Rehnquist in *Connecticut*), instead relying on faulty assumptions that sex offenders have high recidivism rates. Furthermore, Kennedy suggests that making sodomy a registerable sex offense for gays imposes stigma, undermines human dignity, and amounts to state condemnation, but for other sex offenders, this does not seem to be the case. Fischel pointedly suggests, "This is because, for Kennedy, homosexuals are people. Sex offenders are not."[17] Indeed, this may not be an exaggeration, as abundant scholarship documents public attitudes regarding sex offenders as monsters, animals, and generally less than human.[18]

During roughly the same time as sex offenders were becoming the pre-eminent boogeymen, LGBTQ people were being conditionally welcomed into the national community. Though the United States has historically excluded and discriminated against sexual "deviants," the "queer exception" to legal protections has recently begun to fade.[19] One of the earliest "exceptions" to disappear was the bar on gays entering the country, which was repealed in 1990, just months after the BIA affirmed an immigration judge's decision to allow a Cuban man to remain in the United States because of persecution he had faced on account of his homosexual identity. Though the gay movement faced setbacks throughout the 1990s, notably with the "Don't Ask, Don't Tell" compromise of the Clinton administration and a continuing HIV/AIDS crisis, it also garnered several victories, including legal protections in various states and the *Romer v. Evans* (1996) decision by the Supreme Court, ruling that a Colorado state constitutional amendment preventing protected status based on homosexuality or bisexuality violated the equal protection clause. Notably, the following year, the Supreme Court upheld sex offender civil commitment statutes in *Kansas v. Hendricks* (1997). LGBTQ people continued to gain new legal protections and rights in the 2000s, including the striking down of sodomy laws, the enactment of hate crimes legislation, the ability to serve openly in the military, and the legalization of same-sex marriage. By contrast, during the same period, new laws requiring the public registration of sex offenders, community notification, GPS monitoring, and restricted residency, among others, were enacted and largely withstood legal challenge. Thus, as the state retreated from regulating one sexual population, it expanded to more fully encompass another. Notably, though, while things like hate crimes laws and the legalization of same-sex marriage are intended to protect LGBTQ people, they also extend state regulation and penal power in the name of sexuality.

At the same time that sex offenders were increasingly portrayed as the ultimate threat because of the risks they *posed* due to their sexualities, queers were being increasingly recognized as citizens because of risks they *faced* on account of theirs. In an analogous way that sex offenders require legal exceptionalism because of their uniquely dangerous sexual natures, LGBTQ asylum seekers are granted an exception to usual immigration and naturalization practice because of their sexualities and the risk they face because of them, in an illustration of what Jasbir Puar calls "sexual exceptionalism." As she argues, "The contemporary emergence of homosexual, gay, and queer subjects—*normativized through their deviance* (as it becomes surveilled, managed, studied) rather than despite it—is integral to the interplay of perversion and normativity necessary to sustain in full gear the management of life."[20] Key here is that queers are normalized and welcomed into the realm of citizenship *through their sexualities* while a new perverse other is simultaneously created in the form of the sex offender. Nevertheless, risk remains a lens through which even these "accepted" sexual subjects are recognized. Risk assessment, then, works as a mechanism for separating the "good" from the "bad" and therefore also contributes to the proliferation of sexual identities based around risk: the queer asylee, the incurable pedophile, the insatiable rapist, the normal gay.

In what follows, I consider how sexual risk is rendered legally cognizable, what aspects of sexuality are deemed risky, and precisely how risk is calculated within each legal complex in order to show how risk assessment techniques undergird different forms of recognition for sexual subjects.

DEFINING PERSECUTION IN ASYLUM CLAIMS

Adjudicators in both asylum and sex offender law must make risk decisions in terms of particular standards of proof. For asylum claims, that standard is a "well-founded fear of persecution" if the claimant were returned to his home country. However, if a claimant is ineligible for asylum, which is a rather common problem for LGBTQ petitioners for a number of reasons, and must instead seek withholding of removal, the standard is substantially higher. Though courts and legislators do not give concrete quantitative thresholds, the Supreme Court has dictated that the standard for withholding is a "clear probability" of persecution or "more likely than not," which is generally interpreted as a greater than 50% probability.

This higher burden of proof, interestingly, comes through a consideration of risk in some respects. It is often a criminal conviction that renders a claimant eligible only for withholding rather than asylum. If the crime is serious enough, the burden shifts again, this time to a clear probability of torture (as opposed to just persecution) for relief under the Convention against Torture (CAT). Thus, if an immigrant poses a greater potential risk to the United States, as determined by his criminal history, he must meet a higher risk threshold to remain in the country.[21] Indeed, section 208 of the Immigration and Nationality Act (INA) dictates several exceptions to asylum eligibility, including one provision stating that one is ineligible if "there are reasonable grounds for regarding the alien as a danger to the security of the United States."[22] For many LGBTQ asylum seekers, however, the higher burden is often a result of missing the one-year filing deadline for asylum. On its surface this does not seem to reflect a risk concern, but it may in fact be understood that way. The stated reason for imposing the one-year deadline (part of the Illegal Immigration Reform and Immigrant Responsibility Act of 1996) was that any "real" asylum seeker would lodge a claim within a year of arriving. This stated rationale, whether true or not, reflects a purported concern for fraud, a concern that the Trump administration increasingly used in its attempts to curtail the flow of asylum seekers into the United States.

But what exactly does "well-founded fear" or "clear probability" mean? Like all legal standards of proof, they are somewhat subjective. The clearest guidance on this question came with the Supreme Court's decision in *INS v. Cardoza-Fonseca* (1987). In the *Cardoza-Fonseca* case, an immigration judge had ruled that an asylum applicant had not shown that she was "more likely than not" to be persecuted if returned to Nicaragua and was therefore ineligible for asylum. The case hinged on whether "well-founded fear of persecution" (the standard for asylum from section 208[a] of the INA) was equivalent to "more likely than not" to be persecuted (the standard for withholding of removal from section 243[h] of the INA). The court determined that the two standards were different, writing, "One can certainly have a well-founded fear of an event happening when there is less than a 50% chance of the occurrence taking place,"[23] and later determined that

> there is simply no room in the United Nations' definition for concluding that, because an applicant only has a 10% chance of being shot, tortured, or otherwise persecuted, he or she has no "well-founded fear" of the event's happening. As we pointed out in *Stevic*, a moderate interpretation of the "well-founded fear" standard would indicate "that, so long as an objective situation is established by the evidence, it need not be shown that the situation will probably result in persecution, but it is enough that persecution is a reasonable possibility."[24]

The court thus established that even a 10% probability of persecution could qualify as "well-founded fear" for asylum. Yet in its concluding remarks, the court left adjudicators discretion, stating:

> The narrow legal question whether the two standards are the same is, of course, quite different from the question of interpretation that arises in each case in which the agency is required to apply either or both standards to a particular set of facts. There is obviously some ambiguity in a term like "well-founded fear" which can only be given concrete meaning through a process of case-by-case adjudication . . . We do not attempt to set forth a detailed description of how the "well-founded fear" test should be applied.[25]

While setting a general standard, the court refrained from giving specific directions on how to apply that standard. So how do adjudicators actually decide if someone has a "well-founded fear" or "clear probability" of persecution? Before considering how these calculations play out in asylum hearings, it is worth considering what constitutes persecution, for this greatly affects how adjudicators make predictions of future harm.

In addition to determining whether a claimant is truly queer, asylum adjudicators must also decide if the petitioner has suffered past persecution or has a well-founded fear of future persecution. If the adjudicator finds the former, the asylum seeker is granted a presumption of future persecution, and it then becomes the state's burden to rebut that presumption. If the latter, however, the petitioner must prove both a subjective and objective fear of future persecution. The subjective prong depends heavily on the claimant's credibility and whether his narrative is consistent with the objective evidence. Objective proof of future fear of persecution comes primarily in the form of country condition evidence, including expert testimony when available, and will be discussed more thoroughly later in this chapter.

These requirements seem rather straightforward, but they are complicated by the fact that neither the 1980 US Refugee Act nor the 1951 UN Refugee Convention define persecution. Nevertheless, it is widely understood to be "sustained or systemic violation of basic human rights demonstrative of a failure of state protection."[26] Thus, persecution cannot be sporadic incidents but must be sustained persecution by the government or such that the government is unwilling or unable to stop it. US jurisprudence dictates that persecution may be emotional, psychological, or physical and that adjudicators must consider the cumulative significance of experienced harm.[27]

The 1990 *Toboso-Alfonso* decision established that sexual orientation could be the basis for a PSG and thus that one could be persecuted for one's sexuality. However, LGBTQ people may face some dilemmas specific to them in proving persecution. The basis for persecution is often private acts, persecutors are often private actors rather than the state, and sexual assault often constitutes at least part of persecution claims. LGBTQ asylum seekers are therefore unlikely to resemble the paradigmatic claimant; that is, a man persecuted by his government for overt and public political actions and beliefs.[28] But case law has established that all of these things can constitute persecution, and, in theory, these precedents should apply equally to LGBTQ asylum seekers.[29] Nevertheless, it often seems like a rather subjective decision whether certain harmful acts rise to the level of persecution, and, indeed, this likely accounts for some of the considerable variation in asylum grant rates between jurisdictions and even between immigration judges within the same court.[30]

Having considered the ambiguity of the term "persecution," how, then, do adjudicators actually decide if a claimant has met the required burden of proof? Unlike the sex offender civil commitment trials I will discuss in the next chapter, asylum hearings do not rely on any quantitative evidence that provides a numerical estimate of future risk. Rather, the process is more holistic and qualitative, and to a significant extent relies on the judgment of the adjudicator. But judges do sometimes express a desire to be able to more accurately calculate risk, as the Seventh Circuit did in a 2016 case when it wrote, "If we could balance the magnitude of the risk times the probability of its occurrence against the cost of offering a few additional procedures, or a few more years, in the United States, we would."[31] In the absence of the ability to make such a calculation, however, the court deferred to the immigration judge's denial of relief.

Regardless of the precise process, the risk assessment is the single most important part of an asylum hearing, for it determines whether the claimant will be allowed to remain in the United States or removed to his home country. As such, the risk assessment ultimately serves as the key mechanism for recognizing the LGBTQ asylum seeker as a sexual subject eligible (or not) for the rights of citizenship. He will either be deemed a legitimate asylum seeker and potential US citizen due to the risk he faces from his home country (and the relatively low risk he poses *to* the US) or simply an illegal alien. The 2010 case of Lucas Velez illustrates this idea. Velez was found to be credibly gay and to have a subjective fear of future persecution, but the immigration judge (and ultimately both the BIA and Eleventh Circuit) determined that the abuses of queer people in Velez's home country of Colombia did not meet the threshold of persecution—that is, that Colombia was not "risky" enough for queers. In its decision, the Eleventh Circuit wrote:

> At his original hearing before the Immigration Judge ("IJ"), Velez called an expert witness who testified about the practice of police, paramilitary groups and guerillas attacking "undesirables," including sexual minorities, called "social cleansing." Velez also submitted Country Reports for 1995, 1998 and 2000 to 2006 and numerous articles documenting violence against homosexuals in Colombia and social cleansing. The IJ determined that this evidence showed isolated incidents of private violence against members of the gay community, but did not establish that Velez himself would more likely than not be persecuted upon his return to Colombia.[32]

Where another judge may have found "social cleansing" campaigns to indicate a pattern or practice of persecution against sexual minorities, this judge did not. Without the requisite level of risk, Velez was denied his status as a queer asylee and instead simply deemed an illegal alien and presumably deported. Indeed, findings of insufficient risk of persecution or torture are the single largest reason for denials in cases in the appellate archive, accounting, at least in part, for 59% of denied appeals. This is often true even for claims from countries where the same court previously or subsequently granted relief to a different claimant.

Individualizing Risk Determinations

As the above discussion suggests, even though decisions about persecution are highly dependent upon broad social and cultural conditions in a given country, asylum determinations are ultimately individual-level decisions and generally must be narrowly framed to apply only to the particular applicant. Technically, judges can grant claims based on a "pattern or practice" of persecution against a certain group of people in a given country, but judges generally avoid such declarations because of what is often referred to as the "floodgates" problem. Former BIA judge Lory Rosenberg put it this way: "The thing is that the big fear that pervades the Board and the whole EOIR [Executive Office for Immigration Review] in the asylum area is the fear of floodgates, right? . . . So, it's like when we were doing Chinese one-child cases, which was going on a lot . . . the huge fear is that anybody could come to the United States and say, 'I had one child and I wanted to have another child and they would have forcibly sterilized me if I stayed in China.'"[33] The same concern prevents government adjudicators from making blanket statements that might suggest that all transgender women from El Salvador, for example, would have a legitimate asylum claim because of a countrywide pattern of persecution against them. This is also why a number of precedential BIA decisions have seemingly strange or unnecessary language characterizing social groups eligible for protection. Rosenberg went on to explain this "floodgate" fear was the reason that the landmark *Kasinga* case (1996) declaring that female genital mutilation (FGM) could be a basis for asylum included language dictating that the claimant had to be politically opposed to the practice.[34] The concern was that, without such language, anyone who had been subjected to FGM could lodge an asylum claim, potentially opening the way for tens, if not hundreds, of thousands of women to migrate to the United States. A similar logic is at play in the recent BIA decision *Matter of A-B-* (2018) issued at the direction of Attorney General Jeff Sessions declaring that domestic violence would no longer be grounds for asylum in the United States.[35]

Thus, like determinations of claimants' sexualities—which are also ultimately individualized decisions—assessments of one's risk of persecution depend on contextualizing an individual life within a broader social context.

CONSTRUCTING RISKY COUNTRIES

Regardless of whether a claimant is found to have suffered past persecution or must prove well-founded fear of future persecution, country conditions evidence is a vital part of any asylum claim for establishing the danger a petitioner would face if returned to his home country. Though a claimant is presumed to face future persecution if he was found to have suffered past persecution, he still must guard against the government's likely argument that the country conditions evidence rebuts that presumption. A claimant must also guard against the argument that he could simply relocate within his own country to avoid localized persecution. This generally requires that an asylum seeker paint his home country as uniformly oppressive and leaves little room for nuance.[36] In other words, asylum hearings are a prime site where the United States is constructed as a liberated space while other countries and their cultures are constructed as backward and oppressive. Key tools in this process are governmental and NGO reports on human rights for sexual minorities.

Human Rights Reports

As discussed in chapter 4, the US State Department Country Reports on Human Rights Practices (the Reports) may be granted substantial, and even determinative, weight in asylum decisions. Asylum officers, immigration judges, the BIA, and appeals courts all generally defer to the Reports unless a critical mass of other sources compels a different decision. Quoting BIA procedural reforms, the Tenth Circuit wrote in *Halmenschlager v. Holder* (2009), "The most common facts about country conditions appropriate for administrative notice are those contained in country reports and pro-files prepared by experienced foreign service officers in the Department of State who are experts on specific regions and countries," before going on to add, "As the courts have recognized, they, the immigration judges, and the Board owe deference to the Department of State on such matters of foreign intelligence as assessments of conditions."[37]

Nevertheless, while they carry considerable weight, the Reports are not wholly determinative in most cases. The Second Circuit has ruled, for instance, that evidence from a Report is not binding on an immigration judge and cannot be used to automatically discredit contrary evidence presented by a claimant, and the First Circuit has said—emphasizing the individualization of risk assessments—that while Reports are generally persuasive, their contents "do not necessarily override petitioner-specific facts—nor do they always supplant the need for particularized evidence in particular cases."[38] Similarly, the Seventh Circuit asserts that "because the State Department's country reports are so general—they may reveal which groups are at greatest risk, but not how much risk and not how the coun-try's forces operate day-to-day—the administrative record needs concrete, case-specific evidence."[39] This is consistent with the argument presented in the previous chapter that determinations of individuals' sexualities in asylum claims depend on contextualizing narrative evidence within larger sociocultural contexts. Case-specific evidence comes most often from the claimant directly but may also be presented by experts, a topic I return to shortly.

However, the Reports are used as one of the primary resources for determining the risk an asylum seeker may face if returned to his home country and are therefore a key piece of how countries are constructed as dangerous to sexual minorities. For example, the 2010 Report for Mexico reads, "While society increasingly accepted homosexual conduct, CNDH and the National Center to Prevent and Control HIV/AIDS stated that discrimination persisted. According to the National Center and the Mexican Foundation for Family Planning, societal discrimination based on sexual orientation was common, reflected principally in entertainment media programs and everyday attitudes."[40] Here, despite increasing legal protections and more acceptance of homosexuality, the culture is portrayed as remaining hostile to queers as evidenced by media and "everyday attitudes." The 2012 Report for Jordan is clearer in outlining a dangerous sociocultural context for LGBTQs:

> Homosexuality is not illegal; however, societal discrimination against lesbian, gay, bisexual, and transgender (LGBT) persons was prevalent. A number of citizens reported sporadic police mistreatment of suspected or actual LGBT persons. Some LGBT individuals reported reluctance to engage the legal system due to fear that their sexual orientation would become an issue. There were reports of individuals who left the country due to fear that their families would punish them because of their sexual orientation.[41]

Again, although homosexuality is legal, social and cultural discrimination makes Jordan an inhospitable country for LGBTQ people. A similar pattern can be observed in a variety of NGO reports on conditions for sexual and gender minorities.

One of the most common tropes for characterizing countries as dangerous to LGBTQ people is through discussions of "culture," which is frequently presented as monolithic, irredeemably "traditional," and existing outside of political-economic factors.[42] As part of its background information on Honduras, a 2009 Human Rights Watch report states, "A culture of deep-rooted patriarchy and religious conservatism creates an atmosphere of intolerance that many times breeds violence."[43] The report continues:

> Machismo in Honduras means that men who do not act like men (or women who are considered somehow not quite women) face hatred and violence for their refusal to conform to normative gender identities. A deep-seated misogyny drives this hatred and enforces gender norms. Religious strictures and legal provisions both reinforce and justify this revulsion and rejection.[44]

The report also extensively discusses legal and structural obstacles faced by transgender and gender-nonconforming people in Honduras, but it ultimately blames much of the violence on prejudice and cultural attitudes. This use of "culture" is especially prevalent in Latin American claims, but culture appears in other guises for other national contexts.

In the African context, concerns with attitudes toward gender also come up, as they did in Amnesty International's 2013 report on LGBTI rights in sub-Saharan Africa: "Men who have sex with men also threaten dominant notions of masculinity where 'real men' are defined through their sexual relationships with women. Men who engage in same-sex sexual activity are often marginalized from the category 'men.'"[45] However, the more widespread use of culture to paint a picture of risk for African countries comprised greater discussion of "traditional culture" and cultural values. In the same report on sub-Saharan Africa, Amnesty International wrote:

> In many countries in sub-Saharan Africa, governments refer to culture and tradition to justify the violation of the human rights of those who are or who are perceived to be lesbian, gay, bisexual, transgender or intersex. Laws criminalizing homosexual activity are a legacy of colonialism, but this has not stopped national leaders from framing homosexuality as alien to African culture.[46]

This is a different deployment of culture than the recourse to "machismo" discussed above, and, indeed, it is one that African leaders sometimes use themselves when publicly decrying homosexuality. The Cameroonian minister of justice, for instance, wrote in 2006 that "by virtue of the African culture, homosexuality is not a value accepted in the Cameroonian society," and a 2008 study found that 80% of South Africans believe that gay and lesbian people are "un-African."[47]

Culture may also refer to popular culture. This comes up with some frequency in Jamaican claims and is echoed in Andrew Reding's 2003 report *Sexual Orientation and Human Rights in the Americas*, where he writes, "In the Caribbean, Jamaica is by far the most dangerous place for sexual minorities, with frequent and often fatal attacks against gay men fostered by a popular culture that idolizes reggae and dancehall singers whose lyrics call for burning and killing gay men."[48]

Reding's report is interesting because it straddles the lines between human rights reporting and expert affidavit, independent research and government intelligence. Reding contracted with the US government for many years to provide research on human rights and a variety of other issues, and he also maintained an affiliation with the World Policy Institute, through which he published his report on sexual rights in the Americas. Though Reding did not position himself as an advocate but as a researcher fulfilling a need for more public information on issues he had been researching privately for the government, as one of the earliest and most comprehensive reports on the status of LGBTQ people in Latin America and the Caribbean, his report became a resource to LGBTQ asylum advocates. Like the human rights reports that would come later from Amnesty International, Human Rights Watch, and others, Reding suggests that "culture" is to blame for much of the discrimination and violence toward LGBTQ people: "*Machista* ideals of manly appearance and behavior contribute to extreme prejudices against effeminate men, and frequently to violence against them. . . . There is a strong social stigma attached to homosexuality, particularly where it comes into conflict with the highly-accentuated and differentiated male and female sex roles prescribed by *machismo*."[49] However, Reding was also careful to point out regional differences, suggest that conditions were improving significantly in many metropolitan areas, and even to contest figures on hate crimes against LGBTQ people in Mexico and Brazil that had circulated widely among LGBTQ advocates and in asylum claims, for which he faced criticism for hurting the cause. Though both sides of that debate have some merit, the reaction by asylum advocates against a call for greater nuance in human rights reporting demonstrates the precarious position asylum seekers from much of Latin America occupy.[50] To present anything less than a one-sided, and possibly reductive, argument is to risk losing the claim.

I realized this issue early in my fieldwork with MIRA when I was tasked with conducting country conditions research. The directions I was given included the stated goal that "our research purpose is to look for news articles and reports on the client's home-country that demonstrate conditions that negatively affect the LGBT/HIV community." I was, however, also instructed to identify sources indicating positive developments and improving conditions, which were to be kept separate from the primary country file, presumably so MIRA attorneys could be prepared for what they would likely face from the government lawyers. These procedures are, of course, unsurprising in our adversarial legal system, where each side is expected—and obligated—to present the strongest case for their client. The government therefore engaged in the same process from the opposing angle, presenting only sources suggesting livable conditions for LGBTQ people. Ultimately, the newspaper articles, NGO reports, and other documents I was assigned to search for provided added context and detail to fill out the picture MIRA wished to create of a claimant's home country, and often included detailed accounts of discrimination, violence, and even murder aimed at LGBTQ people.

In sum, culture is used in a number of different ways to paint countries as "backward" or uniformly hostile toward LGBTQ people, necessary endeavors to win asylum claims. Though certain uses of "culture" are more frequently deployed for particular countries or regions (tradition in Africa;

machismo in Latin America), they are not exclusive to those contexts. Gender attitudes may be discussed for Africa, just as tradition may be considered in Latin America. Nevertheless, the goal is the same regardless: create a portrait of a country that is uniformly dangerous for the asylum seeker. Sometimes, though, documentation is not enough.

Expert Witnesses

When lawyers feel that they cannot put together a convincing enough case with only available documented evidence, they often recruit expert witnesses. Experts provide affidavits containing more detailed country conditions evidence and may also testify in court to support their affidavits. Lawyers typically draw on outside experts in one of two situations. First, existing evidence is unclear or contradictory. Mexico was frequently cited as a prime example of this, and MIRA increasingly seeks out experts when they have Mexican asylum seekers. Mexico legalized gay marriage and adoption and has put in place anti-discrimination laws meant to protect LGBTQ people. From a bird's-eye view, then, Mexico looks like a safe place to be queer. Experts who testify about Mexico, however, argue that the on-the-ground picture does not comport with this view and that the "culture" has been slower to change than the law. As LGBTQ people make legal progress, there may be a significant cultural backlash, or, as is often claimed in asylum cases, those responsible for ground-level protection of LGBTQ people—such as the police—do not enforce the new laws and may even be the persecutors. The second situation in which a lawyer may seek an expert is when limited evidence exists for a country. For instance, if a petitioner comes from Tajikistan, it is unlikely that many NGOs or other organizations will have produced the type of evidence that they have for more populous countries.

Regardless of the specific reasons for seeking an expert witness, the primary goal is to create an image of the claimant's home country as hostile toward LGBTQ people. Like human rights reports, experts also often employ cultural tropes in their statements. For example, an expert affidavit for an asylum hearing I observed for an HIV-positive gay Mexican man opened with the following headline in bold: "'Machismo' motivates Mexico's violence against homosexual men, bisexual men, and transgender individuals." The opening lines of that affidavit go on to state, "The animus that motivates the related persecution and torture of bisexual and transvestite individuals in Mexico is the Latin culture of 'machismo,' an attitude that values 'male-ness' and masculine qualities above all. This set of cultural values is a pretext for perpetrating acts of violence against sexual minorities who 'deviate' from the expected macho standard."[51]

Another expert affidavit stated, "I have observed a pattern of 'institution-alized homophobia/transphobia' that stems from Mexico's very traditional culture around gender and sexuality."[52] In rebuttal to the government argument that conditions in Mexico had improved for LGBTQ people and was evidenced by the massive Gay Pride Parade in Mexico City, one expert responded, "This event may have 'boosted' tourism and the visibility of LGBTQ rights in Mexico but did little in the long term to change cultural attitudes in Mexico."[53] Similarly, sociologist and expert witness Nielan Barnes asserted that government lawyers will often say things like, "They could just go to Mexico City because it's so progressive, and it's got—they could even change their gender on their birth certificate according to a 2003 law in Mexico City that was passed. That's held up as like, 'Oh, that's such a progressive place.'" Her response to this suggestion brings the focus back to culture: "Passing a law and then enforcing it are two entirely dif-ferent things, and one of the things that happens is the uptick in violence, the pushback from the conservative elements in society, particularly the church and such and pro-family groups. And they mobilize."[54] Thus, ex-perts often buttress claims of dangerous cultures, particularly for Latin American countries for which pure legal arguments cannot be easily made because of the decriminalization of homosexuality and even legal protec-tions for sexual minorities.

Immigration lawyers are acutely aware of the need to make these cultural risk arguments for Latin American nations, as attorney Peter Perkowski illustrated when he explained how he refutes government argu-ments that sexual minorities are safe in Mexico: "You just need to point out that the changed country conditions still haven't actually infiltrated the cultural norms to a sufficient degree to change behavior. So just because you can get married in Mexico City doesn't mean you don't any longer have roving hordes of gangs and/or police officers and governmental agents still harassing, beating, torturing, and murdering LGBT people." Perkowski ex-plained that having a country conditions expert was beneficial because it was "very helpful to have kind of set out for the judge the cultural history of Mexico and its macho culture because that's what drives a lot of this violence."[55] Perkowski also relied on published social science research on "machismo" when he couldn't get an expert witness. Immigration attorney Lavi Soloway explained that he believed it was important to bring in cultural factors because simply looking at the legal landscape can be misleading. Whereas the gay movement in the United States worked on changing attitudes for many years before things like same-sex marriage were culturally viable, "They [Mexican LGBTQ activists] actually have gotten a little bit more quickly to a formula that looks like what we have been doing—domestic partnership, domestic partnership adoption. But they haven't changed the public opinion, they haven't changed the environment."⁵⁶ Veteran BIA and immigration judge Paul Schmidt echoed these sentiments, as well. While recognizing that some countries have passed laws protecting LGBTQ people and made some progress, he also said:

> It's progress, but it has to be so fundamental a change that it eliminates the reasonable possibility of harm. And when I look at it . . . these things usually have deep cultural roots. So I think that even when the government acknowledges the problem and tries to deal with it, it doesn't go away any more than passing the Fourteenth Amendment made racial animus and racial [trails off]. You can pass a law, you can set up an office, but if there's a deep cultural antipathy toward LGBT, that isn't going to go away probably for generations. So I'm always somewhat suspicious when a government claims, "Yeah, in the last five years it's changed from dangerous to hunky dory."⁵⁷

Lawyers therefore seek expert witnesses and social science research that can fill in the cultural factors that may be missing from more macro-focused human rights and State Department reporting.

However, social science experts are acutely aware of the statements they are making. My interviewees reported sometimes feeling torn between a desire to help people get out of dangerous situations and the need to be ethical scholars who are true to their research. Speaking about her expert testimony on Honduras, Suyapa Portillo, who is Honduran herself, said:

> And the other thing is just having to say cultural things, you know what I mean? Having to say like there is a culture of my people and—you know it's problematic for us to have to write those things to prove that this is a dangerous society for LGBT folks because I feel like there's a cultural machismo here in the US too, and so how we have to kind of split ourselves into writing functionally to help people get out, you know?

She later explained, "I'm very careful how I say things particularly around machismo. . . . I don't want to say that the culture is inherently machista because that would be inappropriate, and it's not true. And so I say things like—so I cite academic research, you know, that would buttress some things that needed to be said around that without having to say that people are inherently machista, you know?"⁵⁸ All expert witnesses I spoke with suggested that getting this kind of nuance into their testimonies was sometimes difficult because of the expectations of the legal setting. As Barnes explained, "I have to provide sound bites, and I've worked it so I can do that. There's a structure in the questions that I give the lawyers to ask me during my direct [testimony] so that there's a given flow, that I'm not talking too long so that the information is kind of [handed to] them in sound bites so they're being spoon-fed the information."[59] Or as Portillo put it, "They want the short simple answers to the questions."[60] This can cause conflict between scholars' desires to be thorough and detailed in their testimony and the legal system's need to reach a quick and parsimonious conclusion on the risk that a petitioner will face in his or her home country.

This need to make general statements about an entire country may also arise when experts are asked to rebut the idea that an asylum seeker could simply relocate within his home country, as one exchange from a gay Malaysian man's asylum hearing demonstrates:

> JUDGE: What does the Malay government do to discourage homosexuality?
>
> EXPERT: They have recently ratcheted up anti-gay discourse. They publicly say that gays shouldn't visit the country as tourists. They have now set up reeducation camps for students suspected of being gay. They also sent out leaflets to parents with the signs that your kid may be gay and what to do about it.
>
> CLAIMANT'S LAWYER: Is this limited to a particular geographic region of the country?
>
> EXPERT: No, it's pan-Malaysian.[61]

Here, the focus is less about culture and more about the assertion that the asylum seeker would face a substantial risk of persecution regardless of where he lived in Malaysia.

If successful, all of these sources—the claimant's testimony, human rights data, and expert testimony—converge to create a portrait of a risky sociocultural setting to which it would be unconscionable to return the asylum seeker. In the case of asylum, then, sexuality is rendered a risk object only insofar as it puts an individual *at risk* if placed in a certain sociocultural setting. The source of risk is not sexuality, per se, but the sociocultural context of a country. A country's culture, in particular, often features centrally as a source of danger.

How, though, do adjudicators actually *make* the final decision? The next section takes a closer look at the risk determination process and how these various sources of knowledge contribute to it.

MAKING THE DECISION

While asylum decision-makers must make many decisions in the course of adjudicating an asylum claim, the most important is determining the level of risk a claimant would face if returned to his or her home country. If an adjudicator finds that sexual minorities are not persecuted in the claimant's home country or that the claimant himself would not be at substantial enough risk of persecution, the entire claim is lost. The adjudicator could conclude that the petitioner is credible, queer, and even faced violence, but if that violence does not meet the threshold of persecution or if the adjudicator determines that risk to sexual minorities has decreased enough in the claimant's country, the claim will be unsuccessful. As discussed above, the requisite risk threshold for a claimant to receive asylum is "well-founded fear of persecution," which is generally considered to be approximately a 10% probability of facing persecution. By contrast, the required threshold for withholding of removal is "clear probability" or "more likely than not," which is generally considered to be greater than 50% probability. However, as one judge suggested, adjudicators do not necessarily think in terms of probabilities:

> I think that most judges that I know really never thought in terms of the percentages, and that was really a legal construct to say it's a far less significant risk than if you were trying to prove eligibility for withholding of removal. . . . So that's sort of where that standard came from, the *Cardoza-Fonseca* standard. . . . So that's your standard, but it doesn't mean definitely every case where there's a 10% chance, you know.[62]

The judge here suggests ample room for discretion in asylum adjudications simply because any calculations of risk must be done by the adjudicator without any forms of quantitative evidence and with only vague guidelines.[63] Given the legal system's need for objective decisions, how do asylum adjudicators position themselves as objective risk calculators?

Making Subjective Choices into Objective Decisions

In the course of my fieldwork, it became clear quite quickly that different judges had different approaches to adjudicating LGBTQ asylum claims. This was a widely acknowledged fact among MIRA staff, who hoped their cases would be placed with one of the "good" judges. After a particularly close call in a hearing, one lawyer lamented to me that she may have given her colleague a "false sense of security" because she had said the judge presiding over the case was particularly good on LGBTQ cases. "She's good if you do your job," she corrected, but "we can't rely on an IJ [immigration judge] being lenient as our strategy to win." Implicit in her comments was that a different IJ likely would have denied the claim. The assumption that IJs determine asylum claims differently is well supported by large-scale evaluations of IJ outcomes.[64] Judges themselves acknowledged the difficulty of calculating the risk a person might face in the future, partially because of the nature of sexuality: "I think the difference with LGBT cases is that the issue that gives rise to the threat of persecution basically is private conduct, and when the underlying reason for somebody seeking to harm somebody else is something that they're choosing to do in private, it makes it hard to assess objectively what's the risk that they would be harmed for that behavior." Elaborating on this difficulty, the same judge suggested that the nature of persecution against LGBTQ people also complicates risk predictions because "part of the conundrum of LGBT cases is that people are not able to act freely. So if they're going to behave differently how would they be perceived, and what are the chances that they would be harmed, and that's difficult to predict."[65] Thus, as this judge points out, sexuality-based claims may be particularly difficult because part of the persecution they face is being forced to be closeted and may therefore avoid some of the danger they would otherwise face if they were openly queer.[66] Paul Schmidt likewise discussed the difficulty of predicting risk for LGBTQ people because many of them are based on fears of future persecution rather than demonstrated past persecution and pondered aloud during our discussion: "What kind of evidence amounts to a 10% chance that you're going to be harmed and that the government isn't going to be able to protect you?" He went on to explain, "With LGBT cases, since some people, their awareness and they're revealing of their sexuality doesn't happen until they get to the United States, they sometimes don't have that clear evidence of past persecution which gives them a presumption of future persecution. So the prediction becomes more difficult, and the evidence on the country conditions becomes more relevant." His conclusion is to put more weight on country conditions evidence in order to make more generalized risk assessments, but his explanation points to some unique difficulties with predicting risk that other forms of asylum claims do not present.

Moreover, the BIA may employ a different risk determination technique as well, as it did in the case of Miguel Rosiles-Camarena (2013). Quoting from the BIA's decision, the Seventh Circuit wrote, "'In assessing the probability of harm de novo, we may give different weight to the evidence than did the Immigration Judge.' The BIA proceeded to do just that. It accepted all of the IJ's findings of historical fact but disagreed with the IJ about the risk implied by those facts."[67] The court went on to decide that the BIA had committed an error when it substituted its judgment for that of the IJ, but it clearly sympathized with the BIA's desire to create a standardized ruling on whether a given culture (in this case, Mexico) was dangerous for gay men (the BIA believed it wasn't). Citing Ramji-Nogales et al., the court later wrote:

Immigration judges display substantial disparity in evaluating claims for asylum or withholding of removal. See Jaya Ramji-Nogales, Andrew I. Schoenholtz & Philip G. Schrag, *Refugee Roulette: Disparities in Asylum Adjudication*, 60 Stan. L. Rev. 295 (2007). The Board thinks that it is entitled to curtail IJs' divergent approaches and believes that it can do so by determining whether particular countries are, or are not, hostile to particular political or social groups. Indeed, *we have urged the Board to make categorical decisions.*[68]

As of this writing, the BIA has made no such decisions. Absent concrete guidance, adjudicators attempt to "objectify" their decisions in several ways.

The most straightforward instance of this is when the government simply stipulates that some countries are "objectively" bad. As one IJ said, "I mean again some countries' conditions are just so bad . . . sometimes it's clear in an LGBT case that the conditions are bad enough in the home country that anybody who is gay would be at significant risk, so sometimes it's actually an easier case depending on the facts in the home country."[69] This occurs most often with countries where the government overtly punishes, or even kills, LGBTQ people, such as Yemen and Iran. Such cases may go on the "quick docket" in immigration court, where claims can be expedited if the government agrees to the form of relief someone is seeking. This happened for Sarah, a lesbian from Uganda, who received asylum after an approximately fifteen-minute hearing because the government stipulated to the fact that Uganda was simply "objectively" unsafe for her. Outside of these relatively rare cases, adjudicators must use other strategies to legitimate their decisions.

First, IJs often attempt to delineate concrete, objective reasons for their risk determination. Delivering an oral opinion from the bench on an asylum claim by Liu, a gay Malaysian man, one IJ offered an almost bullet-point style list to back up her decision. She began by citing the US State Department Report indicating that there are laws criminalizing sodomy and immoral conduct, though they are rarely enforced. However, the country conditions expert testified that they are sometimes used and were in at least one high-profile case involving the deputy prime minister, who was imprisoned for six years. The expert also testified, and documents corroborate, that police enforce the law extrajudicially and with impunity. At least two speeches in 2012 by the prime minister singled out LGBT people as undesirable. The government has set up reeducation camps for youth; the government condones hate speech and violence. After a lengthy list supporting her determination, the IJ ultimately concluded that "the Court will find that because the respondent is an openly gay Chinese man with effeminate characteristics, he has established well-founded fear of persecution and will grant his request for asylum."[70] Such overt declarations render the decision-making process more transparent. By offering a laundry list of reasons to support a decision, an adjudicator in effect makes what is ultimately a subjective decision resemble something closer to the mechanical objectivity preferred in bureaucratic decision-making. Each step propels any reasonable fact-finder toward one conclusion: that Liu would face persecution in Malaysia. The style of delivery attempts to remove human judgment from the equation, letting the facts speak for themselves.

This strategy can also be seen when adjudicators construct a chain of causality, so to speak, as in the case of Roxanne Isaacs, a lesbian from Guyana. Isaacs's claim for relief depended on her argument that each step in a chain of events was likely to occur. First, she would be identified as a lesbian because of her appearance. Second, she would be arrested and detained by Guyanese authorities because she is a lesbian. Third, she would be tortured (hers was a CAT claim) while in prison. The IJ, however, analyzed each step and concluded that each was not "more likely than not" and concluded that "Isaacs may not establish a claim for CAT relief merely by stringing together a series of suppositions to show that it is more likely than not that torture will result where the evidence does not establish that each step in the hypothetical chain of events is more likely than not to happen."[71] Here, the decision is wreathed in the aura of conditional logic (if A, then B; if B, then C), again in a manner that seems to limit room for subjective judgment.

Another decision-making strategy that can be gleaned from the way judges deliver their opinions is to cite what they perceive to be the most objective sources of information first. We can observe this strategy at work in Liu's case above, where the IJ began her risk assessment by citing the US State Department Report. In the *Rosiles-Camarena* case also discussed earlier, the court stated, "A sound prediction depends on country conditions, not (necessarily) on facts unique to the alien."[72] As Aaron Morris, the Legal Director for Immigration Equality, suggested, adjudicators view some forms of evidence as better than others in making risk determinations:

> I would say there's a tiered system about evidence and why some evidence is better than others. The State Department reports on each country every year. That's probably for better or worse what the US government puts the most reliance on. Sort of a step down on that are other countries like the UK and Canada, which also do similar reports. Similar on that tier of good evidence are really reputable human rights groups like Human Rights Watch

or Amnesty International. But also other really reliable news sources like the BBC or *New York Times*.[73]

This hierarchy of evidence is echoed in one immigration judge's explanation of how she assesses risk: "You go with the reports from various organizations including the Department of State but also including Amnesty International, Human Rights Watch, and there are some others, to see what are current conditions like."[74] Indeed, when specific sources of country conditions evidence are cited, the State Department Reports are by far the most common source. More than a third (38%) of the appellate decisions in my data set explicitly referred to the Reports. At the immigration court level, the Reports were introduced in all twelve cases I observed. When IJs delivered oral opinions from the bench, they frequently cited the Reports, followed by reports from other governments (usually Canada) and well-respected human rights organizations. IJs never explicitly invoked any forms of evidence further down the credibility hierarchy. Like the bullet-point listing of evidence outlined above, tying a risk decision to the US State Department or Amnesty International gives the appearance of removing the subjective judgment of the adjudicator from the final determination.

In other instances, adjudicators attempt to use the purported objectivity of numbers and statistics to legitimate their risk calculations. Advocates frequently argue that Brazil and Mexico continue to be dangerous for LGBTQ people despite legal protections because of the high levels of violence, particularly murder, against them. Specifically, they point out that Brazil and Mexico rank first and second, respectively, for the most murders of LGBTQ people each year. However, some decisions turn these numbers around to support denials of asylum, as the BIA and Tenth Circuit did in the case of Marcelo Halmenschlager, a gay asylum seeker from Brazil:

> The unvarnished fact that 180 homosexuals were killed in one year is not remarkable in a country of over 180 million, particularly when the report does not identify the killings as murder, contains no mention of the reason for the killings or any description of the perpetrators. . . . The reader is left to speculate—were they homophobic killings or were they motivated by other factors (jilted lovers, drug dealing, prostitution, etc.) and only coincidently involved homosexuals.[75]

The Seventh Circuit's *Rosiles-Camarena* decision employs a similar strategy in regard to Mexico. The IJ ruled that Rosiles-Camarena faced substantial risk because 148 people were murdered in Mexico between 1995 and 2006 because of their sexual orientation. The BIA disagreed with this assessment and observed that this amounts to 12 or 13 killings a year in a population exceeding 110 million, at least 2% of which is homosexual, making it unlikely (a risk of no more than 1 in 100,000) that any given gay man would be killed any given year. Expert testimony establishing that "attacks on homosexuals are frequent" does not show the magnitude of risks, any more than expert testimony that "auto accidents are frequent" would imply that a given driver (even one in a high-risk group, such as men under 25) is more likely than not to be injured.[76]

Thus, the BIA couched its decision in the objectivity of numbers, concluding that a 1 in 100,000 risk of being killed does not suffice for withholding of removal. Notably, however, the court remanded the decision to the BIA, reminding it that such numbers must be contextualized and individualized. The court wrote, "For although we have mentioned so far only the statistical risk of death for homosexuals as a group, Rosiles-Camarena contends that he is at greater risk. He is not only gay and HIV positive but also 'out' and planning to live openly with his partner," before clarifying that acts far short of murder may constitute persecution and concluding, "The question for the Board on remand is thus not whether aggregate data imply that Rosiles-Camarena is likely to be killed, but whether the IJ clearly erred in finding that he is more likely than not to be persecuted."[77] The court thus rejected a straightforward statistical calculation of risk, instead ruling that aggregate statistical data can only go so far in determining individual risk. However, the general idea behind statistical inference still finds its way into risk determinations.

Analogical Thinking

Explaining how one decides how at risk an asylum seeker might be, one former immigration judge said, "You do that by comparing them with other people who, to the extent you can ascertain, are similarly situated."[78] This kind of analogical thinking is precisely the logic behind actuarial risk assessment. You look at group-level outcomes—in this case, what happens to LGBTQ people in a particular country—and compare them to the individual case under consideration. The key difference, of course, is that judges' decisions are not quantified in the way actuarial estimates are. While this approach makes sense, it has also led some adjudicators to judge asylum seekers based on individual social visibility; that is, how identifiably queer is the claimant?

This led some judges to employ stereotypes of what they expected gay men to look or act like in order to evaluate whether they would be identified in their home countries for persecution. In the case of Mladen Todorovic (2010), a gay Serbian man, the IJ wrote:

The Court would first note that the respondent says that he is singled out for persecution because he is gay in his home country. The Court studied the demeanor of this individual very carefully throughout his testimony in Court today, and this gentleman does not appear to be overtly gay. The Court does not know whether he is or not, his testimony is that he is overtly gay and has been since he was 17 years old. Be that as it may, it is not readily apparent to a person who would see this gentleman for the first time that, that is the case, since he bears no effeminate traits or any other trait that would mark him as a homosexual.[79]

Similarly, in *Razkane v. Holder* (2009), the IJ wrote that Tarik Razkane's "appearance does not have anything about it that would designate [him] as being gay. [He] does not dress in an effeminate manner or affect any effeminate mannerisms," and further decided that Razkane had not "shown that it is more likely than not that he would be engaged in homosexuality in Morocco or, even if he was, that it would be the type of overt homosexuality that would bring him to the attention of the authorities or of the society in general."[80] These two decisions evince a risk determination process dependent specifically on whether the claimants would be singled out as identifiably queer.

Indeed, this is not a strategy limited to judges. Claimants and their lawyers often point to gender nonconformity as a risk factor. As immigration lawyer Aneesha Gandhi explained, "They'll say when I was a kid I was bullied and beaten up, and we want to make sure we put that information in and then we have to kind of connect why are we putting this information in. Well, why did they do that to you? What was it about you that they didn't like? And a lot of them will say I liked to do girl things . . . the way I walked was more girly or I liked to play with girls instead of boys."[81] Likewise, Maria, a lesbian asylum seeker from Mexico, testified that she had a hard time growing up because she had four brothers, all of her friends were boys, she preferred to play with boys, and kids teased her because she was "different," calling her things like "marimacha," a derogatory slang term for lesbian. José Lopez, a bisexual Salvadoran asylum seeker, claimed he was raped because of his feminine appearance.[82] Thus, appealing to gendered stereotypes is often a strategy used to demonstrate that a claimant would be at increased risk. This may be particularly true when a petitioner has not experienced past persecution and is making a future persecution claim, perhaps based on changed life circumstances, such as transitioning genders. Heather McClure suggested that

future persecution cases are really tricky and, in that case, it might be particularly important that the applicant come into that courtroom cross-dressed; you know, dressed as a transgendered [*sic*] person, because if they're willing to do that in a US court of law, which is so extraordinarily formal, and they're willing to withstand the looks or the, you know, whatever response they may get, then it's more believable to the court that they would be willing to do that in their home country.[83]

The assumption, then, is that being openly trans would increase their visibility and therefore their risk.

However, this individual visibility standard is not, in fact, how adjudicators are supposed to assess risk. The cases cited above—*Razkane* and *Todorovic*—were both struck down by appellate courts for unacceptable uses of stereotypes.

Commenting on this use of stereotypes to assess the risk LGBTQ claimants may face, Lory Rosenberg explained:

> There are terrible stereotypes, and some are stereotypes, but some of them do reflect some historical reality. Like are gay people more likely to go out to bars and put themselves in the way of harm? Or, you know, are gay people going to be making a lot of noise going down the street outside of bars and so provoking the police, that kind of thing? Are people sexually loose? That kind of stuff. There's all these stereotypes and prejudices that I think attach that it's really important to clarify.[84]

For Rosenberg, then, while stereotypes of gay sexual promiscuity may be damaging and irrelevant, others—such as the idea that LGBTQ people may gather in highly visible spaces, such as gay bars—may be relevant to assessing the risk a petitioner may face. In fact, at least one appellate court has ruled that being persecuted for attending gay bars may be tantamount to being persecuted for being gay.[85] Former immigration judge Ingrid Lawson likewise suggested that some stereotypical thinking was not the result of prejudice, but rather an attempt to determine one's risk:

> I don't believe that the people who've been criticized for making comments that might be deemed as kind of stereotypical are actually guilty of stereotypical thinking. I think more they're trying to assess what's the actual risk of harm being inflicted. So if a person is a very out person as opposed to kind of a very conservatively dressed person who . . . somebody would be shocked in knowing that they actually were gay then I think it goes to objectively what's the risk of harm being inflicted on them if they return to a situation where gay people are really at risk.[86]

Despite her reasoning, this is still the incorrect standard. Rather, her analogical approach introduced at the beginning of this section is a more acceptable way to predict risk. Picking up on some of the cases where judges had employed an individual visibility requirement, the USCIS–Immigration Equality training for asylum officers corrected, "Some adjudicators mistakenly believe that social visibility or distinction requires that the applicant 'look gay or act gay.' In this context, social visibility or distinction does not mean visible to the eye. Rather, this means that the society in question distinguishes individuals who share this trait from individuals who do not."[87] Thus, individual visibility may become *a* factor in risk determinations for some claimants, such as those who are visibly gender nonconforming, but it cannot be *the* determining factor.

In sum, asylum adjudications determine risk through a holistic process dependent on the trained judgment of judges who are afforded significant professional discretion. Judges consider evidence ranging from macro-level human rights and political conditions in claimants' home countries to individual-level information about applicants' personal circumstances. Risk is therefore rendered legally cognizable primarily through the subjective assessment of individual judges. In other words, judges are the risk assessment tools in asylum hearings. However, judges do try to make their decisions appear as objective as possible by explicitly listing forms of evidence viewed as more objective and reliable, engaging in analogical thinking, using logical inference, and sometimes drawing on the authority of numbers. Importantly for this analysis, sexuality is not the "risk object"—the source of harm—at all. Rather, the claimant's home country and culture are constructed as the risk object. Sexuality, in these calculations, is a risk factor; indeed, it is the *primary* risk factor. Even though sexuality is not the explicit target of risk calculations for asylum decisions, the risk faced on account of one's sexuality is the principal mechanism for constituting LGBTQ asylum seekers as legal and sexual subjects before the state. As the next chapters illustrates, this process is quite different for sex offenders whose sexuality *is* the source of danger.

8: SEXUAL PREDATORS AND THE CONSTITUTION OF DANGEROUS INDIVIDUALS

"It's basically malpractice not to use them. I know some people don't like to use them, and I think that's crazy. When we go with our gut, we may as well be flipping a coin," explained Michael Kleppin, a sex offender therapist and evaluator in Illinois, to a room of about fifty therapists, lawyers, and probation, parole, and police officers who had gathered to learn about recent changes to Illinois's standards for the treatment and evaluation of sex offenders. But what is so crazy that not using it would be malpractice? Kleppin was referring to actuarial risk assessments, like the Static-99, Minnesota Sex Offender Screening Tool (MnSOST), and Rapid Risk Assessment for Sexual Offense Recidivism (RRASOR), all tools designed specifically to be used with sex offenders. Although some clinicians continue to believe that their intuition, honed over years of working with sex offenders, is a better predictor of an offender's risk, studies consistently show that actuarial assessment outperforms clinical evaluation. As Kleppin pointed out in his presentation, clinicians who use unstructured clinical judgment are no better than chance (and sometimes worse) at predicting whether a particular offender will recidivate. By contrast, studies of the Static-99 put its predictive accuracy at about 70%. Because of the substantial difference in predictive power, many states now require that evaluators use certain actuarial tools when assessing sex offender recidivism risk for a range of legal decisions, from sentencing and probation to determining whether an offender should be civilly committed indefinitely.

In contrast to asylum risk determinations discussed in the previous chapter that rely on the subjective "trained judgment" of immigration judges, sex offender risk evaluations take a more mechanical, quantitative approach to assessing risk through the use of actuarial techniques—though as I will discuss below, considerable professional discretion often finds its way into these evaluations, as well. Greater data availability in comparison to the asylum setting make these more sophisticated techniques possible, but the greater visibility of sexual assault as a social problem and the greater need for communication across institutions also push risk determinations for sex offenders to more closely resemble what Porter calls "mechanical objectivity."[1] Despite these differences, risk assessments for sex offenders similarly serve to constitute legal and sexual subject positions. Just as judgments of the risk that an asylum seeker will face persecution determine whether he will gain access to the national community and the rights of citizenship, so, too, do decisions about a sex offender's risk of sexual recidivism determine his civil rights and liberties and the level of access he will have to civil society.

This may seem like an exaggeration or inapt comparison, but closer inspection shows it is quite appropriate. Although sex offenders are (typically) US citizens, courts have carved out many legal exceptions to their constitutional rights to privacy, due process, and double jeopardy, among others. Unlike other violent offenders, sex offenders are subject to public registration, residency restrictions, restrictions on free movement, prohibitions from using social media and sometimes the Internet at all, and many other curtailments of basic civil liberties. Decisions about the extent of such restrictions—including how long one must register, who must be notified of the ex-offender's presence, and where one can live—are often made through risk assessment. These constraints on the everyday rights of people who have been convicted of sexual crimes are generally justified by questionable claims of exceedingly high rates of recidivism and assertions that such policies protect the wider community from the unique danger sex offenders pose. Protecting the public is certainly a worthwhile goal, but studies suggest that most of these laws have little or no effect on rates of sexual assault and may even increase risk by preventing ex-offenders from reintegrating into communities. Nevertheless, the purported risk posed by sex offenders, especially those deemed "sexual predators" (a formal legal designation in many states), continues to drive public policy and legal decision-making.

The most striking example of how risk determines sex offenders' access to citizenship is illustrated by SVP laws that allow for the indefinite civil commitment of some sex offenders. As explained in the introduction, SVP statutes are aimed at the "worst of the worst" and allow the state to seek the indefinite civil confinement of a sex offender after he has served his full criminal sentence. Although civil commitment programs are supposed to be treatment facilities, in practice many offenders receive little to no treatment, and civil commitment often ends up being a de facto life sentence without the accompanying criminal conviction.[2] A risk assessment can therefore serve to remove a sex offender from civil society forever. Put another way, it determines whether he will ever again have access to many of the most basic rights of citizenship.

Because of its parallels with asylum determinations vis-à-vis access to citizenship, in this chapter I concentrate on SVP adjudications. Specifically, I analyze how sexual risk is rendered legally cognizable, precisely how risk is calculated, and how risk determinations constitute the figure of the "sexual predator" as a particularly dangerous person requiring exceptional social control measures. First, I want to briefly consider the standards of proof employed in SVP proceedings and how they are interpreted and operationalized.

PREDICTING THE FUTURE
"BEYOND A REASONABLE DOUBT"

Just as petitioners must prove a "well-founded fear of persecution" in asylum claims, the state must prove that a sex offender is likely to sexually reoffend in SVP trials. However, unlike asylum law, which has one uniform standard for "well-founded fear" nationwide, the standard of commitment varies across the country. Depending on the jurisdiction, a sex offender must be "likely," "more likely than not," or "substantially probable" to sexually recidivate. Courts in many states have attempted to clarify what these terms mean, but often their clarifications leave considerable room for interpretation. Compounding the confusion, SVP laws also have standards of proof that are distinct from the standards of commitment. Whereas standards of commitment apply to risk (i.e., how likely is this person to sexually reoffend?), standards of proof apply to the totality of the trial (i.e., did the state prove that this person is an SVP?). Standards of proof also vary across jurisdictions, with most states adopting the "beyond a reasonable doubt" standard of criminal trials, though some states use lower standards typical of other civil proceedings. See table 8 for a summary of the standards of commitment and proof for all jurisdictions that have enacted SVP laws. Because I am concerned with risk determinations, I will mostly focus on standards of commitment for the remainder of this chapter.

What Is a Standard of Commitment?

In Illinois, a sex offender must be found to "suffer from a mental disorder that makes it substantially probable that the person will engage in acts of sexual violence" in order to be adjudicated a "sexually violent person."[3] In Minnesota, by contrast, an offender must be "likely to engage in acts of harmful sexual conduct."[4] And Missouri offers yet another standard, stating that an offender must be "more likely than not to engage in predatory acts of sexual violence."[5] But what do all of these various terms mean? Is "substantially probable" the same as "more likely than not"? Is "likely" a higher or lower threshold than "more likely than not"? Many state courts

TABLE 8. Standards of commitment and proof for civil commitment of sex offenders.

State	Standard of commitment	Standard of proof
Arizona	Likely	Beyond a reasonable doubt
California	Likely	Beyond a reasonable doubt
Florida	Likely	Clear and convincing
Illinois	Substantially probable	Beyond a reasonable doubt
Iowa	Likely	Beyond a reasonable doubt
Kansas	Likely	Beyond a reasonable doubt
Massachusetts	Likely	Beyond a reasonable doubt
Minnesota	Likely	Clear and convincing
Missouri	More likely than not	Clear and convincing
Nebraska	Likely	Clear and convincing
New Hampshire	Likely	Clear and convincing
New Jersey	Likely	Clear and convincing
New York	Likely	Clear and convincing
North Dakota	Likely	Clear and convincing
Pennsylvania	Likely	Clear and convincing
South Carolina	Likely	Beyond a reasonable doubt
Texas	Likely	Beyond a reasonable doubt
Virginia	Likely	Clear and convincing
Washington	Likely	Beyond a reasonable doubt
Wisconsin	Likely	Beyond a reasonable doubt
Federal	Unclear in statute	Clear and convincing

have tried to provide some definitional clarity to these terms, but others have refused to offer any guidance. Moreover, among those that have tried to clarify matters, no consistent definition of "likely" has emerged.

The California Supreme Court case *People v. Superior Court (Ghilotti)* (2002) provides one instance of such an attempt. In considering whether state evaluators had misinterpreted the meaning of "likely" to engage in sexually violent conduct, the court took the opportunity to clarify the term. Ghilotti, the offender, argued that "likely" should be understood as "'highly likely,' or at least 'more likely than not,'" while the state asserted that "likely" "does not mean 'probable' or 'more likely than not,' but refers to 'a significant chance, not minimal'; something less than 'more likely than not' and more than merely 'possible.'"[6]

After consulting several sources on the definition of "likely"—including the *Oxford English Dictionary*, legal dictionaries and thesauruses, common usage, legal usage in the United Kingdom, legislative intent, and other court decisions using a "likely" standard—the court ultimately disagreed with both parties and instead offered its own interpretation. The court concluded:

> . . . *"likely* to engage in acts of sexual violence" . . . connotes much more than the mere *possibility* that the person will reoffend . . . the statute does not require a precise determination that the chance of reoffense is *better than even.* Instead, an evaluator applying this standard must conclude that the person is "likely" to reoffend if . . . the person presents a *substantial danger,* that is, a *serious and well-founded risk,* that he or she will commit such crimes if free in the community [italics in original].[7]

Thus, in California, "likely" can mean something less than 50%, though it is unclear precisely what a "serious and well-founded risk" might be. Presumably individuals could genuinely disagree over such terms. But applying the "well-founded" principle from asylum law would suggest that even a probability of recidivism as low as 10% could qualify an offender for civil commitment in California.

Illinois provides another example. The Second District Appellate Court of Illinois in *People v. Hayes* (2001) ruled that "substantially probable," the standard of commitment in Illinois, "means 'much more likely than not,' a standard higher than or equal to the 'likely' standard found constitutional in *Hendricks.* However, we emphasize that this definition cannot be reduced to a mere mathematical formula or statistical analysis."[8] The court's assertion that the definition cannot be reduced to a quantitative calculation is significant here because recidivism probabilities on actuarial assessments very rarely exceed 50%. As Illinois evaluator Dr. Richard Travis pointed out, "If you look at the recidivism [on] the actuarials, especially the Static-99R and the Static-2002R, a person can be very high risk, and yet when you look at their absolute risk, which is the probability assigned that this person will be charged or convicted of a sexual offense within a certain amount of time, it's below 50%."[9] This is likely why a number of courts that have considered the issue echo the Illinois court's contention that risk cannot be determined only through a statistical estimate, as the Kansas Supreme Court did in 2011 when it wrote: "Nor is there support for suggesting that if an actuarial test is used, a particular percentage or category of risk must be shown on the actuarial risk assessment test before an offender may be characterized as a sexually violent predator."[10] Similarly, in 2002 the Massachusetts Supreme Court declared:

> While likely indicates more than a mere propensity or possibility, it is not bound to the statistical probability inherent in a definition such as "more likely than not," and the terms are not interchangeable. To conclude that

likely amounts to a quantifiable probability, absent a more specific statutory expression of such a quantity, is to require mathematical precision from a term that, by its plain meaning, demands contextual, not statistical, analysis.[11]

The North Dakota Supreme Court was the clearest in stating that by refusing to specify a clear threshold, it was preserving the discretion of courts and evaluators. The court wrote in 2002: "This definition prevents a contest over percentage points and the results of other actuarial tools, and allows experts to use the fullness of their education, experience and resources available to them in order to determine if an individual poses a threat to society."[12]

In a move that seems to parallel the asylum context, courts assert the need for context in making SVP determinations. Interestingly, however, "context" in the SVP complex is quite different than "context" in asylum hearings. Rather than the social context demanded in asylum hearings, "context" in this instance consists of situating an offender's diagnosis and risk assessment within his overall biography. Carol Heimer's schematic distinction between "cases" and "biographies" is helpful here: "Bureaucratic routines act on standard objects; legal systems abstract cases from the rest of life; standardized commodities with a single cost and price are bought and sold in markets. All of those acts are also done by people who are born, grow up, work, form families, sicken, and die. All acts in bureaucracies, legal processes, or markets are, then, both instances of general categories and pieces of people's biographies."[13] While cases do the necessary work of excluding certain information and standardizing legal processes, they can never be completely removed from the context of one's biography. In other words, cases can never be fully dehumanized. Developing this insight in relation to the criminal history component of the Federal Sentencing Guidelines, Mona Lynch argues that "instead of transforming defendants into a set of criminal history points that help to determine sentence assignment from a table, the quantified criminal history provides another opening to a qualitative, ideographic narratively based debate about the moral makeup of the juridical subject to be punished."[14] Something similar is at work in SVP proceedings, where adjudicators want both the authority of numbers and the ability to interpret those numbers as they see fit in the context of an offender's biography. Thus, as I will discuss further below, although actuarial risk assessment tools are understood by most to be objective, discretion is pervasive at many points in the SVP adjudication process, including in deciding how to operationalize terms such as "likely" and "substantially probable."

By refusing to give firmer guidelines, courts and legislatures open the way for significant discrepancies, not only across jurisdictions, but also from trial to trial and juror to juror. In one study of actual jurors who served on SVP juries, researchers found that 81.7% of jurors believed that a 15% estimated chance of recidivism meant that an offender was "likely" to reoffend, and more than half (53.6%) believed that even a 1% chance of reoffense indicated a "likely" recidivist.[15] The researchers concluded that jurors tend to view risk more in terms of the severity of potential harm than in terms of statistical probability and that when laws grant jurors discretion in defining tolerable risk, jurors find even statistically low degrees of risk intolerable.

This low-risk tolerance is reflected in the success rates of states that seek to commit sex offenders. When I asked evaluators how often someone they believed to be an SVP was found by a court to be so, they invariably responded by saying nearly always. My exchange with Dr. Kim Weitl, an Illinois and Missouri SVP evaluator, is illustrative:

AUTHOR: How often is your recommendation actually the way that the court decides?

DR. WEITL: Pretty much always. In Missouri I think I had a 100% accuracy just because, especially in the early days . . . there were very few courts in the land that were going to say no when you're saying this guy is dangerous because he clearly is.[16]

Similarly, Dr. Travis said in response to the same question, "From the ones that I've followed up on or that I have knowledge of it's about 90 to 95% of what I recommend."[17] In perhaps the most measured response to that question, Dr. Donya Adkerson, a treatment provider and occasional SVP evaluator, said, "The courts routinely respect my opinion, and I think it goes with my recommendations much more often than not."[18] Margaret Menzenberger, Assistant Attorney General for the state of Illinois who has been with the SVP unit for over ten years, told me that she had only ever had one case where an offender was found not to be an SVP. (I subsequently observed one of her SVP trials in which the offender was found not to be an SVP, bringing her total to at least two now.) Certainly, these people could be exaggerating their success rates, and several suggested that courts went with their assessments because they were "very good at what [they] do" or because they "really rely on the science." However, audit studies suggest that they are likely telling the truth. One study in Texas found that juries committed 100% of the twenty-six offenders tried during the study period and that this resembled the history of the Texas SVP law: only one jury had ever found an offender not to be an SVP.[19] Other reports indicate that 95% of SVP petitions are granted in Florida, and about 80% are granted in Minnesota.[20]

Given this information, though, how is risk actually determined in SVP trials? How is a person's sexual risk gauged in order to determine whether he meets the loosely defined "likely" standard? Whereas in asylum hearings, a country and its cultural setting become the source of risk and an individual's sexuality a risk factor, in SVP trials, the individual is constituted as risky and the community as at risk from him. Through the diagnosis of mental disorders and the prediction of future sexual risk, forensic psychologists and courts coproduce the legal identity of the "sexually violent predator" as a distinct type of person, a unique risk object. Forensic psychology lends support to this legal construction by providing mental health diagnoses and actuarial risk assessments that serve as the basis for durable social and sexual identities for SVPs. Each SVP trial provides an opportunity to reinforce collective understandings of sexuality and sexual violence through the legal constitution of an individual SVP. The aggregate effect is to constitute "sexual predators" as permanently pathological and indefinitely dangerous.

CONSTITUTING THE SEXUALLY VIOLENT PREDATOR

A primary way that psychologists contribute to the construction of the SVP is through diagnosing offenders with mental abnormalities that become the basis for permanent legal and social identities. Drawing on the legitimacy of the *DSM*, forensic psychologists can authoritatively dictate medicalized identities that courts readily accept. Because the *DSM* provides explicit diagnostic criteria, adjudicators generally accept these diagnoses as objective and reliable. Nevertheless, debate continues within the "psy" professions around whether certain personality patterns or behaviors— such as rape—qualify as mental disorders and also around the accuracy of particular diagnoses. As Dr. William Marshall, a well-regarded researcher and treatment provider, commented, "We need to realize when looking at these diagnoses applied in SVP settings . . . for example, pedophilia diagnosis, the inter-rater agreement . . . is .6. Inter-rater reliability for an important decision should be .8 or better. This is an important decision so .6 is nowhere near it. For [paraphilia] 'not otherwise specified' it's .4, which is even lower. And the other possible diagnosis is sexual sadism which is .4. So it is nowhere near meeting the criteria for reliability."[21] Similarly, commenting on the controversy around the "paraphilia not otherwise specified, nonconsent" diagnosis for SVPs, researcher and treatment provider Dr. Robin Wilson said:

I think it is overdiagnosed, and I think one of the reasons why it's overdiagnosed is because the American Psychiatric Association has completely abdicated its responsibility to give us a reasonable criterion set with which to actually make the proper diagnosis. So the fact that they just continue to say, "Nope, nope, nope," basically leaves practitioners out in the woods searching for the boundaries of what they can use to make this diagnosis.[22]

By refusing to include some form of a nonconsent or rape paraphilia in the *DSM*, the APA, Wilson suggests, is contributing to the problem of inconsistent diagnosis. Nevertheless, psychiatric diagnoses carry considerable authority in both the legal and public spheres and serve as one basis for constructing SVPs, and, by extension, all sex offenders, as permanently pathological. In fact, today many forensic psychologists consider paraphilias, such as pedophilia and sadism, to be akin to sexual orientations. As Dr. Isabel Davis, an Illinois SVP evaluator, explained:

> I look at arousal on a spectrum, and it's just not male, female. We extend out to male/male, female/female, so if you extend it farther, in my estimation . . . the person could have arousal to children. . . . In that regard, it becomes a lot more difficult to—we don't look at changing it. We look at intervening on it so that the person does not act on it against children. It has to be an ongoing intervention.[23]

Similar statements often appear in court decisions, as in the SVP hearing of Mark Broer in Washington State: "The trial court rejected the testimony of Dr. Wollert, that Broer's pedophilia is in remission. The court relied upon the testimony of Dr. Wheeler that paraphilias do not spontaneously remit and that Broer's condition is chronic and enduring, as well as Dr. Spizman's testimony that the current thinking is that pedophilia never goes into remission."[24] This legal-scientific conception of pedophilia both draws support from and itself supports lay opinions of pedophilic sex offenders. In one study of lawyers who deal with sex offenders, sociologist Jamie Small found, "Unlike other criminals, respondents categorize pedophiles as uniquely deviant. They perceive them to be incorrigible. The pedophile is unrehabilitative because his sexual urges are a core part of his being."[25]

In fact, however, most child molesters do not exhibit significant arousal patterns to prepubescent children or meet the *DSM* diagnostic criteria for pedophilic disorder.[26] Rather, their offense was situational and not necessarily an indicator of a pattern likely to be repeated. In other words, not all "pedophiles" are unrehabilitative, nor is a sexual urge to molest children a "core part" of their sexual being. As evaluator and treatment provider Dr. Adkerson explained, "It is common for people in media in current culture to refer to anyone who molests a child as a pedophile, and it's just not the case. There are pedophiles who molest. There are pedophiles who don't molest. And there are people who molest children that are pedophilic, and there are people who molest children who aren't pedophilic."[27] Yet lay understandings of the term "pedophile" as a distinct type of person are reinforced by the *DSM* definition of paraphilias as enduring arousal patterns and, specifically, the designation of pedophilia as akin to a sexual identity such as gay or straight. The *DSM-5* even refers to pedophilia as a "sexual orientation," though the editors later issued a correction saying that it should read "sexual interest."

This view of sex offenders, and especially pedophiles, as unique and particularly monstrous highlights the way that our culture grants excessive weight to sexual matters. This cultural view colors our penal approach to sex offenses, as exemplified in the exceptional measures we take to control them, such as Megan's Law and GPS monitoring. As Karl Hanson, co-creator of the Static-99, pointed out, part of his rationale for creating an actuarial instrument specific to sex offenders was precisely because of this view in the penal system: "The standard practice, and it's still the standard practice in many of our jurisdictions, is to automatically override sex offenders into a high-risk category for correctional management purposes, just because they're sex offenders."[28] In creating the Static-99, he was partially working to dispel the myth that sex offenders are inherently more dangerous than other offenders simply because their crimes involved sex. While this approach may have gained some traction in Hanson's native Canada, in the United States, separate risk instruments for sex offenders serve mostly to reinforce the idea that sex offenders are special kinds of criminals.

Significantly, the Supreme Court's *Hendricks* ruling (1997) established that treatment was not necessary to make SVP civil commitment constitutional. In its decision striking down the SVP statute, the Kansas Supreme Court wrote, "It is clear that the overriding concern of the legislature is to continue the segregation of sexually violent offenders from the public. Treatment with the goal of reintegrating them into society is incidental, at best. The record reflects that treatment for sexually violent predators is all but nonexistent."[29] Accepting the conclusion that treatment for SVPs might not exist, Justice Clarence Thomas, writing for the majority, stated simply, "We have already observed that, under the appropriate circumstances and when accompanied by proper procedures, incapacitation may be a legitimate end of the civil law."[30] Indeed, the Kansas statute's preamble plainly states, "In contrast to persons appropriate for civil commitment under the [general involuntary civil commitment statute], sexually violent predators generally have anti-social personality features which are unamenable to existing mental illness treatment modalities and those features render them likely to engage in sexually violent behavior."[31] This language is echoed verbatim in several other SVP statutes across the country, including those in Florida, Iowa, New Hampshire, and Washington. Such statements make it clear that rehabilitation is not a priority, and it seems that it wasn't even seriously considered at the time these statutes were enacted. Rather, legislatures and courts alike agreed that they were dealing with a permanently pathological person, not a dynamic individual. Though individualized assessment was required to commit an SVP, the legal actors involved clearly believed that the individual would remain a danger indefinitely. These understandings are further bolstered by the use of static risk assessment instruments, which I return to shortly.

As noted previously, the *Kansas v. Crane* (2002) decision also helped to solidify forensic psychologists' pivotal role in determining whether an offender suffers from a "mental abnormality" that affects his volitional control.[32] Perhaps even more importantly, though, this case highlights the importance of psychological predictions of "dangerousness" for sexual predators. A psychiatric diagnosis, though certainly serving as the basis for a permanent penal and social identity, is not enough to designate someone an SVP. Rather, the mental abnormality must also predispose an offender to future sexual violence, and, per *Hendricks*, psychologists must be able to separate SVPs from more typical recidivists. This was particularly an issue in *Crane* because exhibitionism is not typically considered an extremely dangerous disorder. His commitment therefore depended to a larger extent on his antisocial personality disorder (APD) diagnosis. Research suggests, however, that a substantial portion of the male prison population—perhaps upward of 60%—could be diagnosed with APD.[33] An APD diagnosis alone, then, may be insufficient to commit an offender, as it may not properly distinguish SVPs from other offenders.[34] A psychologist's prediction that an offender will continue to be dangerous indefinitely, however, can be more determinative in labeling someone an SVP.

ACTUARIAL RISK ASSESSMENT AND THE DESIGNATION OF DANGEROUSNESS

Predictions of dangerousness constituted an important part of sexual psychopath commitments, but the subjectivity of these predictions led to widespread concern about the validity of the process. However, while the new generation of sex offender civil commitment statutes were being enacted, forensic psychologists were also creating what were presented as more objective means of assessing future dangerousness in the form of quantitative risk prediction tools. Hanson developed the first of these instruments in 1997, and soon thereafter he and David Thornton created the Static-99, which is now the most widely used actuarial risk assessment (ARA) tool for sex offenders in the United States.

Although actuarial techniques use group-based risk prediction, I sug-

gest that the turn to actuarialism is continuous with earlier attempts to indi-
vidualize punishment and the "will to know the criminal" and is consistent
with efforts at clinical risk prediction during the "sexual psychopath" era.[35]
Indeed, SVP evaluations resemble the parole system, which might be considered the epitome of individualized justice. ARA, however, is seen as a
purer and more objective view of the individual by both courts and forensic
psychologists. As I will show, though, courts appear to want the purported
objectivity of numbers *and* the discretion of clinical judgment when dealing
with sex offenders. As such, while courts draw on the authority of numbers
to legitimate their decisions, they also couch those numbers within larger
narratives of deviance where the numbers largely serve to justify an a priori
conclusion about the moral character of the offender. Before taking a more
in-depth look at how ARA constitutes the SVP as a legal and sexual subject,
I first want to briefly consider the creation of actuarial instruments for sex
offenders and, specifically, the development of what is now the most widely
used actuarial tool for sex offenders worldwide: the Static-99.

Dangerous by Design?

The use of actuarial methods in the penal domain dates back to the early
twentieth century, when University of Chicago sociologist Ernest Burgess
designed an instrument for the state of Illinois to predict the likelihood
that a prisoner would be successful on parole.[36] However, actuarial tools
were not widely used in the United States until the 1980s and 1990s,
when instruments were designed to predict violent recidivism and the
individual risk of prisoners, the results of which were often used for sentencing decisions and to sort prisoners into different security levels.[37] ARA
tools specifically for use with sex offenders began being developed in the
mid- to late 1990s. Two of the earliest were the Minnesota Sex Offender
Screening Tool (MnSOST), created in 1995 by a team of researchers for the
Minnesota Department of Corrections, and the Rapid Risk Assessment for
Sexual Offense Recidivism (RRASOR), introduced in 1997 by Hanson, a
researcher for Public Safety Canada. Though both tools showed promise,
the MnSOST required considerably more information about the offender
and more training for coders than the four-item RRASOR, which could
generally be completed with minimal training using information found
in most offenders' records.[38] Nevertheless, both instruments were used
to some extent by forensic psychologists and treatment providers, and
some clinicians continue to use these tools. But both have been falling into
disuse since the introduction of the Static-99 in 1999 (and subsequently
the Static-2002, as well as both of their revised versions, the Static-99R and
Static-2002R). Because the revised and updated versions have only been
changed to reflect new weightings of certain items and updated recidi-

vism estimates based off of newer samples, my discussion of the Static-99 largely applies to the revisions, as well.

The Static-99 created by Hanson and Thornton is a ten-item actuarial scale that is a combination of the two researchers' respective scales: Hanson's RRASOR and Thornton's Structured Anchored Clinical Judgement (SACJ). Items from the RRASOR include prior sex offenses, age at release, victim gender, and relationship to victim (related or unrelated). The other six items came from the SACJ and were relationship status (ever lived with a partner for at least two years?), prior non-sexual offense convictions, index non-sexual violence (i.e., was the offender convicted of a non-sexual offense at the same time as his sexual offense), prior sentencing dates, convictions for noncontact sex offenses, and any stranger victims. As Hanson and Thornton explained in their article introducing the Static-99, "Many of the variables used in the Static-99 can be grouped into general dimensions that are plausibly related to the risk of sex offense recidivism, such as sexual deviance, range of available victims, persistence (lack of deterrence or 'habit strength'), antisociality, and age (young)."[39] However, selection of the variables was not guided by theory, but rather on the basis of observed correlations with recidivism. Hanson has acknowledged this possible shortcoming, writing, "None of the items were intended to measure psychologically meaningful constructs; they were selected purely on the basis of empirical relationships with recidivism and ease of administration."[40] He has also forthrightly acknowledged that the Static-99 factors were chosen in part for administrative ease and because the information used for scoring the Static-99 is generally recorded in administrative records. Indeed, the instrument's low administrative burden likely accounts in part for the Static-99's widespread uptake.

But as Hanson suggested, the timing of an evaluative study of five actuarial instruments likely also aided the Static-99's ascent: "The next thing that happened is that Howard Barbaree did the comparison of four or five risk scales that were there, and Static-99 came out on top. This was a fluke, right? Because one of them's got to come out on top."[41] In fact, the RRASOR came out on top, with a receiver operating characteristic (ROC) of 0.77, followed closely by the Static-99 with an ROC of 0.70, but the difference was not statistically significant.[42] However, subsequent studies have shown the Static-99 to perform better than the RRASOR, and Hanson and others from the Static-99 workgroup have publicly recommended against continued use of the RRASOR because its norms have not been updated in line with the best available data and statistical techniques. The Barbaree study also showed the MnSOST not to be a statistically significant predictor of sexual recidivism, precipitating its decline in use. Interestingly, some studies have also shown other ARA instruments to be more predictive than the Static-99. One study found that the Violence Risk Assessment Guide (VRAG) and

Sex Offender Risk Appraisal Guide (SORAG), an offshoot of the VRAG, were both more predictive of sexual recidivism than the Static-99 (though the differences were not statistically significant for all samples).[43] Notably, however, the VRAG and SORAG require much more in-depth information about offenders to be fully scored, including phallometric test results and a psychopathy score from the Hare Psychopathy Checklist–Revised (PCL-R), both of which are unavailable for many offenders and have also faced significant criticism regarding their validity. Administrative ease, data availability, and its acceptably high predictive ability, then, have allowed the Static-99 to edge out its competition to become the most widespread sex offender ARA instrument in use today.

Because of its widespread uptake, the Static-99 is also continually revised. In 2002 a new version called the Static-2002 was introduced, which made small changes to the group norms and recidivism predictions but did not perform significantly better than the Static-99. As Hanson explained: "We expected the 2002R to be sufficiently better than the 99 that it could replace it. It didn't turn out that way. It was a bit better, and I still think it's a bit better, but not hugely so."[44] In 2008–9, both the Static-99 and 2002 were re-normed using new and much larger samples of offenders. Importantly, the new norms incorporated four samples from the United States, partially blunting the criticism often levied against the instruments in US courtrooms that the samples used to norm the tools were all based outside of the United States (the original samples were all from the UK and Canada). Lastly, in 2012 both the Static-99 and 2002 became the Static-99R and Static-2002R (for "revised"), with changes to the weighting of the age variable that allowed risk scores to decrease as offenders aged, in line with data suggesting that the likelihood of sexual recidivism significantly decreases with age.

Because of the advances in predictive ability of ARA for sex offenders, ARA is now widely accepted by courts. Many psychological professionals now echo Dr. Kleppin's sentiment from the beginning of this chapter that it is simply unethical not to use ARA given its much better accuracy compared to clinical judgment, especially for such important decisions as SVP determinations. This is not to say that ARA comes with no downside. The Static-99, for example, is the quintessential black box. The creators have provided information on the populations used to develop and norm the instrument and derive recidivism rates, and have extensively discussed why they chose certain variables over others. However, the algorithm and weighting behind the deceptively simple scoring check sheet (see appendix 1) remain proprietary, and the creators have refused to turn over certain data sets to other researchers for re-analysis. Moreover, many ARA instruments, including the Static-99, lack a theoretical foundation, have low inter-rater reliability, and can sometimes act as cover allowing professional discretion and bias to enter legal proceedings disguised as objective quantitative calculations. Before delving more deeply into these issues, I want to consider how ARA technologies are actually used in making risk determinations of sex offenders and how these predictions serve to constitute the SVP.

Locating Risk in the Sexually Violent Predator

Legal scholar Eric Janus asserts: "As constructed by the predator laws, risk tells us something essential—rather than accidental—about the person. This characteristic—sometimes called 'dangerousness'—is portrayed as a stable ingredient of the person, a part of him even if it is not now visible."[45] Risk assessments that consider only static or unchanging factors, such as the Static-99, reinforce this conception because one's risk level can never change if only historical factors are considered.[46] This design gives the impression that risk is fixed indefinitely in the very person of the SVP. Court determinations that conclude that an offender *is* a "sexually violent predator" assign an identity label, not merely a punishment for criminal behavior. Expert affidavits further attest to this. As one Illinois evaluator wrote in his report to the court for an SVP hearing: "It is this examiner's opinion, to a reasonable degree of psychological certainty, that Mr. Lowe is dangerous—his mental disorders make it substantially probable that he will engage in acts of sexual violence."[47] In this formulation, Jordan Lowe's dangerousness is part of his makeup, a characteristic of him as a person. But this construction of the sexual predator has spillover effects for all sex offenders. Megan's Law, for instance, is premised on the assumption that treatment of sexual offenders is futile and that they will remain dangerous—indeed, that they are guilty not just of bad behavior but of being bad people.[48]

The notion that sexual offenders are inherently bad or dangerous is further evidenced by the rarity with which SVPs are released from custody. Minnesota and Missouri, for instance, are facing ongoing legal battles over their civil commitment programs because of the way their programs have been enacted. Missouri has never released an SVP since the inception of its program in 1999. Minnesota has released only a handful since its program began in 1994 and currently has the highest per capita rate of civilly committed sex offenders of any state in the country. Both programs have been accused of providing insufficient treatment and unclear paths for "patients" to progress toward release. An expert evaluation of the Minnesota program prepared for the court attests to these complaints.[49] As Michael Miner, one of the contributing experts in the Minnesota case, commented:

We were twenty years into it in Minnesota and . . . this clearly appears to be an indefinite commitment program; this does not appear to be a treatment program since nobody seems to be successful. You know, what's the problem here? Is it that we truly have a bunch of intransigent people and, therefore, we can expect this to continue to grow? Or is there something wrong with both the way the law is written and the way it's implemented?[50]

Miner went on to explain, as he did in his expert affidavit to the court, that he believed it to be an issue of both how the law was written and implemented. A 2007 report on SVP commitment programs nationwide likewise found that only about 10% of those committed since 1990 had been released by 2006.[51] As Miner's comments and SVP release data suggest, despite ostensibly being treatment programs, SVP programs appear to be aimed more at containing those who are viewed as "intransigent" rather than malleable or amenable to rehabilitation.

When they are released, offenders in general, and SVPs especially, face increased surveillance and severely curtailed liberties on where they can live and work, and even whether they can use a computer. Many face lifetime registration on public sex offender registries and often must notify the community of their presence. These often-lifelong restrictions promulgate the idea that sex offenders are incurable deviants permanently possessed of a pathological sexuality. Ideas of enduring sexual pathology certainly draw support from many sources—including cultural stereotypes—but forensic science provides a powerful tool to reinforce these views, particularly when courts are searching for a rationale to treat sex offenders in exceptional ways. Quantified risk estimates offer perhaps the best justification for the notion that sex offenders are indefinitely dangerous. Unlike the "yes" or "no" dangerousness determinations of the sexual psychopath era, risk estimates are probabilistic, meaning there is rarely, if ever, a situation in which an offender would be deemed to have no risk. Thus, regardless of the numerical estimate, courts can use actuarial risk assessments as justification for the assumption that sex offenders will *always* be risky.

The 2016 decision by the Seventh Circuit in *Belleau v. Wall* illustrates this idea. Belleau had been declared an SVP by the state of Wisconsin due to two prior sexual assault charges involving children. After ten years in prison and five years of civil commitment, Belleau was released from custody based on the opinion of a psychologist that he was no longer more likely than not to commit future sexual assaults. Using the Static-99R, the psychologist estimated that Belleau's risk of recidivism was 16% at the time of his release from civil commitment and 8% at the time of his appeal. In Belleau's appeal, he argued that Wisconsin's requirement that all sex offenders released from civil commitment wear a GPS ankle bracelet twenty-four hours a day for life was unconstitutional. The district judge agreed that the statute was unconstitutional, precipitating an appeal to the Seventh Circuit, which reversed the district court. As part of its reasoning, the court cited the evaluating psychologist, who stated that "it is well understood in my profession that pedophilia in adults cannot be changed."[52] The court leaned heavily on the belief that sex offenders remain dangerous forever and used Belleau's actuarial scores to substantiate it, writing: "And even if we credit the 8 and 16 percent figures, the plaintiff can't be thought just a harmless old guy. Readers of this opinion who are parents of young children should ask themselves whether they should worry that there are people in their community who have 'only' a 16 percent or an 8 percent probability of molesting young children."[53] The court later added, "There is the further problem that the 16 percent figure is just a guess, and the even more serious problem that the figure implies that of every six pedophiles with character-istics similar to those of the plaintiff in this case one will resume molesting children after his release from prison."[54] Thus, the court simultaneously minimized the actuarial prediction as "just a guess" and held it up as proof that sex offenders are always dangerous, suggesting that the court desires the aura of objectivity that comes from quantification but the latitude to in-terpret science as it sees fit. It sustained this logic with an unsubstantiated assertion drawn from a Supreme Court decision wherein the court said that "the risk of recidivism posed by sex offenders is frightening and high."[55] Under the rationale followed by this court, then, a probability of recidivism as low as 8% may certify that someone remains a sexual danger.

The quantification of risk in this scenario allowed the court to impute an enduring risk to almost any sex offender in a way that earlier subjective "yes" or "no" dangerousness determinations did not. Such probabilistic measures of risk create a policy climate aimed not just at reducing risk but at eliminating risk altogether, resulting in practices like civil commitment meant to remove certain sex offenders from civil society indefinitely (and perhaps permanently), residence restrictions for former offenders, and lifetime monitoring and registration. But actuarial risk assessment shapes and reinforces current policy aims in another way, too: by constructing the "sexually violent predator" as the biggest risk to society and thus as the subject needing the most resources.

Many sex offender statutes define "sexual predators" only as those who offend against strangers, excluding intrafamilial and other offenders known to the victim from the category. For example, the federal Wetter-ling Act defines predatory behavior as "an act directed at a stranger, or a person with whom a relationship has been established or promoted for the primary purpose of victimization."[56] Actuarial risk assessment tools, such as the Static-99, give scientific backing to these legal definitions by classi-fying "stranger" offenders as more dangerous than non-stranger offenders. Some recidivism studies do, in fact, show that incest offenders may be less likely to reoffend than other types of offenders, but we also know that intra-familial abuse is the least likely type of sex crime to be reported.[57] Even when the assault is not within the family but the perpetrator is still known to the victim, the crime is substantially less likely to be reported.[58] Because actuarial tools are based only on offenders who have been convicted of a crime, they cannot capture this reporting disparity. Moreover, the factors scored on the Static-99R simply may not accurately reflect the seriousness of one's crime if it took place within the family. For instance, a married thirty-five-year-old man who sexually abused his two daughters over the course of many years would receive a score of 0 on the Static-99R, placing him in the lowest-risk category. By contrast, a single thirty-five-year-old man who once fondled an unrelated boy would receive a score of 3, pushing him into the next highest risk category. Depending on the way the assessment is scored, he may receive a 4, placing him in the "moderate-high" category. In other words, according to the Static-99R, a man who abuses his own daughter(s) over the course of many years would be considered less of a risk than a man who once touched an unrelated boy. For this reason, many would advocate not using such tools for intrafamilial offenders. However, such results reinforce the dominant cultural perception that "stranger danger" is the greatest risk when it comes to sexual assault and allows us to easily construct strangers as "sexual predators" through the use of risk prediction tools. Notably, the "stranger danger" trope is highly racialized and typically calls to mind a man of color (usually Black) jumping out of the bushes to attack a (White) woman. The "sexual predator" moniker similarly dehumanizes, portraying offenders as uncontrollable animals, not unlike the "super predator" discourse of the 1990s that centrally featured Black men.

How Accurate Is Actuarial Assessment?

In addition to creating an image of sex offenders as indefinitely risky and incapable of change, actuarial assessments have been criticized for a number of other issues, prime among them is that they are not as highly predictive as many would like for making life-altering decisions. Most estimates of the predictive accuracy of the Static-99R put it at around 70%, leading some to be skeptical of its use for civil commitment decisions. Speaking of the Static-99, William Marshall, a well-regarded researcher and clinician, commented:

> If you look at the area under the curve, for example, the risk assessment instruments, the best ones, have a .71. A .5 is chance, right? So .71 is not exactly something that's gonna get you a Nobel Prize, but it's significantly better than chance. . . . They've had a very, I think, significant impact in the eyes of the law, particularly in courts. But I think they're a bit exag-

gerated in their—I mean nobody who testifies in these cases explains that, you know, .5 is chance and these are at .71. So we're looking for 1.0, so don't get too excited. But they present them as if they're knockdown, unfortunately.[59]

Thus, while Marshall acknowledged the advances over clinical prediction that actuarial assessments represent, he was also skeptical of using such technologies for major decisions.

Oftentimes defense attorneys will use these critiques to highlight the shortcomings of actuarial assessments in civil commitment trials, as Jordan Lowe's attorney did in the following exchange with the state's expert witness:

DEFENSE: You used the Static-99R. That doesn't tell you anything about Mr. Lowe personally, does it? Just the group he's assigned to, right?

EXPERT: Yes.

DEFENSE: What is the error rate of that test?

EXPERT: The area under the curve is 0.71.

DEFENSE: So three out of ten are wrong?

EXPERT: Yes.

DEFENSE: And then there are different groups and different estimated risks for each group, but the developers don't give any objective criteria for choosing which group to assign someone, right?

EXPERT: Right.

DEFENSE: For the routine group, a score of 7 has a recidivism rate of 18.8% over five years, and the high-risk, high-needs group has a rate of 37.9% over five years. Which group did you use for Mr. Lowe?

EXPERT: High risk, high needs.

DEFENSE: So a 30% risk, but they're wrong 30% of the time?

EXPERT: Yes.[60]

In this case, the defense counsel's tactics were successful, and in a rare turn of events, Lowe was found by a jury not to be an SVP. However, in many more instances, despite such deconstruction of actuarials, courts and juries still find sex offenders to be unacceptably risky, as in the case of *U.S. v. Shields* (2011), where the court wrote:

The question of Shields's risk of future offense was by no means an easy one. As each of the experts who testified at trial acknowledged, there is no crystal ball that an examining expert or court might consult to predict conclusively whether a past offender will recidivate. At best, offenders can be located, by means of an actuarial tool, within a population of individuals that share certain characteristics and that studies have shown to recidivate at a particular rate. These tools are, as the district court's appointed expert cautioned, "moderate" predictors of risk.[61]

The court continued on to acknowledge that Shield's attorney "effectively elicited testimony highlighting the shortcomings of the actuarial tools," but interestingly that "the court granted 'little weight' to the raw scores returned by the experts' actuarial tools, and focused instead on the experts' evaluation of certain 'dynamic factors' (age, treatment history, and ongoing deviant behavior) that tailor the actuarial risk assessment to an offender's individual circumstances." The court's use of dynamic factors suggests that adjudicators may rely less on numerical estimates provided by actuarials and more on an expert's overall opinion and embedding raw numbers within larger narratives of criminality that are used to justify indefinite confinement.

In fact, the creators of the Static-99 suggested in their article introducing the instrument. "It is likely that actuarial risk scales can improve on Static-99 by including dynamic (changeable) risk factors as well as additional static variables." They then stated:

Static-99 does not claim to provide a comprehensive assessment, for it neglects whole categories of potentially relevant variables (e.g., dynamic factors). Consequently, prudent evaluators would want to consider whether there are external factors that warrant adjusting the initial score or special features that limit the applicability of the scale (e.g., a debilitating disease or stated intentions to reoffend). Given the poor track record of clinical prediction, however, adjustments to actuarial predictions require strong justifications. In most cases, the optimal adjustment would be expected to be minor or none at all.[62]

As I will discuss in the next section, many evaluators have taken seriously the warning that the Static-99 is not a comprehensive assessment. They have taken less seriously the admonishment that optimal adjustments should be minimal or none.

NASCENT DYNAMISM?

Although only static instruments are typically introduced in SVP proceedings, researchers have developed dynamic assessments for sex offenders. The most popular is the Stable-2007, though it is designed for use with offenders living in the community. However, evaluators often use it as a guide for assessing dynamic risk factors in SVPs in what they label an "adjusted actuarial approach." All of my interviewees reported using this approach, rather than a "pure" actuarial approach, in order to customize their assessments to individual offenders. Explaining his adjusted actuarial approach, Illinois SVP evaluator Dr. Aaron Barton stated that he begins with the Static-99R and then, he explained, "I see where that data takes me, and I incorporate it with the rest of the case-specific data and then make a determination. I don't make adjustments to those instruments. I let those instruments run their course and whatever risk category they suggest, I take that into consideration."[63] Similarly, Illinois evaluator Dr. Kim Weitl said:

> I actually like using them for what I like to call the baseline, kind of a starting ground. So if the guy starts at the moderate low, say, then I've got a lot of work to do to get him up to more likely than not, which means a lot of other aggravating factors. Hanson's meta-analysis has identified a bunch of risk factors that aren't included in the actuarials. So, if I have a lot of those, maybe he's got a lot of victims that he got caught with, then I can maybe pull him up. But if he's scoring on a six or moderate high, I don't have to do a whole lot . . . that's my starting point, in my mind anyway. I think in that way, they're priceless. They're objective measures. . . . So, it's kind of nice, it's just kind of comfortable as an evaluator to have that as a baseline.[64]

Thus, actuarials serve as the first step in an individualized assessment process. All evaluators I spoke with were confident their adjustments were warranted, and almost all mentioned something of Hanson's or another researcher's meta-analysis of risk factors, as Dr. Weitl did above, in justifying their methods. That is, evaluators seem by and large to believe they are compensating for a limitation of static instruments by making individualized adjustments. However, a meta-analysis of three studies to have compared a straight actuarial approach to an adjusted actuarial approach found that a straight actuarial approach was more predictive in all three studies.[65] One of the included studies even found that clinical adjustments had an inter-rater reliability of less than chance. In essence, adjusted actuarial approaches may simply be allowing the biases of clinical assessment into the risk evaluation process under the guise of objective actuarial technologies, in effect black-boxing discretion. Interestingly, courts seem to evince a strong willingness to afford adjusted actuarial approaches determinative weight, perhaps because adjustments are most often necessary to reach the standard of commitment.

As the Fourth Circuit Court of Appeals stated in the case of Andrew Sheradin in 2012, "As we have previously explained, the determination of a particular individual's risk of recidivism may rely not only on actuarial tests, but also on factors such as his participation in treatment, his ability to control his impulses, and his commitment to controlling his behavior."[66] Even more clearly stating its reliance on factors outside of the static risk instruments, the Fourth Circuit in *U.S. v. Perez* (2014) wrote:

> Although the district court recognized and considered the statistical rates of recidivism based on the various actuarial scales, the court explained that it "affords them less weight than respondent's past and current conduct, and the testimony of the experts as a whole." The district court noted that each of the testifying experts identified several factors as indicative of Perez's lack of volitional control, including Perez's impulsivity, failure to cooperate while on supervised release, and his brazen and risky behavior despite previous legal sanctions. The district court also gave significant weight to Perez's lack of sex offender treatment and his apparent denial of pedophilic sexual interest.[67]

As the court notes, Perez's past conduct played a large role in its decision, not unlike the way that criminal history has become the primary factor in determining the risk and character of other types of offenders.[68] These data indicate that courts routinely weigh additional static and dynamic factors external to actuarial assessments in arriving at their final determinations. In the case of sex offenders, these factors rarely seem to decrease risk, but rather are used primarily to present an offender as *more* dangerous than his actuarial scores would suggest.

Rather than using dynamic factors to paint a picture of an individual capable of change, evaluators generally used these factors to generate risk estimates high enough to meet the legal requirements for civil commitment. In Illinois, for instance, the state must prove that an offender is "substantially probable" to sexually reoffend, which is interpreted to mean "much more likely than not." However, the Static-99R and Static-2002R very rarely produce a probability of recidivism above 50%, meaning that evaluators *must* boost their risk estimates using dynamic factors to meet the legal threshold of commitment. Consequently, all of the evaluators with whom I spoke justified their recommendations for commitment based on an upward adjustment of the initial actuarial estimate, generally justified by dynamic criminogenic factors, such as deviant sexual preferences (often identified through use of the controversial penile plethysmograph), impulsivity, and poor problem-solving skills. Defense attorneys attempt to turn dynamic factors in the other direction, arguing, for instance, that treatment has lowered an offender's sexual risk. These arguments are rarely accepted, suggesting that although dynamic factors are used to individuate, they rarely work to create a portrait of a dynamic risk subject. Rather, because sexuality is seen as fixed and as the source of danger for

SVPs, rehabilitation is understood to take an extremely long time and may never be possible.

Another justification for upward adjustments is that actuarials only predict recidivism for up to ten years, but SVP trials must account for an offender's likelihood of reoffending over the course of his entire life. As Illinois evaluator Dr. Edward Spencer wrote in his assessment of Jordan Lowe, "Unlike assessments of recidivism, the statutory threshold for dangerousness is not time limited. Therefore, actuarial predictions of risk, however more accurate than predictions from other kinds of risk assessment, are nonetheless conservative and underestimate risk." Dr. Spencer proceeded to state, "With a score of 7 [on the Static-99R], Mr. Lowe is 5.25 times more likely to recidivate than the typical offender," and "Mr. Lowe's estimated five-year risk is 24.0%; at ten years his estimated risk increased to 33.8%."[69] It is notable (though not unusual) that Dr. Spencer, like SVP proceedings more generally, commits the ecological fallacy—making inferences about Mr. Lowe based on the group to which he belongs. Though this is a misinterpretation of how actuarials work, it is a further indication of the belief that ARA provides an unbiased view of the individual. In the remainder of his fifty-five-page report, Dr. Spencer justified his conclusion that Mr. Lowe is an SVP by constructing a detailed narrative of Lowe's life, and particularly his criminal history, which has historically been understood as a prime means of knowing the individual offender.

Further indicating that actuarialism is driven by a "will to know" the offender is that both the Static-99R and Static-2002R now require evaluators to place offenders into one of four groups—each of which has different risk estimates—based on their individual dynamic and criminogenic needs. As Dr. Spencer's report explains, "Estimating an individual's risk to engage in further acts of sexual violence with the Static-99R requires calculating his relative risk (i.e., his Static-99R score), and then determining which sample provides the most appropriate absolute risk." Dr. Spencer goes on to explain that the "routine sample" is the default, but if "there are reasons to believe the offender being assessed is not typical, then it would be appropriate to use the recidivism rates from Preselected or Non-Routine Samples. Such use, however, requires justification. If an offender has sufficient dynamic or criminogenic needs, it is reasonable to use Pre-Selected or Non-Routine norms."[70] Dr. Spencer elected to place Lowe in the "High Risk/High Needs" group because of the extensive evaluation process that eliminates 96–98% of all offenders from commitment and because a court had already found probable cause to believe that Lowe was an SVP.

As some interviewees pointed out, the step of determining which group to compare an offender to is another point where evaluator bias may enter. Dr. Travis suggested: "Each evaluator comes to things with their own perspectives, their own flexibilities and rigidities, and we're all different. I hate to say that sometimes it comes down to who's the evaluator, but sometimes it comes down to who's the evaluator and how do they see things. . . . [Some are] just more prone to see that people are dangerous than I am."[71] Dr. Karen Franklin, a clinical psychologist and critic of civil commitment laws, asserted:

> It's not necessarily the raw score, but it's how do you interpret that score? Like how much weight do you place on it? And then there's been these huge controversies over—and it's really technical—but like what norms do you compare this person to? So let's say this person gets a six or a five or something on the Static-99. Do you compare them to this group of people with "high-risk norms," or do you compare them to kind of the aggregate of all the data that has been selected on the Static-99? If you compare to the high-risk norms, you're gonna get a high-risk guy. So that's been one of the things is that the government evaluators will always use the high-risk norms, which are less stable, less accurate.[72]

The end result of all of these machinations is generally to constitute the figure of the "sexual predator" as a permanently pathological and indefinitely dangerous individual incapable of rehabilitation. In summing up the decision-making process, former Clinical Director of Florida's SVP program, Dr. Robin Wilson, said:

> One of the great difficulties in most civil commitment programs is that there should be a bar. And if you're above that bar, then you meet criteria, and you should be in the civil commitment center. If you're below that bar, you should be released to the community. The difficulty is that the bar to get in is relatively low; the bar to get out is relatively high. Theoretically, they should be identical, right? You either meet criteria or you don't. It shouldn't be differential depending on what it is that you're trying to accomplish. So it's relatively easy to civilly commit people; it's relatively difficult to release them.[73]

As this quote intimates, once an offender is deemed an SVP through the dual processes of psychiatric diagnosis and actuarial risk assessment, his legal and sexual identity is largely cemented.

In this chapter, I have argued that the figure of the "sex offender," and particularly the "sexual predator," is constituted jointly through legal and scientific mechanisms as permanently pathological and indefinitely risky. Through the diagnosis of paraphilias and the designation of dangerousness on account of those diagnoses, SVPs are given a durable legal and sexual identity. In the legal complex of SVP adjudications, violent sexual behaviors, such as child molestation and rape, cease being only criminal acts and become instead the basis for a sexual identity akin to gay or straight. Though both diagnosis and risk prediction are seen as rather objective because of their seemingly clearly delineated criteria and, in the case of ARA, the quantified language of probability, I have shown how both processes allow clinical judgment and possibly bias to enter the assessment process in often subtle and unrecognized ways. For instance, ARA is widely seen as a huge step forward in risk prediction, but courts rely on, and forensic psychologists employ, an "adjusted actuarial" approach that may cloak subjective discretion in the guise of numbers. Similarly, the diagnosis of "paraphilia not otherwise specified" that is generally used for rapists has an inter-rater reliability of less than chance, yet it has been accepted by most courts that have heard SVP cases because of the scientific legitimacy granted by the DSM. But data from the Illinois SVP program suggest racial bias in this diagnosis. That is, despite accounting for only 26% of the SVP population, Black men comprise 62% of PNOSN diagnoses. This suggests a greater tendency to medicalize rape as the basis for the indefinite detention of Black men, or a greater likelihood of Black men being convicted of rape in the first place, or both.

CONCLUSION

Risk assessments increasingly guide decision-making regarding criminal justice and wider governance issues, yet relatively little attention has been devoted to considering how risk assessments, understood as particular types of state "grids of intelligibility," constitute sexual subject positions. But sexual governance, no less than other state decision-making, appears to be increasingly structured by risk. In both SVP adjudications and asylum determinations, sexual subjects' access to citizenship is ultimately dictated vis-à-vis risk. In other words, whether they will be recognized as legitimate rights-bearing citizens by the state depends on the risk they pose and/or the risk they face. Juxtaposing these two risk assessment practices demonstrates that risk is not an ontological state or a preexisting and fixed quality of people, places, or objects. Risk is a historically and institutionally specific way of imaging and dealing with particular issues.[74]

Further, risk is emergent in relations between actors and institutions. Particular risk assemblages are actively constituted and reconstituted in interactions between actors and the institutions charged with rendering them legible and manageable by the state. Different discourses, technologies, actors, and institutional settings come together to give rise to divergent strategies for making sexual subjects knowable via risk. Risk discourses and practices are always imbued with moral meaning and shaped by cultural and political factors.[75] This is evident in the legal settings analyzed here where courts often invoke "science" to justify decisions or authorize commonsense understandings of phenomena. In drawing on a mix of expert and non-expert knowledges, courts create new risk assemblages that are neither scientific nor anti-scientific.[76] Thus, as Mariana Valverde and colleagues suggest, "Risk assessments that were originally developed in a scientific context lose much of their scientificity as they are reworked into an assemblage whose logic is not scientific."[77] That is, the law may adapt science to its own needs while also drawing on cultural common sense and politicized discourses, ultimately producing hybrid risk assemblages that give us the dual figures of the sexual predator and the LGBTQ asylum seeker.

Of course, these risk assessment processes are quite different. Risk determinations in asylum proceedings depend on qualitative evaluations of a country's risk to a particular asylum seeker on account of his sexuality. Although judges attempt to make their decisions appear as objective as possible, they clearly depend on the subjective judgment of that adjudicator. By contrast, risk evaluations of sex offenders use quantified actuarial estimates of sexual recidivism to determine an offender's potential risk to a community. The quantification of risk and the "mechanical objectivity" of actuarial tools seems to take subjective judgment out of the equation, but as I have shown, substantial discretion remains in this process, though it is often black-boxed to a significant extent.

These distinct risk adjudication processes undergird different forms of recognition of sexual subjects before the state. Where the asylum seeker may be recognized as an imperiled sexual subject in need of benevolent state protection, the sex offender faces the prospect of being labeled a "sexual predator" and a permanent risk to his community in need of constant state surveillance. These risk determination processes thus fit within the broader epistemic logics of their respective institutional domains. The risk an asylum seeker faces can only be discerned by placing him in the context of a specific country and estimating what risk that setting will pose to him, similar to how narrative accounts of sexual identity development had to be placed in a particular cultural context. The risk a sex offender may present to his community, conversely, is decided through an individualized process that largely disregards social context, like what we saw regarding courts' determinations about sex offenders' sexualities.

Regardless of these differences, both processes reify symbolic boundaries around the category of citizen and make risk a central element in constructing that boundary. In the conclusion, I will consider what these practices suggest about the shifting meanings of sexual citizenship in the twenty-first century and their significance for state governance of sexuality.

CONCLUSION: SEXUALITY, SCIENCE, AND CITIZENSHIP IN THE TWENTY-FIRST CENTURY

The respondent has stated that his family became aware of his homosexuality after his convictions for possession of child pornography and sexual assault of a twelve-year-old child. However, in no way can homosexuality be equated with child molestation and pedophilia. I submitted evidence to the court today that it's harmful to homosexuals when society attempts to paint pedophiles as homosexuals rather than as sexual predators. In this case, I would argue that there is little objective evidence in the record establishing that the respondent is homosexual, but there is evidence in the record establishing that he is a pedophile and sexual predator, and I think it's very important to make that distinction. It's nothing short of offensive to attempt to equate the two.

DHS ATTORNEY CLOSING ARGUMENT IN
REMOVAL PROCEEDINGS FOR ACHMED HASSAN,
CHICAGO IMMIGRATION COURT, OCTOBER 2014

Sorting Sexualities has argued that the techno-legal classification practices that state actors engage in naturalize social distinctions along the lines of sexuality and engender new subject positions and forms of social control based around those classifications. One result of these practices has been the extension of rights for certain LGBTQ people. Another has been the concomitant escalation of punishment and surveillance aimed at sexual offenders. Nowhere was this more clearly crystallized during all of my fieldwork than in the closing argument offered by the state's attorney in Achmed Hassan's removal proceedings, in which Hassan sought protection under the Convention against Torture (he was barred from both asylum and withholding of removal because of his criminal convictions). Hassan feared returning to his native Pakistan because, he contended, his conviction for sexual assault of a boy would out him as gay. It had already occasioned his coming out to his family, who had begun receiving threats intended for Hassan from anonymous strangers. Hassan argued, both in immigration court and to state prosecutors earlier, that the boy had told Hassan he was eighteen years old, but in an attempt to avoid an even longer prison sentence, Hassan struck a plea deal, as most criminal defendants do. However, in another common turn of events, Hassan was not informed by his defense lawyer that his plea deal would also mean his removal from the United States after he served his sentence.

Hassan's removal proceedings provided a dramatic enactment of the clash between the penal and welfare logics I have outlined in the preceding pages. But it was the DHS lawyer's closing statement that also brought into sharp focus the competing epistemic logics and divergent classification practices described in *Sorting Sexualities*. The attorney's argument hinged on the assertion that pedophilia was distinct from homosexuality, a contention that is now cultural commonsense but until very recently would have been controversial itself. But more than that, she seemed to argue that pedophilia was, in fact, a distinct kind of sexual orientation itself, and even if one exhibited attraction exclusively to males, it still bore no relation to homosexuality. In her formulation, homosexuality meant that one was attracted to *men*, in the sense connoted by law, that is, eighteen years of age or older. And in a rare moment of the legal complexes of asylum and sex offender law bleeding into each other, she drew on the work of psychologists who have made the strongest arguments for pedophilia as a distinct sexual orientation to make her case. Nevertheless, the judge ultimately granted Hassan deferral of removal under the CAT. Somewhat ironically, the judge determined that his gayness was insufficient to grant his claim; rather, it was his criminal convictions for sexual assault that put him at heightened risk of torture.

Hassan's case brings together many of the themes of this book—the politics of expertise and classification, the deployment of state power through knowledge claims, the cultural boundaries of citizenship—and gives us the opportunity to revisit its central arguments and consider what they mean beyond the asylum and SVP courtrooms.

SEXUALITY AND EPISTEMIC LOGICS

Sorting Sexualities began by asking how "the state" attempts to objectively measure sexuality for the purposes of classification and state action. In the preceding pages, I have argued that the state does so in multiple ways. In fact, to ask how the state as a unified entity categorizes sexual subjects is an unanswerable question, just as asking how "law" or "science" know sexuality is misguided. The state, law, and science are all massive social institutions made up of numerous organizations and actors that have different (and sometimes competing) goals, practices, and guiding assumptions. As such, the way these entities know is multiple and organizationally specific.

Techniques of knowing are dependent on what I have called "epistemic logics," or hybridized ways of approaching measurement, classification, and knowing that are formed through the interplay of cultural, political, and institutional forces. Epistemic logics vary across state institutions and are highly dependent upon the knowledges and technologies that inform state legal decision-making in a given arena. As we have seen, anthropologists understand sexuality rather differently than psychologists, and when these disciplines inform decisions, they do so in quite distinct ways.

I demonstrated that asylum adjudicators favor narratives of sexual identity development and "coming out" as evidence of one's sexuality. In this way, sexuality is understood as knowable only through indirect indicators that must be placed in particular social and cultural contexts. Asylum adjudicators have recognized nascent social constructionist arguments regarding gender and sexuality, including acknowledging that sexuality can be fluid and may change over the life course and that sexual acts and identities have different meanings in different cultures. This approach to knowing sexuality suggests a particular ontology of sexuality as well, one that does not necessarily assume a fixed inner sexual essence inherent in the body. Rather, it allows for social influences on sexuality and sexual identity.

SVP adjudications, conversely, depend much more heavily on direct bodily evidence, such as the polygraph and penile plethysmograph, and other forms of objective measurement, including actuarial risk assessments. These are understood to be direct measures of sexuality in the SVP legal complex. Rather than being indicators in need of context, technologies like the PPG are believed to be objective measurements that are universally applicable. Such methods suggest a more essentialist understanding of sexuality that views it as emanating from the individual body. There is little room for social or cultural context. The measurements simply speak for themselves.

The different forms that risk assessment takes in these two domains both flow from and reinforce institutionalized means of knowing sexual subjects and are primary ways of defining the bounds of proper sexual citizenship. The quantified, actuarial approach to risk assessment found in SVP trials is consistent with the broader epistemic logic of that legal arena, which assumes that sexuality and sexual risk can be objectively measured through direct indicators and inscription devices. Actuarial assessments are viewed as providing an unbiased view of the individual in much the same way as one's criminal history has historically been understood in the justice system. Subjective professional discretion, however, is still present at numerous points throughout the risk assessment process for sex offenders, from determining what "likely" to reoffend means to deciding how to interpret an offender's quantitative risk estimate.

This procedure looks quite different in the asylum context and is more in line with the overall epistemic logic of that arena. Lacking the kind of data that would allow adjudicators to make quantified risk predictions, immigration judges instead engage in a risk determination process that more closely resembles "trained judgment" and trusts decision-makers to be able to render unbiased decisions based on their professional experience. To make their decisions appear as objective as possible, adjudicators typically invoke authoritative sources—such as the US State Department, recognized human rights organizations like Amnesty International, and academic experts—to bolster the credibility of their predictions. But like the risk assessment process in SVP trials, asylum hearings also allow considerable subjectivity, for instance, in operationalizing "well-founded fear." The Supreme Court has given some guidance to adjudicators in recognizing when fear may be "well-founded" (i.e., as little as a 10% chance can qualify) in a way that courts have largely not done for civil commitment standards for sex offenders. Like risk assessments of sex offenders that privilege a view of risk as emanating from individuals, though, risk assessments of countries that see danger as a product of social factors in asylum hearings clearly resonate with the broader epistemic logic of the legal complex. Regardless of their differences, both processes make risk a central frame through which to *know* sexual subjects vis-à-vis the state.

Decisions about which knowledges will guide state officials are both practical and political. The institutional need to decide if a sex offender poses a risk to the community necessitates a form of knowledge trained on the individual, while the need to determine the risk that an entire country may pose to an asylum seeker would seem to require a very different approach. Yet, as I have shown, skirmishes over professional jurisdiction, credibility struggles, and political maneuvering affect state knowledge-making as much as practical institutional needs.

By shifting the focus to knowledge-making about sexuality in institutions that have been largely ignored by other STS scholarship—including the social sciences, law, and the many branches of the state—I have attempted to open new theoretical and empirical lines of inquiry. Analyzing the deployment of knowledges and technologies in these many settings offers greater leverage for understanding sexual knowledge-making in its various forms. Moving beyond the case of sexuality suggests that the concept of epistemic logics has general utility for theorizing the relationship between state institutions and non-state expert actors in relation to state knowledge. Neil Fligstein and colleagues' recent analysis of why the

Federal Reserve failed to predict the financial crisis of 2008 provides one example.[1] They argue that the Fed failed to anticipate the crisis because its primary cognitive frame was macroeconomic theory. They therefore demonstrate the central importance of epistemic logics and non-state experts in guiding state action without centering expertise as a critical factor. In his comparative study of punishment in the United States and Germany, Joachim Savelsberg has similarly argued that the "nation-specific institutionalization of knowledge construction and domination must be taken into consideration in order to more fully explain the macro outcome of criminal punishment decisions."[2] Lisa Stampnitzky's examination of "how experts invented terrorism" *does* highlight the importance of the interaction between state institutions and non-state experts in guiding state action, demonstrating more directly how the concept of epistemic logics offers explanatory power in a range of settings.[3] As a theoretical heuristic, epistemic logics can provide a more precise lens through which to theorize these disparate state-society interactions and leads to important questions for study. Under what circumstances do various modes of knowing predominate? What consequences do these different knowledges and technologies have? How, and under what circumstances, do these different ways of knowing diffuse throughout the social world and with what effects?

Sorting Sexualities has begun to answer these important questions by analyzing the knowledge practices that undergird policy-making and the adjudication of sexuality-related issues. The close examination of these knowledges in both asylum and sex offender law provides a fuller understanding of how the state legitimates forms of social control, creates sexual knowledge, and categorizes individuals for subsequent state action. Specifically, I have argued that state legal institutions depend on non-state experts to create measurement and classification schemas for sexual subjects so state officials can make subsequent governance decisions regarding those subjects. More than that, I have suggested, in line with sociologist Gil Eyal, that we must reconceptualize expertise, not as the possession of individuals, but as a characteristic of a network of actors. This shift in focus is necessary if we are to capture the multiple and hybrid knowledges that inform state decision-making in the realms of LGBTQ asylum and sex offender law—and beyond. In these cases, this also means dissolving the always permeable and arguably artificial division between "state" and "society."

INSURGENT OR COMPLICIT EXPERTISE— DOES IT MATTER?

This raises a set of questions in relation to the expert actors and networks who offer their knowledge in both the asylum and SVP legal complexes.

Under what circumstances do particular kinds of knowledge intervene in policy or legal issues and actually have an effect? When are those knowledges likely to support state goals versus challenge them? When are challenges likely to be successful? We can glean at least partial answers to these questions based on the preceding analysis of the networks of expertise in the asylum and sex offender legal complexes.

I have characterized forensic psychology as a kind of complicit expertise given its support of the goals of the state legal apparatus. Conversely, I labeled the hybrid expertise of the asylum network insurgent expertise because it more directly challenged the prevailing legal classification practices of the state. Both, however, were responding to cultural shifts that had engendered different types of legitimacy crises within various arms of the state. These crises provided openings for epistemic entrepreneurs to offer new ways of accomplishing the tasks the state needed done. This is most clear in the case of forensic psychology with its challenge to the prevailing institutionalized psychiatric expertise of the time. As psychiatry fell out of favor with both the public and the state because of its poor track record of managing sex offenders, and the APA subsequently refused to endorse new SVP statutes, forensic psychologists stepped in to fill the void. Not only did they assert that the APA was wrong in many of its views on the treatment and evaluation of sexual offenders; they also offered what seemed to be more objective methods of assessing and classifying offenders. In this case, their challenge to psychiatric expertise was successful because it directly offered the means of accomplishing a task that the state wanted done, and it did so in a way that was likely to quell many of the concerns with the subjectivity of diagnosis and risk assessment for offenders.

The story for asylum is both similar and different. The legal and human rights activists who started forming the network of expertise that would eventually get semi-institutionalized within the state immigration apparatus responded to what they perceived as a legitimacy crisis in the processing of LGBTQ asylum claims. While the state was less concerned with this issue than the management of sex offenders, some asylum offices and key actors within the State Department began to recognize the unmet need represented by this new area of asylum law. These parallel developments suggest that an unmet need to accomplish a task coupled with an institutional opening are two key pieces that allow new epistemic actors to gain footholds and begin spreading their way of knowing. This also suggests that to be successful some sympathetic actors within the state are necessary, particularly when challenging state goals. But asylum actors did not press for the wholesale overturning of prevailing policy or procedure. Rather, they adopted a practice of "generosity" and strategically used boundary objects to graft their ways of knowing onto the state's own. In much the same way that health social movement actors have been successful by fashioning themselves into "lay experts" and insinuating themselves into key organizational positions, asylum actors learned both the ways of the state *and* educated themselves in social scientific theories of gender and sexuality and thus were able to bring those two schools of thought together.[4] Forensic psychologists similarly pursued a process of generosity, albeit in a different manner. Namely, rather than demanding exclusive control over their professional mandate or terms like "mental abnormality," they conceded some authority to legal actors and evinced a willingness to work within the bounds dictated by the law. In essence, they subordinated themselves to the needs of the state in exchange for professional authority and jurisdiction. In this way, it was very much a hybrid exchange, a two-way street that cannot be neatly separated into a "legal" or "state" mode of knowing, on the one hand, and a "psychological" way of knowing, on the other. Rather, a network of expertise bridges such divisions.

Thus, both strategies were successful but in quite different ways and with different effects. Why, for instance, did the asylum network challenge state practices when forensic psychology did not? To the extent that a field or expert network is wholly (or almost wholly) dependent upon the state for its professional standing, we should expect it to be complicit with state goals. Conversely, as a discipline becomes more independently established and depends less on the state for its professional jurisdiction, it becomes more likely to openly challenge state policies. This is exemplified by organized psychiatry's willingness to lend its expertise to state efforts to identify and control "sexual psychopaths" in the early to mid-twentieth century when psychiatry was still a discipline in its infancy and struggling to gain professional authority. By the 1990s, psychiatry was firmly established and no longer needed that professional toehold. Similarly, the asylum expertise network—comprising lawyers, human rights activists, and social scientists—is largely independent from the state. The human rights and social science experts who testify in asylum proceedings do not depend on state contracts for their livelihoods (as many forensic psychologists do) nor for their professional identities. Forensic psychology, conversely, was a field still in formation in the early 1990s and seeking greater professional legitimacy. The law conferred that legitimacy in exchange for forensic psychology's willingness to adapt to the law's institutional needs.

That being said, both insurgent and complicit forms of expertise tend to grant more legitimacy to state institutions via technocratization. Certainly, there are instances wherein technocratization delegitimates, and the level of (de)legitimacy of a given state policy or institution will vary across audiences for various reasons.[5] For instance, if forensic psychologists suddenly started employing the PPG to assess the sexualities of asylum seekers, that would delegitimate the process in the eyes of many (as we saw with the Czech Republic), even though this would represent an instance of technocratization. When it comes to contested social issues—such as those around sexuality—technocratization may be more likely to delegitimate state action in the eyes of some than when more "settled" techno-science is brought to bear on issues. However, even this proposition is tenuous if we consider things like climate change, on which the vast majority of scientists agree, but which remains politically unsettled.

Indeed, Robin Stryker suggests that the "settled" or "unsettled" nature of the science brought to bear on legal and policy decisions should affect the extent and effectiveness of technocratization. In her formulation, "settled" science should result in more effective policy implementation and higher levels of technocratization. I suggest, however, that the "settled" status of the science matters less than the extent to which science and law are co-produced and become engineered together in such a way that they appear more and more inseparable over time. In other words, though the science may be unsettled or controversial in certain domains—such as the techno-scientific disciplines from which it is drawn—the techno-*legal* claims that are created in the process of adjudicating sexuality become more settled, more true, as they are deployed as the basis for legal decisions. This is the nature by which epistemic logics operate. They naturalize certain forms of hybrid knowledges that are seen as true in their own interstitial institutional spaces. Those knowledge claims may diffuse beyond their limited institutional spheres, at which point they may become the basis for considerable controversy.

SEXUALITY FORMATION/RACIAL FORMATION

A central contention of *Sorting Sexualities* has been that these different ways of knowing support different forms of state power and approaches to governance. Through a framework of coproduction, I have shown that state institutions depend on knowledge to govern (and to legitimate that governing) and, conversely, that forms of knowledge require social supports. Knowledges are anchored to institutional practices just as institutional practices are guided by forms of knowledge. These divergent knowledges and classification practices make possible and legitimate different forms of governance.

For instance, if sexuality is inherent to an individual, as the epistemic logic in the SVP domain suggests, then it is legitimate to confine or "treat" those with dangerous sexualities. A logic that sees sexuality as the possession of an individual body makes for easier assignations of pathology and criminal blame and suggests that the proper course of action may be to punish or treat that individual. A feminist epistemology of sexual violence would more likely suggest that sexual offenders are not the product of individual pathology but of a broader social ill that socializes men in particular ways. Such an outlook would call for rather different interventions than the ones we currently employ.

By contrast, the epistemic logic of the asylum arena suggests that sexuality is the joint product of an individual and his social setting. This is more consistent with the governance goals of the asylum complex, which seeks to provide humanitarian relief to those fleeing from oppressive social contexts. An epistemology that takes cultural factors seriously also makes sexual identities unfamiliar to American adjudicators more easily intelligible. Rather than seeking to assign blame or pathology to an individual, this epistemic outlook more readily allows for the identification of dangerous countries or cultural settings. The forensic psychological and anthropological forms of knowledge deployed in SVP and asylum law, respectively, thus support and legitimate the prevailing institutional governance goals of their legal complexes.

Processes of classification are inevitably also processes of boundary-making and identity formation. Classification and measurement practices crystallize cultural changes, but they can also engender social change, in part through creating new social identities and subject positions. The LGBTQ asylum seeker did not exist as an identity until its ascription in legal discourse. And as I have shown elsewhere, asylum advocates have used the indeterminacy of the law in conjunction with their social scientifically informed perspective on sexuality to expand categories of legal protection beyond the "homosexual" man initially granted relief under that body of law.[6] As chapter 1 demonstrated, the "sex offender" category has undergone similar changes over the course of the twentieth century. Technologies like the PPG and actuarial risk assessments enact sexual subject positions and create new sexual identities, such as the sexual predator and the pedophile.

Essential to all of these classifications is risk. Risk increasingly structures decisions regarding sexual citizenship. Whereas non-normative sexualities of all kinds were once a priori excluded from the realm of citizenship, today it is increasingly risk rather than sexuality, per se, that demarcates the boundary between citizen and noncitizen. Whether they are the qualitative/clinical risk determination processes of asylum law or the quantitative/actuarial approaches of SVP law, risk assessments fundamentally determine sexual subjects' potential entry into the national community and their access to the rights of citizenship.

Decisions about who is part of the nation inevitably revolve around collective notions of moral worth, and thus questions of citizenship are central to creating social cleavages and their concomitant inequalities. Historically, race and gender have represented two of the starkest divides in how the United States has defined citizenship, but sexuality has been interwoven with both of these. Indeed, sexual formation and racial formation—despite their different genealogies—share many commonalities, and though sociologists have been slow to consider the role of law and the state in sexual formation, adopting the tools of critical race scholars can help us see how their insights apply similarly to sexuality.

Michael Omi and Howard Winant define racial formation as "the process by which social, economic and political forces determine the content and importance of racial categories, and by which they are in turn shaped by racial meanings."[7] As I have argued in this book, political, social, and institutional forces have been central in determining a range of sexuality-related issues, whether it is the type of expertise that will inform legal decision-making or the level of scrutiny different sexual subjects will be subjected to before the state. The salience and valence of sexuality has likewise waxed and waned with economic pressures, social movement mobilization, and presidential administrations. These social forces pushed homosexuality out of the realm of sexual deviancy and criminality and eventually created a wholesale shift in our cultural understanding of the danger posed by queer people, such that queer people are generally no longer seen as a threat to the nation, but rather as a group in need of protection from others who would do them harm. Yet these protections have come through strategic appeals by the gay and lesbian movement to core American values—marriage, family, military service—a strategy that queer studies scholar Lisa Duggan calls "homonormativity."[8]

Notably, homonormative politics is a highly racialized (and classed) politics, which draws our attention back to the ways that sexuality and race are so often mutually constitutive. Sexualization is simultaneously a process of racialization (and vice versa), and these dual processes inform the boundaries of citizenship. That is, even though a subject may not be White, professing a "proper" sexual narrative to the state can serve to discursively (and conditionally) repatriate "proper" sexual citizens into the realm of Whiteness, a phenomenon that Jasbir Puar points out is dependent on an "ascendency of whiteness."[9] Conversely, those who are White may experience a "descent" from Whiteness through a racialized classification process that expels sexual deviants from the province of proper sexual citizenship. This is most evident in the case of pedophiles, who are often imagined as White but lose many of the protections that their Whiteness would otherwise provide when the state officially labels them "sexual predators" and strips them of many of the traditional rights of (White) citizenship.

Note, for instance, the way the DHS lawyer above is careful to distinguish the figure of the deserving homosexual asylee from the sexual predator pedophile. Such dehumanizing moves are indicative of attempts to expel certain subjects from the boundaries of citizenship or even the category of "human" itself. As Sylvia Wynter contends, there are different "genres" of human: the human, the not-quite-human, and the not-human.[10] Sexual predators, regardless of their race—but emphatically so for people of color accused of such crimes—are relegated to the not-human genre. This is not simply a cultural trope (though we must not discount the power of cultural stereotypes) but a de jure form of distinction. The US Supreme Court has delineated considerable legal exceptions specifically for sex offenders, and even the lowest-risk offenders are subjected to extreme deprivations of civil liberties, such as the ability to live with their families or use the Internet (often even when their crimes did not involve it). Some face such severe spatial restrictions that they are rendered homeless by the law, even as other statutes *require* them to maintain a permanent address or risk breaking another set of laws. Our punitive policies, in short, have created a permanent underclass of sex offenders who are closely surveilled and chronically unable to reintegrate into society, putting them at higher risk of recidivism. Sound familiar? It's not a dissimilar story from what we have done to Black neighborhoods. We have created situations in which the very existence of racialized others is a crime.

Asylum tells a story that is at once more optimistic and not, but one that shows a parallel process of racialization/sexualization. Asylum offers an important route to citizenship for some queers of color. Yet this acceptance is premised on the ability of these subjects to offer a narrative of persecution and identity that are acceptable to the US legal system, and, as noted in chapter 2, the primary beneficiaries of asylum have historically been individuals of eastern European descent, suggesting that there are still advantages to being White in the asylum-claiming process. Certainly, the asylum process for sexual and gender minorities has improved significantly since its inception in 1990, and some criticisms of the process that suggest that claimants must come prepared to offer the court a story of an immutable Western identity appear hyperbolic. But some narrative trajectories are certainly easier for US adjudicators to comprehend, and those without legal representation are less likely to be able to craft a story that fits the US legal context. We should remember this is not a problem with the asylum process specifically, but a broader issue with the US legal system's ability to comprehend complexity, as critical race scholars have noted for some time.[11]

These problems do present special issues for some queer subjects, though. As I've noted elsewhere, transgender claimants do not seem to be granted as much flexibility in their identity development narratives as sexual minorities.[12] Courts tend to privilege one particular way of being trans that includes one's recognition at a very early age that they were "in the wrong body" and desired to transition to the "opposite" sex. Similarly, issues continue to arise for queer women when adjudicators privilege the ability to be publicly "out" about one's sexuality or public experiences of persecution that women are less likely to have than men because of the interlocking nature of gender and sexual oppression. Women, including queer women, are more likely to experience forced marriage, female genital mutilation, honor killings, and the like at the hands of their families and communities rather than by state actors, meaning their persecution may be viewed as less severe or legitimate than men's by some legal actors.

The progress that was achieved by asylum seekers and their advocates came under direct and sustained attack by the Trump administration. We saw this in the Muslim ban and Trump's attempt to end asylum as we know it by executive fiat (a move likely to be struck down by courts), as well as by such decisions as *Matter of A-B-* (2018). That decision, issued by former Attorney General Jeff Sessions, stated that fleeing domestic violence or gang violence would no longer be grounds for asylum. Though none of these have been direct attacks on sexual orientation–based asylum, they are sure to affect LGBTQ people. Queer women, for instance, are likely to be negatively affected if domestic violence no longer counts as persecution.

Finally, even if asylum for LGBTQ people remains completely unaffected, it still creates a foil against which Trump and his nativist colleagues can compare those they demonize as "illegal" and "criminal." See, they will insist, we let in *these* people. The others are simply undeserving criminals and fraudsters. Even as the US government itself breaks the law by interning thousands of asylum seekers and denying others the ability to even lodge a claim, it will hold up some asylees as "proof" of the United States' sexual exceptionalism.

SEXUALITY AS TECHNOLOGY

Sorting Sexualities has argued that sexuality is central to state governance and that the state, in conjunction with non-state expert actors, is also central to the formation of sexuality as an identity and regulatory category. Yet I have focused predominantly on two issues that directly affect only a small fraction of people—asylum and SVP determinations. The focus on these two issues demonstrates with startling clarity how sexuality is a vector for the state's intimate probing of individual lives and bodies. Although I have chosen two relatively circumscribed issues for their analytic purchase, we should not be fooled into thinking that these are isolated or unimportant topics.

First, let's consider the cases at hand. Sexual orientation–based asylum directly affects several thousand individuals each year, but the broader asylum and refugee governance apparatus directly touches tens of thousands of lives every year. And not only do the knowledge practices examined in this book affect the entire system, but the immigration system itself has been centrally structured around sexuality and heteronormative notions of kinship since its inception in US law and policy. This means, for instance, that family reunification—still the single largest source of migration to the country—is limited for LGBTQ migrants. This was especially true before the legalization of same-sex marriage in the United States, but many LGBTQ migrants, especially asylum seekers, come from countries where such unions are still not possible, meaning that when they immigrate, they may not be able to petition to have their partner, or possibly even children, join them. Same-sex partners petitioning for asylum may have to lodge separate complaints, meaning that even if one receives asylum, the other may not. Thus, while LGBTQ asylum law may at first blush seem a narrow issue, it is embedded within a larger system of sexual regulation that encodes policies—even those not explicitly governing sexuality—with broad cultural resonance.

A parallel story can be found in SVP law. Though SVP laws likewise directly affect only a sliver of the population, they represent the much larger phenomenon of an escalating "war on sex" that has given rise to hundreds of new laws aimed at regulating sex and sexuality in its many forms.[13] This war has criminalized a wide range of "sexual" acts—such as public urination or sex between consenting minors—and contributed to ballooning public sex offender registry rolls, which now include nearly a million names. Research shows that public registries and other extra measures taken to control ex-offenders, such as residency restrictions, have negative consequences not just for the individuals directly implicated, but also for their families, whether it is stigmatization by association or the inability of one's father or partner to live in the family home.

Beyond these direct effects, the highly public and salient nature of criminal and civil sanctions against sex offenders and the public discourse surrounding them creates an often-misleading cultural climate regarding sex crimes. For instance, most public debate until recently has portrayed sex crimes as being perpetrated by dark, shadowy figures who jump out of bushes and forcefully abduct or assault women and children. Things like sex offender registries and public notification reinforce this notion by positing that if only we *knew* there were sex offenders in our midst, we could better protect ourselves and our children. These ideas give rise to a certain image of sex offenders in the cultural imaginary that is inaccurate and contributes to a misalignment between the actual social problem of sexual assault and our policy response to it. The #MeToo movement has begun to change these perceptions, but our policy has yet to evolve signifi-cantly. Like asylum, then, SVP law is part of a much broader apparatus of security aimed at regulating sex and sexuality that contributes to cultural ideas about sexuality that have resonance far beyond the confines of the courtroom where SVP trials are adjudicated.

We can see these knock-on effects in legislation such as FOSTA-SESTA (Fight Online Sex Trafficking Act, Stop Enabling Sex Traffickers Act), a recently passed federal statute purportedly aimed at combating sex traf-ficking that in reality has further endangered the very people it was meant to protect and shrunk or eliminated online spaces where marginalized sexual communities could meet. FOSTA-SESTA makes online platforms liable if they knowingly abet sex trafficking. But the statute is so vague as to how this will be enforced that many online spaces have simply shuttered their doors rather than risking civil and criminal penalties. This has meant the shuttering of outlets like Craigslist personals, Backpage, and other venues that sex workers were able to use to screen clients and maintain their own safety. It has also resulted in the end of a variety of online plat-forms where marginalized sexual communities were able to connect and communicate, including spaces for trans and queer people, furries, and the BDSM community. The popular blog site Tumblr, for instance, had long been a space where people could create and curate sexual content unavail-able in more mainstream outlets. Due to FOSTA-SESTA, however, Tumblr decided to change its rules to no longer allow anything it deemed porno-graphic content, effectively eliminating the large online communities that once flourished through the site.

In sum, I am suggesting that we think of sexuality as a more than an identity or ontological state. Rather, we should conceptualize sexuality as a technology—that is, as a tool that can be deployed to sort people, order lives, extract labor, partition space, create subject positions—in short, to wield power. Michel Foucault's classic statement on *scientia sexualis*, or sexual science, foreshadows such a conceptual move. Foucault argued that the modern West sought to unearth the "truth" of sexuality through its scientific study and deployed these "truths" for a number of political ends: controlling women's and children's bodies, disciplining sexual devi-ance, optimizing the population.[14] "Public hygiene" campaigns and state-sponsored racist eugenics policies serve as some of the clearest examples of these practices in action. In short, sexuality (often paired with race) has long been a political technology used in the service of social control, though sociologists have been slow to recognize its significance. Conceptualizing sexuality as a technology, however, compels us to shift from thinking of sexuality as merely a state of being to a consideration of *what can be done* with and through sexuality.

My suggestion here parallels critical STS scholars of race—such as Ruha Benjamin, Wendy Hui Kyong Chun, and Beth Coleman—who have similarly argued that race is a technology, and we must think about how race is used as such.[15] It's no coincidence that I draw on the thoughts of critical race scholars to theorize sexuality. As I have argued, race and sexuality have historically been, and continue to be, tightly intertwined. Though their histories and trajectories differ, our modern conceptions of both race and sexuality can be traced to the period of European colonization when sexualized racial stereotypes were used to justify colonization, domination, and often extermination of racialized others.[16] Moreover, the effectiveness of race as a technology stems, in part, from its multivocality. Whether biology- or culture-based notions of race, their malleability allows them to adapt to prevailing social, political, and economic circumstances. As Ann Laura Stoler explains:

> The ambiguity of those sets of relationships between the somatic and the inner self, the phenotype and the genotype, pigment shade and psychological sensibility are not slips in, or obstacles to, racial thinking but rather conditions for its proliferation and possibility. . . . The force of racisms is not found in the alleged fixity of visual knowledge, nor on essentialism itself, but on the *malleability* of the criteria of psychological dispositions and moral sensibilities that the visual could neither definitively secure nor explain.[17]

Stoler's argument parallels the one I have been making about sexuality throughout this book. Namely, whether sexuality is understood to be an essential element of one's biological makeup or a cultural attribute of a group, identifiable via some bodily indicator or only through cultural context, it draws its power as a technology from its malleability, its ability to adapt to current political and social needs. Sexuality as a political technology thrives even under—perhaps especially under—conditions of uncertainty. Its polyvalence means it can at once be used to constitute certain subjects as *at risk* and others as *a risk*, one a citizen, another a pariah.

These technological deployments of sexuality, then, can come in a range of forms, from the seemingly benign to the overtly punitive. The constant barrage of Andrew Christian advertisements I receive on Facebook, for instance, result from an algorithm that has identified my tastes and Internet search history as fitting those of a gay man. What seems superficially to be a rather innocuous attempt at targeted marketing may, as STS scholars remind us, actually end up reifying pernicious stereotypes, such as the idea that the LGBTQ community is wealthy and White.[18] That LGBTQ people are not predominantly wealthy or White—but, in fact, are more likely to be of color and lower socioeconomic status than non-LGBTQ people—means that LGBTQ people are also more likely to face forms of technological discrimination that disproportionately affect poor people and people of color, such as credit scoring.

It's likewise not difficult to imagine a not-so-distant scenario in which LGBTQ people could be identified through facial recognition or algorithms drawing on "big data" (e.g., your shopping and web browsing history) and charged higher insurance premiums because of research showing that sexual and gender minorities have poorer health outcomes than their straight, cis counterparts. It makes no difference that these health disparities are likely the result of stigma, societal discrimination, and worse access to health care. Such social ills are likely to be essentialized, as in notions of inherent Black criminality that continue to make the rounds in certain intellectual and policy circles.

At the individual level, facial recognition algorithms are likely to misgender or fail to recognize trans and gender-nonconforming people. It's easy to envision a future where airport security routinely selects trans people for extra screening or bars them from traveling at all because a facial recognition algorithm flags them as suspect—the high-tech version of allowing only a "male" or "female" marker on one's identity documents. Yet we know that even long-used biometric measures, such as fingerprints, can yield inaccurate results that are often compounded by race and gender.[19] Should we expect different results as we race to develop new biometric technologies, like facial recognition and iris scans, particularly when we consider that the algorithms powering these technologies continue to be trained using predominantly White bodies by White male engineers?

Facial recognition for sexual minorities could be even more dangerous in other contexts, especially when we consider the fact that the most highly developed facial recognition algorithms currently belong to a Russian tech firm, where the authoritarian government is persecuting LGBTQ people and turning a blind eye to the detention, torture, and murder of queers in Chechnya. In 2017 a Stanford professor ignited ethics debates when he published research claiming to be able to identify whether someone was gay or straight by using a facial recognition algorithm using "deep neural networks." Shortly after that, he was invited to present his research to none other than the highest ranks of the Russian government, including the Russian prime minister. In an interview with the *Guardian* where the researcher, Michal Kosinski, recounted how honored he was to be invited to Russia, he professed that he also believed that IQ and criminality could be deduced using facial recognition, a stark reminder of that ways that social differences can easily be essentialized through technology.[20] It's not so different, in fact, from the way twentieth-century eugenicists likewise claimed to be taking advantage of new data sources to merely describe social realities.[21]

And, of course, if facial recognition technologies gain widespread acceptance, it would be no surprise if they were deployed at ports of entry to immediately assess any asylum seekers who claimed to be queer or if they were used to identify "true" pedophiles for civil commitment. The simple truth is that a future in which these technologies are used is inevitable—indeed, it is already here. Customs and Border Patrol is experimenting with facial recognition technology at some ports of entry.[22] The Trump administration called for the development of an algorithm that could immediately assess any migrant's risk.[23] The FBI is at work on its Next Generation Identification initiative, a biometric database that could consist of voice data, iris scans, palm prints, and more, and would be populated not just with law enforcement data but data from commercial databases, social networking sites, security cameras, and more.[24] Whatever shape these new technologies take, they *will* be contoured by sexuality, as well as other axes of social difference like race and gender.

My hope is that this book will serve as a call to sociologists, legal scholars, and science and technology studies scholars alike to think more deeply about sexuality's place in the social world. For too long, to the extent that any of these fields have devoted much attention to sexuality at all, it has mostly meant studying gay men and perhaps lesbians, usually White. It is time we shift the analytical lens to think of sexuality more broadly—to the ways it structures our lives and our worlds and intersects with other axes of difference—and not just for those of us who happen to be queer. Sexuality as a technology of social organization, domination, and resistance is everywhere. Our job is to start recognizing it.

ACKNOWLEDGMENTS

Researching and writing this book has been a very long journey, and more people than I can probably remember have helped me along the way. Foremost among those was Steve Epstein, whose guidance and intellectual generosity helped shape this project and make it a success from beginning to end. Héctor Carrillo's expertise and continuous support from my first day of graduate school likewise helped me get this project off the ground all those years ago. I still remember the first time I met Laura Beth Nielsen when she shouted from the back of the room at my first departmental reception, "Everything has to do with the law. Come talk to me!" I did, and the rest is history. I am also grateful to Wendy Espeland, who was always willing to chat with me about nascent ideas or offer incisive feedback on my work. As a University of California Chancellor's Fellow, I was lucky enough to get to work with Val Jenness, whose mentorship and ability to deal with my near-constant anxiety about the job market should earn her a Nobel Prize of some sort. Thank you also to David John Frank, Alex Cho, Irene Vega, Chris Seeds, Lee Cabatingan, and Bryan Sykes, who supported me in so many ways during my time at UCI. This book would never have existed without the support of these folks or the support I received from the Department of Sociology, the Gender & Sexuality Studies Program, and the Legal Studies Program at Northwestern University. I will be forever grateful for the time to conduct research and write uninterrupted that I was afforded through dissertation fellowships from the Sexualities Project at Northwestern and the American Council of Learned Societies.

I would be remiss not to mention the people who made it possible for me—as a pretty naive first-generation student—to get through (or even into!) graduate school. Joey Sprague's feminist mentorship meant more to me than she will probably ever realize, and I can't imagine my scholarly journey without her. Joane Nagel was likewise pivotal to my success in graduate school and my budding as a young scholar. I have always been a bit of a perfectionist, and as Joane once pointed out with a wry smile, I was a somewhat "high maintenance" advisee. Yet she always read draft after draft of my papers, teaching me everything from how to organize a research paper and make a sound argument to the nitty-gritty of how to write interesting sentences. She was relentless in making me a better writer and scholar, and I love her dearly for it. Bob Antonio and Bill Staples were also instrumental to my success as I transitioned into sociology, and I am so grateful for their advice and open doors.

I am also appreciative of the many groups who allowed me to present my (sometimes questionable) work-in-progress and offered invaluable feedback. These include the Culture & Society Workshop, Gender & Sexuality Studies Colloquium, and Science in Human Culture Workshop at Northwestern University; the Departments of Sociology at the University of Kansas, Northwestern University, UC Irvine, and UC Davis; the Department of Criminology, Law & Society at UCI; and the Gender & Sexuality and Migration Working Groups at UCLA.

Thank you also to the many people who offered thoughts on various aspects of my work, listened to me vent, and generally kept me sane while I wrote this book. Wendy Griswold, Jess Meyer, Vincent Yung, Becca DiBennardo, Robin Bartram, Patrick Grzanka, Trevor Hoppe, Chrysanthi Leon—thank you all. Finally, thank you to those people nearest and dearest to me who made this journey possible. My parents, who supported me even when I left a lucrative career to study something they'd never even heard of. My platonic soulmate, Lindsay, whose unwavering friendship for twenty-plus years means the world to me. My partner, Kellen, who read drafts, listened to me ruminate for hours about ideas and worries, and was always there when I needed him—I cannot express enough gratitude. And of course, my fur babies, Appa and Pabu, whose love cuddles were a key component of writing this book.

APPENDIX 1: STATIC-99R CODING FORM

Question Number	Risk Factor	Codes		Score
1	Age at release from index sex offence	Aged 18 to 34.9		1
		Aged 35 to 39.9		0
		Aged 40 to 59.9		−1
		Aged 60 or older		−3
2	Ever lived with a lover	Ever lived with lover for at least		0
		two years?		1
			Yes	
			No	
3	Index non-sexual violence: Any convictions	No		0
		Yes		1
4	Prior non-sexual violence: Any convictions	No		0
		Yes		1
5	Prior sex offences	Charges	Convictions	0
		0	0	1
		1, 2	1	2
		3–5	2, 3	3
		6+	4+	
6	Four or more prior sentencing dates (excluding index)	3 or less		0
		4 or more		1
7	Any convictions for non-contact sex offences	No		0
		Yes		1
8	Any unrelated victims	No		0
		Yes		1
9	Any stranger victims	No		0
		Yes		1
10	Any male victims	No		0
		Yes		1
	Total Score			

Translating Static-99R Scores into Risk Categories

Score	Label for Risk Category
−3 through 1	Low
2, 3	Low-Moderate
4, 5	Moderate-High
6+	High

APPENDIX 2: METHODOLOGY

I drew on a range of sources to generate my analysis: legal decisions, NGO and government documents, news coverage, interviews with various actors involved in both LGBTQ asylum and sex offender law and/or advocacy, and ethnographic observations in multiple settings, including immigration court, criminal court, NGO offices, governmental meetings, and professional conferences. These various data necessarily speak to different parts of the story I tell in this study, and sometimes one source tells a different story than another. This is precisely why I drew on multiple kinds of data. Official recorded accounts, such as those found in legal decisions, often tell only a small part of the story and conceal important aspects. In these instances, interviews and ethnographic observation can (and did) help fill in the gaps. For example, judicial decisions regarding sex offenders generally make no mention of how the penile plethysmograph affects legal decision-making. Yet in observing SVP trials and talking with evaluators, I learned that phallometric testing sometimes underwrites expert testimony in these hearings even though the technology itself is not generally admissible in court. By triangulating these multiple sources—documentary, interview, and observational—I was able to check one against the others, and use findings from one source to guide data collection and/or coding of others. In this way, both my data collection and coding were iterative processes. Coding of documents sometimes suggested new questions to ask interviewees, while my ethnography sometimes indicated things I should be attentive to when analyzing documents, and so on.

DOCUMENT ANALYSIS

I drew on a range of documentary sources, primarily consisting of legal decisions, but also including NGO and government documents, legal statutes, news coverage of asylum and sex crimes, and academic texts. Because asylum decisions are not publicly available unless they are appealed,

I was limited in the cases I could select. Decisions at the immigration court level are audio-recorded, but no transcript is generated unless the case is appealed to the BIA. At this point, the case still does not become public unless the BIA chooses to publish its decision, which it does with only a handful of precedential rulings each year. In the case of LGBTQ asylum, only one precedential decision has been published by the BIA—*Toboso-Alfonso* (1990), the first decision to grant a gay man withholding of removal. Asylum seekers can also appeal to a US Circuit Court of Appeals if they are denied relief by the BIA. At this point, the circuit court's judgment becomes public, and these are the primary decisions I used for this study. To collect these rulings, I used LexisNexis, an academic database that catalogs legal decisions. I searched the database in several different ways to ensure that I was locating all relevant cases. I began by conducting searches using the following keywords: gay, homosexual, homosexuality, sexuality, sexual orientation, sexual preference, and lesbian. For each search, I used the "search within results" function to search for the keyword "asylum." Additionally, I conducted searches using each keyword in conjunction with "asylum" (e.g., gay AND asylum). Ultimately, this process produced 184 LGBTQ asylum decisions, which I believe to be the entire universe of cases as of the time of my search.

I took a similar approach to locating legal decisions regarding sex offenders. But because there are many more sex crimes cases (including lower court decisions, unlike asylum) and I was interested in particular aspects of the law (e.g., civil commitment, risk assessment, use of technology and expertise), I modified my search techniques. I used the "core terms" search feature in Lexis to find cases containing "civil commitment" and "sexual," which returned 1,754 cases.[1] I selected all four US Supreme Court cases for analysis. I then narrowed the search to only cases from 1990 to 2015—the same time frame for which I had asylum decisions—and selected all 66 rulings from US Circuit Courts of Appeal. I next filtered for only US District Court cases ($n = 239$), sorted the results chronologically, and then selected the first case and every tenth subsequent case for a final sample of 24 decisions. I subsequently repeated this search, limiting it to only include judgments from Illinois ($n = 31$), which I used as a case study.

To analyze the use of technologies in legal decision-making about sex offenders, I also conducted searches specifically focused on polygraphs and penile plethysmographs. I tried many methods of finding cases dealing with polygraph issues with sex offenders, but most procedures returned many hundreds of cases that were irrelevant. I ultimately used a search that looked for "polygraph" in the case overview and "sexual" as a core term, and limited results to US Circuit Courts of Appeals decisions, resulting in 60 cases for analysis. Far fewer cases concerned phallometric testing (whose use as a keyword returned no results). Searching for "plethysmograph" in the case overview returned 73 cases for analysis, comprising both US Circuit Courts of Appeal and state-level appellate courts. My final sample of cases dealing with various facets of sex offender law included 258 court decisions, ranging in scale from US District Courts and state-level appellate courts to the US Supreme Court.

I chose to focus on appellate decisions for two primary reasons. First, they are readily available and allowed me to generate a large sample of cases from a range of jurisdictions. This allowed me to analyze legal decision-making both at the federal level and across the patchwork of state sex crimes statutes. Second, and more importantly, appellate courts set standards for lower courts. Because I was interested in general rules and processes through which state legal institutions render sexuality legible for governance, appellate courts were the ideal settings to examine, for they set those standards and review the procedures that lower courts use. Nevertheless, to account for the fact that most of the "action" of law does not occur in appellate cases, I supplemented my legal analysis with in-depth qualitative interviews and extensive ethnographic fieldwork.

INTERVIEWS

I conducted 41 interviews with lawyers, activists, judges, administrators, researchers, and expert witnesses for both asylum and SVP hearings. Detailed information on interviewees is included in table 9. I selected interviewees based on their centrality to the field, expertise on particular topics, or experience in either asylum or SVP law, or some combination of these factors. I identified most interviewees through my fieldwork or background research, but some were suggested by other interviewees. I tailored interviews depending on the interviewee's professional position (e.g., I asked different questions to expert witnesses than to judges), and I sometimes made adjustments to questions for subsequent interviews based on my experiences with informants, what Mario Small calls "sequential interviewing." Interviews generally lasted about one hour and were audiorecorded and later transcribed for coding. I conducted interviews either in person (preferably) or over the phone.

ETHNOGRAPHIC OBSERVATIONS

The final component of my methodological tool kit involved multi-sited ethnographic observations. From July 2013 to July 2015, I worked with Midwest Immigrant Rights Advocates (MIRA), a nonprofit organization that advocates for and provides legal representation to LGBTQ asylum seekers

TABLE 9. Interviewee information

Name	Position, Organizational Affiliation	Interview Date
Donya Adkerson	Psychologist, private practice	2/22/2016
Cori Alonso-Yoder	Immigrant Justice Clinic	7/17/2018
Evan Asher	Psychologist and SVP evaluator	4/13/2016
Nielan Barnes	Sociologist, California State University, Long Beach	6/11/2016
Aaron Barton	Psychologist and SVP evaluator	6/22/2016
Isabel Davis	Psychologist and SVP evaluator	4/11/2016
Julie Dorf	Human rights expert, founder of International Gay and Lesbian Human Rights Commission (IGLHRC)	8/2/2016
Nathan Edwards	US government researcher	8/2/2016
Karen Franklin	Psychologist, private practice	8/30/2016
Aneesha Gandhi	Immigration lawyer, National Immigrant Justice Center	1/24/2014
Susanne Goldberg	Professor of Law, Columbia University	10/31/2016
Guy Groot	Psychologist, Illinois Sex Offender Management Board	5/19/2016
Neil Grungras	Immigration lawyer, Organization for Refuge, Asylum and Migration (ORAM)	1/13/2016
Karl Hanson	Psychologist, Canadian government	9/8/2016
Michael Jarecki	Immigration lawyer, private practice	2/7/2014
Shan Jumper	Clinical Director of Illinois SVP Program	2/29/2016
Arjun Kapoor	Psychiatrist, private practice	12/12/2015
Richard Krueger	Psychiatrist, Columbia University	9/8/2016
Ingrid Lawson	Retired Immigration Judge, US Department of Justice	11/20/2014
William Marshall	Psychologist, private practice	8/22/2016
Heather McClure	Anthropologist, formerly with Midwest Human Rights Partnership for Sexual Orientation	6/2/2016
Margaret Menzenberger	Assistant Attorney General, State of Illinois SVP Division	6/16/2016
Michael Miner	Psychologist, University of Minnesota	9/8/2016
Shannon Minter	Legal Director for the National Center for Lesbian Rights	8/16/2016
Aaron Morris	Immigration lawyer, Immigration Equality	8/14/2013
Stephen Murray	Independent scholar, expert witness in asylum hearings	6/14/2016

(continued)

TABLE 9. *(continued)*

Name	Position, Organizational Affiliation	Interview Date
Victoria Neilson	Immigration lawyer and former Legal Director of Immigration Equality	8/14/2013
Peter Perkowski	Immigration lawyer, private practice	2/11/2014
Suyapa Portillo	Assistant Professor of Latino Studies, Pitzer College	8/18/2016
Ashley Reed	Paralegal, National Immigrant Justice Center	1/24/2014
Lory Rosenberg	former BIA judge	5/18/2017
Paul Schmidt	former immigration judge and BIA member, retired	5/25/2017
Michael Seto	Psychologist, University of Toronto	11/7/2017
Lavi Soloway	Immigration lawyer, co-founder of Immigration Equality	6/3/2016
Amanda Sullivan	Paralegal, National Immigrant Justice Center	1/24/2014
Daniel Tenreiro	Immigration lawyer, private practice	9/16/2013
Richard Travis	Psychologist and SVP evaluator	3/8/2016
Kim Weitl	Psychologist and SVP evaluator	5/31/2016
Alyssa Williams-Schafer	Coordinator for Sex Offender Services, Illinois Department of Corrections	11/23/2015
Robin Wilson	Psychologist, private practice, formerly employed by Florida SVP program	4/7/2017
Keren Zwick	Immigration lawyer, National Immigrant Justice Center	1/24/2014

and has a national presence on queer immigration issues. I aided with various aspects of case preparation—mostly country conditions research and small administrative tasks—in exchange for being able to observe their weekly case update meetings, in which the staff would meet to discuss ongoing cases, new intakes, and other issues facing the organization. Through MIRA, I was also able to observe twelve asylum hearings in the Chicago immigration court. After my formal fieldwork period ended in 2015, I continued to check in with MIRA and occasionally returned to their offices for updates on cases that were ongoing from my time there.

My fieldwork for the sex offender legal complex took place from September 2015 to November 2017 and occurred in a range of settings. I observed the bimonthly meetings of the Illinois Sex Offender Management Board (SOMB), which is tasked with implementing aspects of state sex offender policy, including setting standards for the treatment and evaluation of sex offenders in state custody and making recommendations to the state legislature on policy needs. I also attended the 2015 annual meeting for the Association for the Treatment of Sexual Abusers (ATSA), the 2016 biannual meeting of the International Association for the Treatment of Sex Offenders (IATSO), the 2016 biannual meeting of the Illinois chapter of ATSA, and a risk assessment and evaluation training held by the SOMB in 2017. In addition to many informal conversations at these events, I also attended scholarly presentations, social events, and conducted some interviews at these conferences. Finally, I observed two "sexually violent persons" (SVP) trials in Chicago.

In all of these settings, I routinely maintained field notes concurrently and typed more extensive notes as soon as possible after being in the field. Unlike some field settings where carrying a notebook around and constantly scribbling notes in it would make the researcher obvious and perhaps intrusive, in these contexts, most participants were doing the same thing, and my note-taking therefore did not seem out of place at all. Moreover, participants in my two long-term field sites—MIRA and the SOMB—knew that I was a researcher and agreed to my presence.

CODING

I coded documents, interview transcripts, and field notes through an iterative holistic coding method, using both inductive and deductive approaches. Initial coding themes were generated deductively and focused on subjects drawn from my theoretical framework, such as sexual narratives, evidence of sexuality, diagnosis, risk assessment, expert statements, and uses of technology. With these overarching themes in mind, I inductively generated many subcodes for each category.[2] For example, within the broad theme of "evidence of sexuality" in the asylum context, subcodes included stereotypes, gender nonconformity, corroborating letters, sexual experiences, and romantic relationships. Similarly, in the sex offender context, the "uses of technology" theme contained many subcodes, including "use of polygraph" and "use of PPG," which each had many subsubcodes regarding admissibility, reliability, and specific uses (e.g., was it used for treatment, evaluation, or risk assessment?). Codes sometimes also overlapped. Sexual narratives, for instance, were coded as "evidence of sexuality," but they were also coded as "sexual narratives" for a separate analysis of the structure of the narrative (e.g., did it follow a typical "coming out" narrative?).

Other themes emerged inductively on subsequent readings of my materials. This was particularly true for various legal standards that I was not initially thinking about, such as legal requirements to meet the threshold of persecution in asylum. Indeed, while I was initially concerned with risk assessment practices for sex offenders, this was not a topic that I originally coded for in the asylum context. Rather, as I repeatedly read asylum judgments, I came to realize that determining whether a petitioner would face persecution if returned to his or her home country *was* a form of risk assessment. This also led to me developing codes around country conditions information, their sources, their credibility, and their legal admissibility in asylum hearings. This process ultimately resulted in approximately 150 distinct codes.

NOTES

INTRODUCTION

1. Political sociologists often refer to "the state" in their studies of state institutions, and I do so provisionally and for analytic ease throughout this introduction. However, I do not mean to imply that I view the state as a monolithic or unified entity. Rather, I view the state as a constellation of institutions, actors, and discourses that may have conflicting goals at times and certainly vary in their practices. I similarly refer to "law" and "science" this way at times, though I also consider these to be multifaceted institutions comprising many organizations and actors.

2. See Lee (1993), Loveman (2014), Marx (1998), Thompson (2016).

3. Puri (2016, 150).

4. This is a pseudonym, as are all names of asylum seekers, sex offenders, and other actors identified in my fieldwork. I use the actual names of most interviewees because they granted permission to be identified.

5. Notably, the primary Chicago immigration courtrooms look quite similar to this, though on a smaller scale.

6. Because of the looser rules governing the admittance of hearsay evidence in SVP trials, however, evaluators are allowed to discuss penile plethysmograph results in these settings.

7. Freedman (1987); Terry (1999).

8. Here I am conceptualizing of cultural schemas as "generalizable procedures applied in the enactment/reproduction of social life" (Sewell 1992, 7), or, more concretely, as "ordered, socially constructed, and taken-for-granted framework[s] for understanding and evaluating self and society, for thinking and for acting" (Blair-Loy 2001, 689).

9. Friedland and Alford (1991, 248–49).

10. Knorr Cetina (1999, 1).

11. Much of the preceding discussion of epistemic logics would seem to apply to the concept of civic epistemologies, which Sheila Jasanoff defines as "the institutionalized practices by which members of a given society test and deploy knowledge claims used as a basis for making collective choices" (Jasanoff 2005, 255). These collective "knowledge-ways" define what counts as expertise and objectivity, among other things, in specific contexts. However, Jasanoff conceptualizes civic epistemologies as characterizing whole societies (also see Miller 2008). With the idea of epistemic logics, I suggest that civic epistemologies are not unified but rather that ways of knowing vary across institutions within the same country.

12. I am using the concept of cultural frames slightly differently than I used cultural schemas previously. Whereas schemas are generalized frameworks that structure cognition and action, frames are more specific ways of seeing particular objects, events, or, as in the case of sex offenders, groups of people. Thus, the key distinction between schemas and frames as I use them here is scale and generalizability.

13. Beauchamp (2018) and Puar (2007) both show the ways that immigrants, especially non-White immigrants, are often portrayed as potential terrorists.

14. Cole (2000); Lynch (2002); Simon (1998); Simon (2007); Wacquant (2009).

15. Porter (1995) suggests that disciplines exposed to greater public oversight are often pressured into adopting more quantitative approaches to give the impression of objectivity.

16. Valverde (2003, 10).

17. Valverde (2003, 10).

18. On this idea, see Abrams (1988); Mitchell (1999).

19. See Steinmetz (1999).

20. Foucault (2007, 286).

21. On state institutions as anchor points for knowledge creation, see Fourcade (2009). On middle-range analysis of knowledge production, see Epstein (2007).

22. Clemens and Cook (1999); Vaughan (1999).

23. Vaughan (1999, 931).

24. Kunzel (2008, 9).

25. Rubin (1984).

26. The principle of symmetry insists that the same explanations should account for both true and false beliefs (Bloor [1976] 1991).

27. Miller, Keith, and Holmes (2015); Ramji-Nogales, Schoenholtz, and Schrag (2009).

CHAPTER ONE

1. Nathan and Snedeker (1995).

2. Though I concentrate on European and American sexual science, the contributors to Fuechtner, Haynes, and Jones's (2018) volume demonstrate that sexual science was a global phenomenon.

3. D'Emilio (1983); D'Emilio and Freedman (1988).

4. Krafft-Ebing (1965).

5. Krafft-Ebing (1965, 28).

6. Krafft-Ebing (1965, 34).

7. Krafft-Ebing (1965, 369).

8. Rosario (2002); Terry (1999).

9. Kunzel (2008); Rosario (2002).

10. Jenkins (1998).

11. Jenkins (1998).

12. Jenkins (1998, 21).

13. Leon (2011); Terry (2013).

14. Kunzel (2008, 47).

15. Chauncey (1994).

16. Terry (1999).

17. Jenkins (1998); Terry (1999).

18. Freedman (1987); Terry (1999).

19. Terry (1999).

20. Terry (1999, 275).

21. Leon (2011).

22. Leon (2011).

23. Cole (2000); Jenkins (1998).

24. Jenkins (1998).

25. We might also consider this to be an illustration of what philosopher Ian Hacking (1995) has called "looping effects." That is, labeling humans often engenders responses from those subjects, who may react against, embrace, or change the meaning of the categories into which they have been placed. Classification may therefore become a dialectical relationship between "top-down" and "bottom-up" forces that results in shifting meanings of categories over time.

26. Terry (1999).

27. Terry (1999).

28. Terry (1999).

29. Hooker (1957).

30. Jenkins (1998).

31. Waidzunas (2015).

32. Drescher (2015).

33. In an effort to de-pathologize non-normative yet consensual sex practices, such as BDSM (similar to the move to "sexual orientation disturbance"), the *DSM-5* now only considers paraphilias to be disorders if they cause one distress or involve nonconsenting persons.

34. De Orio (2017).

35. Jenkins (1998, 125).

36. Nathan and Snedeker (1995).

37. The release of convicted child molester Earl Shriner from prison in 1987 resulted in the passage of first contemporary SVP law in Washington State.

38. Foucault (1990).

39. This idea is central to sociologist Tom Waidzunas's work on sexual "reorientation" therapy. Through an examination of credibility struggles between the LGBT and "ex-gay" movements, Waidzunas shows that the APA has declared studies using phallometric testing to be the most objective and scientific while discrediting as unscientific those using self-report. This is, of course, very different than the asylum context that I will analyze throughout this book, where phallometric evidence is rejected in favor of self-report, highlighting the importance of institutional context for making knowledge claims.

40. Somerville (2000).

41. Rosario (2002); Terry (1999).

42. Rosario (2002).

43. Terry (1999).

44. Rosario (2002).

45. Hegarty (2003); Rosario (2002).

46. Hooker (1957).

47. Alder (2007).

48. Waidzunas (2015, 64).

49. Waidzunas and Epstein (2015).

50. Seto and Kuban (1996); Seto and Lalumière (2001).

51. See Alanko et al. (2016).

52. Poeppl et al. (2013); Schiltz et al. (2007).

53. On differences in brain structure, see Savic and Lindstrom (2008). For a critique of such brain science, see Jordan-Young (2011).

54. Cantor et al. (2004).

55. Lalumière, Blanchard, and Zucker (2000).

56. Seto (2012).

57. Annemarie Mol suggests that objects are enacted through practices on an ongoing basis. As she writes, "Objects come into being—and disappear—with the practices in which they are manipulated. And since the object of manipulations tends to differ from one practice to another, reality multiplies" (2002, 5). In her examination of atherosclerosis, Mol argues that the disease is *enacted* differently in the outpatient clinic (where it manifests as pain in a patient's legs) than in the pathology lab (where it is occluded arteries under a microscope), and yet these multiple objects hangs together as atherosclerosis. The conception that will matter at any given moment depends on the socio-material setting in which it is enacted.

CHAPTER TWO

1. Stryker coins and develops the idea of technocratization in a series of articles (Stryker 1989, 1994, 2000).

2. Camic, Gross, and Lamont (2011, 3).

3. On the politics of classification, see Bowker and Star (1999); Espeland and Stevens (1998); Timmermans and Epstein (2010). On the centrality of classification to state-making, see Appadurai (1996); Carroll (2006); Desrosières (1998); Emigh, Riley, and Ahmed (2016); Loveman (2005); Thompson (2016).

4. Scott (1998, 2). Scott's wide-ranging survey of state-initiated social engineering asserts that a central problem of statecraft is legibility and that the state uses scientific methods to create simplified maps of intelligibility to administratively order nature and society and render them amenable to measurement and intervention.

5. An extensive literature considers the political nature and uses of censuses. See Anderson and Fienberg (1999), Desrosières (1998), Emigh (2002), Kertzer and Arel (2002), Lee (1993), Loveman (2014), Nobles (2000), Skerry (2000).

6. Loveman (2014); Marx (1998); Nobles (2000); Thompson (2016).

7. Bourdieu (1994, 13).

8. Anderson ([1983] 1991); Lee (1993); Loveman (2014); Nobles (2000); Thompson (2016).

9. Loveman (2014) has pointed to the importance of specialized actors and institutions *within* the state, and others have gestured to the importance of non-state expertise without developing it further (e.g., Lara-Millan 2017). Emigh, Riley, and Ahmed (2016) have given the most attention to non-state experts—or "census intellectuals" in their terms—in state information-gathering efforts, arguing that they are vital for transforming commonsense categories into official state classifications. But their study looks at only one grand state-building project, censuses, without examining the role that experts play in the day-to-day classification projects of state bureaucracies, which arguably constitute the bulk of the state's classification work. And the historical nature of their study does not allow us to examine how non-state experts function in contemporary states. Finally, the non-state expert actors they identify—clergy, magistrates,

and learned gentleman—are considerably different than the credentialed and, in many ways formally institutionalized, social science actors discussed in this study.

10. Carroll (2006); Eyal (2006); Ezrahi (1990); Mukerji (1989, 2009).

11. Carroll (2006)

12. Brint (1994); Fischer (2009); Hilgartner (2000); Jasanoff (1990).

13. Golan (2004); Jasanoff (1995).

14. Cole (2001); Jasanoff (1990); Lynch et al. (2008).

15. Loveman (2005, 1653, 1652).

16. Latour and Woolgar (1979); Shapin (1994, 1995).

17. Sarat, Douglas, and Umphrey (2007, 1–2). Mariana Valverde and colleagues have similarly shown in a number of studies that legal knowledges are hybrid—drawing on political rationales here, ethical ones there, science as needed, and a heavy dose of legal knowledge—and, moreover, that many local epistemologies exist in various legal complexes (Levi and Valverde 2001; Moore and Valverde 2000; Valverde 2003).

18. Jasanoff (2008, 762) similarly suggests: "So thoroughly are these institutions [science and law] enmeshed that close investigation of various dimensions of legal practice (e.g., evidentiary hearings, advisory committee meetings, patent litigation), and the actors who engage in them, is as likely to shed light on the production of scientific knowledge as studies of laboratory science-in-the-making or of scientific controversy."

19. Sarat, Douglas, and Umphrey (2007, 19).

20. Bourdieu (1987) has suggested that the law is the state's official means of knowing.

21. Latour (2010).

22. Some scholarship, for instance, posits an incommensurable "culture clash" between law and science stemming from law's focus on "process" and science's ethic of "progress" (Goldberg 1994). Other scholars evince a strong concern that the adversarial legal process allows "junk science" to influence decision-making and that judges and juries do not have the knowledge to determine what should rightfully count as expert evidence (Faigman, Porter, and Saks 1994; Huber 1991). It may be true that "junk science" makes its way into courtrooms. But I am less concerned with adjudicating truth or "real" science than I am with examining precisely how certain ways of knowing come to be seen as valid in legal proceedings and how those epistemic practices affect social reality. Tenuous scientific claims may become "more true" as they circulate through society (Gieryn 1999).

23. Silbey (2008).

24. Research has shed light on the ways that science and law coproduce notions of expertise (Golan 2004; Lynch 2004), causation (Bal 2005; Jasanoff 2002), forensic evidence (Cole 2001; Lynch et al. 2008; Lynch and Jasanoff 1998), and the very boundaries of law and science (Jasanoff 2008; Silbey and Ewick 2003).

25. Though Jasanoff (2004) has provided the most comprehensive synthesis of the idea of coproduction, many studies illustrate the concept. Notable examples include Bowker and Star (1999), Carroll (2006), Mukerji (1989), Scott (1998), and Shapin and Schaffer (1985).

26. Jasanoff (2004, 3).

27. Foucault develops his idea of the inextricability of power and knowledge throughout his work, but see especially Foucault (1977, 1980, 1990).

28. Jasanoff (1995); Solomon and Hackett (1996).

29. Jasanoff (1995, 10).

30. Valverde (2003).

31. Moore and Valverde (2000).

32. Cole (2001).

33. Jasanoff (1995, 44).

34. *Frye v. United States*, 293 F. 1013 (D.C. Cir 1923).

35. *Daubert v. Merrell Dow Pharmaceuticals*, 509 U.S. 579 (1993).

36. Solomon and Hackett (1996).

37. Stryker (1989, 1994).

38. Some scholars have found support for the notion that social science impacts legal decisions (Acker 1990; Fiske and Borgida 2008), but others argue that social science findings have little or no effect (Lempert 2013; Nelson, Berrey, and Nielsen 2008). Hull (2017) offers a review of social science as it has applied to same-sex marriage decisions and concludes that the effect of social science in these legal decisions remains unclear. Also see Mertz (2008) for an excellent overview of socio-legal work on social science in the law.

39. Adams and Light (2015); Ball (2014); Falk (1994); George (2016); Levit (2010); Powell, Quadlin, and Pizmony-Levy (2015); Yoshino (2015).

40. Diamond and Rosky (2016); Goldberg (2002).

41. Haney López (2006); Pascoe (2009); Sohoni (2007).

42. Zylan (2011).

43. Puri (2016) borrows and develops the notion of "state effect" from Timothy Mitchell to suggest that sexuality provides one mechanism by which the notion of a unified, singular "state" that stands apart from civil society is maintained.

44. Bernstein (2010). Also see Chapkis (2003, 2005).

45. Foucault (1997); Puar (2007); Stoler (1995).

46. Puar (2007, xi).

47. See Canaday (2009); Luibhéid (2002); Somerville (2005). Critics note that citizenship continues to be largely heteronormative, that legal gains for gays and lesbians, such as marriage and military service, simply reinforce heteronormative values, and that such protections largely accrue to the most privileged gays and lesbians (Brandzel 2005; Cossman 2007; Puar 2007).

48. Cantú (2009); Epps, Valens, and González (2005).

49. Canaday (2003, 2009).

50. Wacquant (2009, 209).

51. Hoppe (2016); Jumper, Babula, and Casbon (2012).

52. On the criminalization of Blackness, see Alexander (2010). On Black sexuality, see Nagel (2003).

53. Douard and Schultz (2013); Lynch (2002).

54. Small (2015).

55. Citizenship is more than a legal status conferred by the state. It is also about belonging to a community, and it is significant at multiple levels, from the national to the local (Epstein and Carrillo 2014; Glenn 2010; Joppke 2007). As Evelyn Nakano Glenn (2010, 2) suggests, "Citizenship is constructed through face-to-face interactions and through place-specific practices that occur within larger structural contexts." However, this dissertation largely focuses on citizenship as a legal status conferred by the state and as a symbolic boundary demarcating inclusion in the nation.

56. Hoppe (2014); Norton (2013).

57. *State of Iowa v. Valin* 724 N.W.2d 440, 442 (Iowa Sup. Ct. 2006).

58. Baker and Simon (2002).

59. Feeley and Simon (1992).

60. Harcourt (2007).

61. Daston and Galison (2007).

62. The 1980 Refugee Act also formalized a system through which individuals arriving in the United States could seek asylum. It did this, in part, by adopting the 1967 Protocol Relating to the Status of Refugees, which states that countries cannot deport those with a reasonable fear of returning to their home countries without fully evaluating their asylum claims.

63. It is important to note that appeals can generally only be made based on errors of law, not errors of fact.

64. Several of my interviewees felt that queer claims were not treated significantly differently than other claims. Some scholars, however, contend that the "credibility" requirement is particularly difficult for LGBTQ asylum seekers (Lewis 2014; Millbank 2009).

65. Information on the total number of successful asylum claims comes from the US Office of Immigration Statistics (Mossaad 2016). The percentage of claims under the PSG category was provided to me by Talia Shiff, who obtained the data through a Freedom of Information Act request.

66. Ramji-Nogales, Schoenholtz, and Schrag (2009).

67. Leon (2011).

68. Halperin and Hoppe (2017). On the idea of sex panics as particular kinds of moral panics, see Herdt (2009) and Lancaster (2011).

69. Perhaps the most notable change required by the Adam Walsh Act (AWA) is the suggested tiering system of offenders based on offense type rather than calculated risk. That is, whereas some states use risk assessment methods to assign offenders to a "risk tier" for registration and notification purposes, the AWA mandates that states use a three-tier system based on offense or lose some of their federal funding for law enforcement. As of 2015, seventeen states are in compliance with the AWA, though according to the National Conference of State Legislatures, several states have elected to remain noncompliant because compliance would cost more than the loss of federal funds. Of the noncompliant states, some still use offense-based classification, but others employ risk-based classification of offenders.

70. Leon (2011, 29).

71. Chauncey (1993); Cole (2000); Sutherland (1950).

72. McGrath et al. (2010). This pattern is notably reversed in Canada, where 88% and 10% of programs report using the PPG and polygraph, respectively. These figures do not count nonresidential treatment programs, many of which also require polygraph or PPG testing.

73. Jenkins (1998); Lancaster (2011).

74. Steptoe and Goldet (2016). This number does not include sex offenders committed under other similar programs, such as Illinois's Sexually Dangerous Persons law, which allows for the civil commitment of sex offenders prior to a criminal conviction.

75. *Kansas v. Hendricks* 521 U.S. 346 (1997); *Kansas v. Crane* 534 U.S. 407 (2002); *United States v. Comstock* 560 U.S. 126 (2010).

76. Some states only allow for bench trials and use lower standards of proof similar to other civil proceedings.

77. *Kansas v. Hendricks* 521 U.S. 346 (1997); *Kansas v. Crane* 534 U.S. 407 (2002).

CHAPTER THREE

1. Jasanoff (2004, 40–41).

2. Collins and Evans (2007).

3. Eyal (2013, 871). Also see Eyal and Buchholz (2010).

4. Eyal (2013, 864).

5. Cambrosio, Limoges, and Hoffman (1992, 345).

6. Cambrosio, Limoges, and Hoffman (1992, 344). Cambrosio and colleagues are, in fact, citing in translation Rip and Groenewegen (1989, 156). This is also reminiscent of Gieryn's (1999) argument that science achieves credibility not in the laboratory but only through how it is taken up "downstream" and, further, that the epistemic authority of science only exists in local and episodic enactments where "sellers" proffer truth and "buyers" choose whether to use or believe it.

7. Though I am using an actor-network-theory-inspired conception of expertise, the idea of preexisting structures is not consistent with the ontological commitments of ANT, and this usage is intentional. Actors do not form networks in a powerless vacuum devoid of already existing structural limitations. Rather, as I suggest, they encounter certain structural barriers that they must navigate, and in some cases displace, in order to successfully create actor-networks that can function to accomplish the desired tasks within some structural limits that cannot be easily altered. As I have argued, however, these networks *can* significantly affect the institutions and structures with which they come into contact, and, indeed, as my data show, this is precisely what forensic psychology and the hybrid expertise of asylum have done. My argument regarding the interaction of institutional structures and networks, then, is more consistent with what Frickel and Moore (2006, 5) call the "new political sociology of science," with its commitment to demonstrating "the ways in which institutions and networks shape the power to produce knowledge."

8. Cole (2000); Freedman (1987); Prentky, Barbaree, and Janus (2015).

9. Burick (1968); Zilney and Zilney (2009).

10. Cole (2000); Kunzel (2017).

11. Grubin and Prentky (1993, 383).

12. Leon (2011).

13. See Group for the Advancement of Psychiatry (1977).

14. Janus (2006); Prentky, Barbaree, and Janus (2015).

15. ATSA was founded as the Association for the Behavioral Treatment of Sexual Abusers, reflecting the dominance of behaviorism at the time.

16. I say "implicitly" because ATSA stated that it did not take a position on the "validity" of the SVP Act but then went on to deconstruct the foundation of the Kansas Supreme Court's decision striking down the act, effectively producing a brief in support of SVP laws. Moreover, the brief is labeled "in support of Petitioner," which in this case was the state of Kansas seeking to overturn the decision of the Kansas Supreme Court. See Brief for the Association for the Treatment of Sexual Abusers Amicus Curiae in Support of Petitioner, 1995 U.S. Briefs 1649.

17. 725 ILCS 207/5 (b).

18. For an elaboration of the containment model, see English (1998).

19. See California Penal Code §§ 290.09, 1203.067, 3008, and 9003.

20. Available at http://www.casomb.org/index.cfm?pid=1231 (accessed July 27, 2020).

21. *Boutilier v. INS*, 387 U.S. 118 (1967). See Canaday (2003) for a detailed analysis of this case.

22. Courts have also deferred to mental health professionals to determine whether a *DSM* diagnosis is necessary in SVP proceedings. The Seventh Circuit, for example, has ruled that "whether a legitimate mental health diagnosis must be based on the DSM is a question for the members of the mental health profession, and, therefore, one to which we do not address ourselves." *McGee v. Bartow*, 593 F.3d 556, 576 (7th Cir. 2010).

23. Many of my interviewees complained about this view of the *DSM*, arguing that the *DSM* is not a "cookbook" but a set of guidelines with significant room for professional judgment. Many expressed frustration with lawyers who cross-examine them based on a "cookbook" view of the diagnostic process and with courts that allow such interpretations.

24. *Kansas v. Hendricks* 521 U.S. 346, 355 (1997).

25. *Kansas v. Hendricks* 521 U.S. 346m 358 (1997).

26. *Allen v. Illinois*, 478 U.S. 364 (1986); *Pearson v. Probate Court of Ramsey Cty.* 309 U.S. 270 (1940).

27. Brief for the Menninger Foundation et al., 1995 U.S. Briefs 1649.

28. Brief for the Association for the Treatment of Sexual Abusers Amicus Curiae in Support of Petitioner, 1995 U.S. Briefs 1649.

29. Brief for the Association for the Treatment of Sexual Abusers Amicus Curiae in Support of Petitioner, 1995 U.S. Briefs 1649.

30. Brief for the Association for the Treatment of Sexual Abusers Amicus Curiae in Support of Petitioner, 1995 U.S. Briefs 1649.

31. Brief for the American Psychiatric Association as Amicus Curiae in Support of Leroy Hendricks, 1995 U.S. Briefs 1649.

32. *Kansas v. Hendricks* 521 U.S. 346, 359 (1997). Notably, the phrase "talismanic significance" is the exact language used in an amicus brief from the Menninger Clinic: "Neither would be it prudent to stake the constitutionality of a State's civil commitment statute on whether that law expressly limited commitment only to the 'mentally ill,' even if the definition of the phrase were left to the State. Such a rule would elevate to talismanic significance the phrase 'mental illness'—in direct contravention of the Court's prudent position that labels or other 'magic words' should not be raised to constitutional significance." Brief of the Menninger Foundation et al., 1995 U.S. Briefs 1649.

33. *Kansas v. Hendricks* 521 U.S. 346, 359, 360 (1997).

34. *Kansas v. Hendricks* 521 U.S. 346, 360 (1997).

35. *Kansas v. Hendricks* 521 U.S. 346, 375 (1997).

36. Though I do not address it at length, forensic psychologists' willingness to participate in SVP adjudications was certainly a bid for professional authority and jurisdiction, as several scholars have asserted about psychiatrist's willingness to do so during the "sexual psychopath" era (Chauncey 1993; Cole 2000; Sutherland 1950). Psychiatry is, of course, in a more secure professional position today than it was in the early- to mid-twentieth century and has less need for this jurisdictional foothold.

37. *Kansas v. Crane* 534 U.S. 407, 411 (2002).

38. Brief for the Association for the Treatment of Sexual Abusers as Amicus Curiae in Support of Petitioner, 2000 U.S. Briefs 957.

39. Brief for the American Psychiatric Association and American Academy of Psychiatry and the Law as Amicus Curiae in Support of Respondent, 2000 U.S. Briefs 957.

40. *Kansas v. Crane* 534 U.S. 407, 411 (2002).

41. *Kansas v. Crane* 534 U.S. 407, 413 (2002).

42. Despite clearer criteria, studies have found the inter-rater reliability of pedophilia diagnoses to be low to moderate. Levenson (2004) found a kappa coefficient of 0.65 for a pedophilia diagnosis, and Seto et al. (2016) found a kappa of 0.59.

43. The *DSM-5* update revised this term to "other specified paraphilic disorder," but I use the *DSM-IV-TR* terminology because the switch did not occur until 2013/2014, so most of my cases use the older term.

44. Levenson and Morin (2006); McLawsen, Scalora, and Darrow (2012).

45. First (2014).

46. Frances and First (2011).

47. See Doren (2002).

48. See Frances and First (2011).

49. King et al. (2014).

50. There is, however, a sizable contingent in the forensic psychological field that supports the idea of "coercive paraphilic disorder," and they have marshaled some empirical support for the concept. See Quinsey (2010); Stern (2010).

51. Author interview with Richard Travis, March 8, 2016.

52. Author interview with Isabel Davis, April 11, 2016.

53. Author interview with Kim Weitl, May 31, 2016.

54. Author interview with Richard Krueger, September 8, 2016.

55. King et al. (2014).

56. *McGee v. Bartow* 593 F.3d 556 (7th Cir. 2010).

57. *McGee v. Bartow* 593 F.3d 556, 580 (7th Cir. 2010).

58. Levenson (2004) found the kappa coefficient for "paraphilia not otherwise specified, nonconsent" to be 0.36. A reevaluation of these data by Packard and Levenson (2006) used statistical techniques more likely to find inter-rater agreement, but still found that the proportion of agreement on that diagnosis to be 0.68. It should be noted that whereas kappa attempts to correct for agreements that are likely to occur by chance, proportion of agreement measures do not.

59. *Brown v. Watters* 599 F.3d 602 (7th Cir. 2010).

60. Antisocial personality disorder (APD) has engendered much the same kinds of controversy as PNOSN because of its ambiguous nature, but even more so because some have estimated that at least 50% of criminals could be diagnosed with APD, and it therefore does not distinguish SVPs from more typical, non–mentally ill criminals.

61. *Brown v. Watters* 599 F.3d 602, 605 (7th Cir. 2010).

62. *Brown v. Watters* 599 F.3d 602, 606 (7th Cir. 2010).

63. *Brown v. Watters* 599 F.3d 602, 607 (7th Cir. 2010).

64. Justice Blackmun's dissent quoting the APA's amicus brief in *Barefoot v. Estelle* 463 U.S. 880, 920 (1983).

65. Harcourt (2007).

66. Harcourt (2007).

67. Author interview with Karl Hanson, September 8, 2016.

68. This move fits readily with the more general trend that Feeley and Simon (1992) call the "new penology," which uses the language of probability and risk rather than clinical diagnosis, focuses on the efficient management of internal system processes rather than rehabilitation, and targets offenders in the aggregate rather than as individuals.

69. See Hanson and Thornton (2000).

70. Author interview with Hanson.

71. Author interview with Michael Miner, September 8, 2016.

72. Author interview with Krueger.

73. Janus and Meehl (1997); Prentky, Barbaree, and Janus (2015).

74. Author interview with Miner.

75. Author interview with Hanson.

76. Prentky, Barbaree, and Janus (2015).

77. The *Frye* standard comes from *Frye v. United States*, 293 F. 1013 (D.C. Cir 1923), which considered the admissibility of an early version of the polygraph. The court established that for expert testimony to be admitted in court, it must have obtained "general acceptance" within the relevant professional field.

78. These include the supreme courts of North Dakota, Iowa, and Illinois.

79. *People of Illinois v. Simons* 213 Ill. 2d 523 (2004).

80. *People v. Simons* 213 Ill. 2d 523, 542 (2004), quoting Janus and Prentky (2003, 1486).

81. *People v. Simons* 213 Ill. 2d 523, 542 (2004).

82. The desire on the part of legal actors to be able to easily trace diagnoses or risk scores back to their source is indicative of what Porter (1995) calls "mechanical objectivity," which implies a check on personal bias by following set rules. Also see Daston and Galison (2007).

CHAPTER FOUR

1. *Matter of Toboso-Alfonso*, 20 I. & N. Dec. 819, 822 (BIA 1990).

2. *Reyes-Sanchez v. United States AG*, 369 F.3d 1239, 1243 (11th Cir. 2004).

3. *Rojas v. INS*, 937 F.2d 186, 190 (5th Cir. 1991).

4. *Nuru v. Gonzales*, 404 F.3d 1207, 1219 (9th Cir. 2005).

5. *Pulisir v. Mukasey*, 524 F.3d 302, 310 (1st Cir. 2008).

6. *Paredes v. U.S. Attorney General* 219 Fed. Appx. 879, 883 (11th Cir. 2008).

7. Author interview with Neil Grungras, January 13, 2016.

8. Author interview with Nielan Barnes, June 11, 2016.

9. Author interview with Ingrid Lawson, November 20, 2014.

10. Author interview with Peter Perkowski, February 11, 2014.

11. Author interview with Paul Schmidt, May 25, 2017.

12. *Gutierrez v. U.S. Attorney General* 576 Fed. Appx. 81, 84 (3rd Cir. 2014).

13. Author interview with Julie Dorf, August 2, 2016.

14. Author interview with Dorf.

15. Author interview with Heather McClure, June 2, 2016.

16. Frank's then-partner sat on the advisory board for IGLHRC.

17. This "common sense" often involved stereotypes of effeminate gay men or "butch" lesbians, as I discuss in more detail in the next chapter.

18. USCIS (2011, 53–54).

19. USCIS (2011, 31).

20. Author interview with Lavi Soloway, June 3, 2016.

21. Author interview with Aaron Morris, August 14, 2013.

22. USCIS (2011, 34).

23. Author interview with Soloway.

24. Author interview with McClure.

25. Author interview with Shannon Minter, August 16, 2016.

26. Author interview with Suyapa Portillo, August 18, 2016.

27. Author interview with Perkowski.

28. *Hernandez-Montiel v. INS*, 225 F.3d 1084 (9th Cir. 2000).

29. *Hernandez-Montiel v. INS*, 225 F.3d 1084, 1093 (9th Cir. 2000).

30. *Hernandez-Montiel v. INS*, 225 F.3d 1084, 1093 (9th Cir. 2000). The court cites Kinsey as supporting the idea that sexual identity is inherent to one's identity as a person. As a behaviorist, Kinsey would not have endorsed such a view, and, indeed, during his lifetime he was an opponent of sexual labels.

31. Legal scholar Joseph Landau (2004–2005) argues that the decision to protect outward displays of sexuality, such as dress and hairstyle, represents a larger shift in asylum jurisprudence toward protecting "performative" aspects of identity. I have made a similar argument regarding courts' nascent recognition of the social construction of sexuality in asylum law (Vogler 2016).

32. Author interview with Barnes.

33. Vogler (2016).

34. I borrow this term from Knorr Cetina (1999, 2).

35. Waidzunas (2013, 4).

36. On political and legal opportunity structures, see McAdam (1982) and Andersen (2005), respectively.

37. Merry (2016).

38. Badgett and Sell (2018).

CHAPTER FIVE

1. http://www.bbc.com/news/world-europe-11954499.

2. Organization for Refugee, Asylum and Migration (2010).

3. https://euobserver.com/lgbti/32349.

4. The full pronouncement is available online at http://www.unhcr.org/4daed0389 .pdf.

5. We should also note, however, that the definition of subjects under scrutiny is partially structured by the law itself, and it may be increasingly untenable to assert a crisp distinction between criminal and immigrants in our current political climate where immigration itself is increasingly criminalized.

6. Knorr Cetina (1999).

7. Knorr Cetina (1999, 63).

8. Knorr Cetina (1999, 106).

9. Foucault (1990, 61–62).

10. Knorr Cetina (1999, 40).

11. Somerville (2000); Terry (1999).

12. Longino (2013).

13. 8 CFR § 1208.13(a).

14. Waidzunas (2015).

15. It is helpful to think of narratives, as Ewick and Silbey (2003) suggest, as collaborative productions between speaker and audience whereby subjective experiences are translated into common vernacular by using known cultural schemas, such as the "coming out" template. Narratives can thus connect the particular to the general.

16. Berg and Millbank (2009).

17. Author interview with Victoria Neilson, August 14, 2013.

18. *Kimumwe v. Gonzales*, 431 F.3d 319, 323–24 (8th Cir. 2005). This particular statement comes from Judge Heaney's dissenting opinion, but the majority also found Kimumwe's sexuality to be credible.

19. Murray (2014, 453).

20. This trope may, of course, reinforce racialist and colonialist notions of "primitive" or "undeveloped" countries, especially when it draws on the idea of a monolithic culture as the cause for oppression. See Cantú (2005) for an extended critique of this tendency in US asylum claims by Latin Americans.

21. Author field notes.

22. Author field notes.

23. On sexual fluidity, the instability of sexual identity categories, and the mismatch between sexual attraction, behavior, and identity, see Diamond (2008); Laumann et al. (1994); Savin-Williams and Ream (2007); Ward (2015).

24. *Pozos v. Gonzales*, 141 Fed. Appx. 629, 632 (9th Cir. 2005).

25. *Matter of Acosta* (United States Board of Immigration Appeals 1985), 233.

26. USCIS (2011:16).

27. Available online at https://immigrationequality.org/asylum/asylum-manual/.

28. Author field notes.

29. Author interview with Neilson.

30. Author interview with Michael Jarecki, February 7, 2014.

31. *Fuller v. Lynch*, 833 F.3d 866, 874 (7th Cir. 2016).

32. I should note that Fuller's case arose in Chicago during my fieldwork and was referred to AIR, though they elected not to represent him because they, too, questioned his credibility, a decision that I believe was reasonable given the available evidence.

33. Polletta (2006).

34. Alexander (2004).

35. The success rate for asylum applicants without legal representation has averaged around 10% or less since 2011, while the success rate for represented applicants has been closer to 60%, though it has dropped precipitously since 2017 with the onset of the Trump administration. Data available through TRAC at https://trac.syr.edu/phptools /immigration/asylum/.

36. Polletta et al. (2011, 115).

37. Berger (2009).

38. Author interview with Minter.

39. *Hernandez-Montiel v. INS*, 225 F.3d 1084, 1089 (9th Cir. 2000).

40. *Hernandez-Montiel v. INS*, 225 F.3d 1084, 1094 (9th Cir. 2000). The range of scholarship regarding sexuality cited is quite remarkable and ranges from legal scholars Susan Goldberg and Kenji Yoshino to anthropologist Gilbert Herdt to sociologist Martin Weinberg to the American Psychiatric Association and even Alfred Kinsey. A particularly notable passage citing an article by legal scholar Naomi Mezey suggests that we must separate the way we speak of sexual acts and sexual identities and, further, that the traditional heterosexual/homosexual binary is too restrictive (1094). The use of social science in *Hernandez-Montiel* is discussed more extensively in chapter 4.

41. *Hernandez-Montiel v. INS*, 225 F.3d 1084, 1094 (9th Cir. 2000).

42. Hernandez-Montiel's brief *did* say that he "may be considered a transsexual," though this seemed largely to be an attempt to make his identity legible to an American

audience. The larger argument—and the one recognized by the Ninth Circuit—recognized Hernandez-Montiel as a "gay man with a female sexual identity."

43. Author interview with Morris.

44. Carrillo (2002).

45. Though one might note that this case could also be misinterpreted to suggest that Latin American sexualities are fully defined along gendered lines, risking a problematic neocolonial rendering of non-US residents as "less modern" or "more traditional others."

46. Author interview with Lawson.

47. Author interview with Barnes.

48. Author interview with Barnes.

49. *Hassani v. Mukasey*, 301 Fed. Appx. 602, 604 (9th Cir. 2008).

50. Organization for Refuge, Asylum and Migration (2010, 7).

51. Author interview with Morris.

52. Author field notes.

53. *Vitug v. Holder*, 723 F.3d 1056, 1060 (9th Cir. 2013).

54. Author interview with Keren Zwick, January 24, 2014.

55. Author interview with Daniel Tenreiro, September 16, 2013.

56. Author interview with McClure.

57. Vogler (2016).

58. *Razkane v. Holder*, 562 F.3d 1283, 1288 (10th Cir. 2009).

59. *Razkane v. Holder*, 562 F.3d 1283, 1286 (10th Cir. 2009).

60. *Matter of S-E-G-*, 24 I&N Dec. 579 (BIA 2008); *Matter of E-A-G-*, 24 I&N Dec. 591 (BIA 2008).

61. USCIS (2011, 16).

62. Author interview with Neilson.

63. *Mockeviciene v. Attorney General*, 237 Fed. Appx. 569, 574 (11th Cir. 2007).

64. *Ali v. Mukasey*, 529 F.3d 478, 491 (2nd Cir. 2008).

65. *Ali v. Mukasey*, 529 F.3d 478, 492 (2nd Cir. 2008).

66. Author field notes.

67. UNHCR (2008, 17).

68. USCIS (2011, 34).

69. This may not be true when it comes to proving injury, however. As Fassin and D'Halluin (2005) note, the body serves as a source of truth in asylum claims for petitioners seeking to prove physical harm as a result of their persecution. Courts may want to see medical documentation and even the scars left by physical assaults. Indeed, Kwame Twumasi demonstrated this during his hearing when he lifted his shirt in court to show the judge scars on his back from being whipped.

CHAPTER SIX

1. Lynch (2019, 8).

2. Kendall (2005).

3. Both the state and defense may present expert witnesses.

4. See for example In re COMMITMENT OF Jacob Sandry 857 N.E.2d 295 (2006); In Matter of the Detention of MICHAEL ALLEN HALGREN 156 Wn.2d 795 (2006). Notably, in other cases where the offender requested that PPG evidence be admitted, courts have denied it. See *North Carolina v. Spencer* 119 N.C. App. 662 (1995); *Garren v. Georgia* 220 Ga. App. 66 (1996).

5. Smith (1984, 61).

6. Smith (2005, 227).

7. Dr. Wood, who had not conducted a clinical interview with Mr. Lowe, gave the additional "possible" diagnosis of sexual sadism disorder, but stated that he needed more information to be sure.

8. Dr. Wood's deposition became the subject of an extensive sidebar, during which the jury was dismissed. So discussion of the PPG was not introduced to the jury. However, it clearly informed Dr. Wood's opinion, at least partially, yet remained unacknowledged as a diagnostic tool.

9. This is comparable to the process that occurs in a scientific lab, as described by Latour and Woolgar (1979). Scientists are confronted with enormous amounts of data that must be turned into ordered knowledge. Also see Star (1985).

10. Latour and Woolgar (1979, 51).

11. Quoted in Lynch et al. (2008, 71).

12. Alder (2007).

13. Balmer and Sandland (2012); McGrath et al. (2010).

14. Alder (2007).

15. Ahlmeyer et al. (2000, 125).

16. For example, in SVP evaluations, state evaluators typically spend only about one to two hours speaking with the offender, if they conduct a clinical interview at all.

17. Illinois has adopted the ATSA guidelines with almost no changes.

18. ATSA (2014, 20–21).

19. *Lile v. McKune* (1998), 24 F. Supp. 2d 1152; *Pool v. McKune* (1999) 267 Kan. 797; *Searcy v. Simmons* (2000), 97 F. Supp. 2d 1055.

20. There are five stages of treatment in the model used by the Illinois civil commitment program. SVPs are sometimes allowed to complete the fifth stage in community treatment under supervised release.

21. Author interview with Donya Adkerson, February 22, 2016.

22. Notably, a "typo" in the *DSM-5* referred to pedophilia as a "sexual orientation." The APA released a correction stating that it should have read "sexual interest."

23. Author interview with Travis.

24. Balmer and Sandland (2012, 613).

25. McGrath et al. (2010).

26. Waidzunas and Epstein (2015, 3).

27. *People v. Sandry* 367 Ill. App. 3d 949, 967 (2006).

28. *People v. Sandry* 367 Ill. App. 3d 949, 975–976 (2006).

29. *People v. Hughes* 338 Ill. App. 3d 224, 233 (2003).

30. For instance, see Diamond (2008).

31. Author interview with Arjun Kapoor, December 12, 2015.

32. See Odeshoo (2004).

33. *United States v. Weber* 451 F.3d 552, 555 (9th Cir. 2006).

34. *United States v. Rhodes* 552 F.3d 624, 627 (7th Cir. 2009). See Tong (2007).

35. *U.S. v. McLaurin* 731 F.3d 258, 259 (2nd Cir. 2013).

36. *Billips v. Virginia* 48 Va. App. 278, 313 (Va. 2007).

37. Author interview with Shan Jumper, February 29, 2016.

38. Fausto-Sterling (2000); Terry (2000).

39. Concern for fraud was one stated reason for implementing a one-year filing deadline for asylum applications during the Clinton administration, and Trump administration officials have cited fraud as rationale for considering further restrictions.

CHAPTER SEVEN

1. Sita Reddy (2002) shows, for example, how American courts pathologize non-American cultures when they accept the "culture defense" by blaming "culture" for individual criminal acts perpetrated by foreign-born "aliens" while rejecting such arguments for US-born minorities. This move also generally coincides with a reductive and monolithic portrayal of foreign cultures.

2. Hannah-Moffat, Maurutto, and Turnbull (2009).

3. Kendall (2005); Raynor and Lewis (2011).

4. Beck (1992, 23; emphasis in original).

5. Douglas and Wildavsky (1982).

6. Rayner (1992, 87).

7. Epstein and Mamo (2017); Esacove (2013); Norton (2013).

8. See, e.g., Vance (1984).

9. Douglas (1992); Hoppe (2017); Lynch (2002); Wald (2008).

10. Canaday (2009); Luibhéid (2002); Shah (2012).

11. Prentky, Barbaree, and Janus (2015, 41).

12. Rose (2002, 212).

13. Hebenton and Seddon (2009, 344).

14. Ericson (2007, 24).

15. Yung (2010).

16. Fischel (2010, 307).

17. Fischel (2010, 307).

18. Cole (2000); Douard and Schultz (2013); Mansnerus (2017); Simon (1998); Small (2015).

19. Kornbluh (2011).

20. Puar (2007, xii; emphasis mine).

21. Notably, criminal history is perhaps the single most widely used metric of risk in the US legal system, as it often forms the basis of sentencing, parole, and bond decisions. See Harcourt (2007); Lynch and Bertenthal (2016); Ryo (2016).

22. 8 USC § 1158.

23. *INS v. Cardoza-Fonseca* 480 U.S. 421, 431 (1987).

24. *INS v. Cardoza-Fonseca* 480 U.S. 421, 440 (1987).

25. *INS v. Cardoza-Fonseca* 480 U.S. 421, 448 (1987).

26. Hathaway and Foster (1991, 104-5).

27. Anker and Ardalan (2012).

28. McKinnon (2016) elaborates on the gendered dimensions of the paradigmatic asylum seeker.

29. For instance, courts have ruled that persecution can be emotional or psychological, as well as physical. See *Mansour v. Ashcroft*, 390 F.3d 667 (9th Cir. 2004); *Stanojkova v. Holder*, 645 F.3d 943 (7th Cir. 2011). For cases determining that sexual assault constitutes persecution, see *Haider v. Holder*, 595 F.3d 276, 287-88 (6th Cir. 2010); *Ndonyi v. Mukasey*, 541 F.3d 702, 710 (7th Cir. 2008); *Boer-Sedano v. Gonzales*, 418 F.3d 1082, 1088 (9th Cir. 2005). For cases establishing that private actors may be persecutors, see *Ornelas-Chazev v. Gonzales* 458 F.3d 1052 (9th Cir. 2006); *Reyes-Reyes v. Ashcroft*, 384 F.3d 782 (9th Cir. 2004).

30. On the wide variation in asylum grant rates, see Ramji-Nogales, Schoenholtz, and Schrag (2009).

31. *Fuller v. Lynch*, 833 F.3d 866, 872 (7th Cir. 2016).

32. *Velez v. U.S. Attorney General*, 360 Fed. Appx. 103, 104 (11th Cir. 2010).

33. Author interview with Lory Rosenberg, May 8, 2017.

34. *Matter of Kasinga*, 21 I&N Dec. 357 (BIA 1996).

35. *Matter of A-B-*, 27 I&N Dec. 316 (A.G. 2018).

36. Cantú (2005); Carrillo (2010).

37. *Halmenschlager v. Holder*, 331 Fed Appx. 612, 621 (10th Cir. 2009).

38. *Tian-Yong Chen v. INS*, 359 F.3d 121, 130 (2d Cir. 2004); *Diaz-Garcia v. Holder*, 609 F.3d 21, 28 (1st Cir. 2010).

39. *Banks v. Gonzales*, 453 F.3d 449, 453 (7th Cir. 2006).

40. US Department of State (2011, 33).

41. US Department of State (2013, 16).

42. Cantú (2009) echoes this point.

43. Human Rights Watch (2009).

44. Human Rights Watch (2009), 15.

45. Amnesty International (2013, 32).

46. Amnesty International (2013, 32).

47. Amnesty International (2013, 33).

48. Reding (2003, 1).

49. Reding (2003, 8-9). Cantú (2005, 2009) singles out Reding for reifying and blaming Mexican culture for gay oppression without accounting for other factors, such as race, class, gender, or globalization.

50. This situation is also illustrated by one expert witness with whom I spoke. Though he has been asked many times to serve as an expert witness for Mexican asylum claims, lawyers have typically withdrawn their request when he explains that to be true to his research, his testimony would be nuanced and include his observations that gay men can live fairly safely in some areas of Mexico.

51. Expert affidavit for Gabriela Martínez case, on file with author.

52. Expert affidavit for Juan Hernández case, on file with author.

53. Author field notes.

54. Author interview with Barnes.

55. Author interview with Perkowski.

56. Author interview with Soloway.

57. Author interview with Schmidt.

58. Author interview with Portillo.

59. Author interview with Barnes.

60. Author interview with Portillo.

61. Author field notes.

62. Author interview with Ingrid Lawson.

63. Notably, this judge openly admits that discretion and subjectivity enter legal decision-making, but as legal scholarship on actuarial risk assessment has demonstrated, discretion is often disguised or black-boxed in these tools (Hannah-Moffat, Maurutto, and Turnbull 2009).

64. Miller, Keith, and Holmes (2015); Ramji-Nogales, Schoenholtz and Schrag (2009).

65. Author interview with Lawson.

66. Marouf (2008) and Southam (2011) make this point, as well.

67. *Rosiles-Camarena v. Holder* 735 F.3d 534, 535 (7th Cir. 2013).

68. *Rosiles-Camarena v. Holder* 735 F.3d 534, 537–38 (7th Cir. 2013), emphasis mine.
69. Author interview with Lawson.
70. Author field notes.
71. *Isaacs v. Holder* 353 Fed. Appx. 515, 517 (2nd Cir. 2009).
72. *Rosiles-Camarena v. Holder* 735 F.3d 534, 538 (7th Cir. 2013).
73. Author interview with Morris.
74. Author interview with Lawson.
75. *Halmenschlager v. Holder*, 331 Fed. Appx. 612, 622 (10th Cir. 2009).
76. *Rosiles-Camarena v. Holder* 735 F.3d 534, 536 (7th Cir. 2013).
77. *Rosiles-Camarena v. Holder* 735 F.3d 534, 539 (7th Cir. 2013).
78. Author interview with Lawson.
79. *Todorovic v. U.S. Attorney General*, 621 F.3d 1318, 1323–24 (11th Cir. 2010).
80. *Razkane v. Holder*, 562 F.3d 1283, 1286 (10th Cir. 2009).
81. Author interview with Aneesha Gandhi, January 24, 2014.
82. Author field notes.
83. Author interview with McClure.
84. Author interview with Rosenberg.
85. *Maldonado v. Attorney General of the United States*, 188 Fed. Appx. 101 (3rd Cir. 2006).
86. Author interview with Lawson.
87. USCIS (2011, 16).

CHAPTER EIGHT

1. Porter (1995).
2. For more on this, see Tolman (2018).
3. Sexually Violent Persons Commitment Act, 725 Ill. Comp. Stat. Ann. 207/5(f) (1998).
4. Sexually Dangerous Person Act, Minn. Stat. 253B.02(18c)(a)(3) (2011).
5. Sexually Violent Predators, Civil Commitment Act, Mo. Rev. Stat. § 632.480(5) (2012).
6. *People v. Superior Court (Ghilotti)*, 44 P.3d 949, 967–68 (Cal. 2002).
7. *People v. Superior Court (Ghilotti)*, 44 P.3d 949, 972 (Cal. 2002).
8. *People v. Hayes (In re Hayes)*, 747 N.E.2d 444, 453 (Ill. App. Ct., 2001).
9. Author interview with Travis.
10. *In re Care & Treatment of Williams*, 253 P.3d 327 (Kan. 2011).
11. *Commonwealth v. Boucher*, 880 N.E.2d 47, 50 (Mass. 2002).
12. *Grosinger v. M.B.K. (In re M.B.K.)*, 639 N.W.2d 473, 477 (N.D. 2002).
13. Heimer (2001, 48).
14. Lynch (2019, 8).
15. Knighton et al. (2014).
16. Author interview with Weitl.
17. Author interview with Travis.
18. Author interview with Adkerson.
19. Boccaccini et al. (2013).
20. Prentky, Barbaree, and Janus (2015).
21. Author interview with William Marshall, August 22, 2016.
22. Author interview with Robin Wilson, April 7, 2017.

23. Author interview with Davis.

24. *In the Matter of the Detention of Mark Broer*, 2005 Wash. App. LEXIS 688.

25. Small (2015).

26. Seto and Lalumière (2001). The Fifth Circuit makes this conflation in *U.S. v. Ortega* 485 Fed. Appx. 656 (5th Cir. 2012).

27. Author interview with Adkerson.

28. Author interview with Hanson.

29. Cited in *Kansas v. Hendricks* 521 U.S. 346, 365 (1997).

30. *Kansas v. Hendricks* 521 U.S. 346, 366 (1997).

31. Kan. Stat. Ann. § 59-29a01 (1994).

32. *Kansas v. Crane* 534 U.S. 407 (2002).

33. Moran (1999).

34. The Seventh Circuit makes just this point in *Adams v. Bartow* 330 F.3d 957 (7th Cir. 2003), ruling that antisocial personality disorder may not be enough to commit someone, but APD in combination with evidence of sexual risk is sufficient.

35. On the idea that actuarialism is consistent with the individualization of punishment and the "will to know the criminal," see Harcourt (2007); Lynch and Bertenthal (2016).

36. Harcourt (2007).

37. Feeley and Simon (1992); Harcourt (2003).

38. Barbaree et al. (2001).

39. Hanson and Thornton (2000, 131).

40. Hanson and Morton-Bourgon (2009, 1).

41. Author interview with Hanson.

42. Barbaree et al. (2001).

43. Harris and Rice (2003).

44. Author interview with Hanson.

45. Janus (2006, 103–4).

46. The newer iterations of the Static-99, the Static-99R and the Static-2002, do allow risk to decrease with age. Dynamic risk assessment tools are also available, but they generally cannot be used with incarcerated individuals. However, most evaluators today will take into account dynamic factors in their overall assessment to some extent, although they will not be reflected in the quantitative recidivism estimates.

47. SVP evaluation of Jordan Lowe by Dr. Edward Spencer, p. 55. On file with author.

48. Hoppe (2016); Simon (1998).

49. Available at http://stmedia.startribune.com/documents/Expert+panel+report +on+sex+offender+program.pdf (accessed January 9, 2017).

50. Author interview with Miner.

51. Gookin (2007).

52. *Belleau v. Wall* 811 F.3d 929, 933 (7th Cir. 2016).

53. *Belleau v. Wall* 811 F.3d 929, 933–34 (7th Cir. 2016).

54. *Belleau v. Wall* 811 F.3d 929, 934 (7th Cir. 2016).

55. *Smith v. Doe*, 538 U.S. 84, 103 (2003). For an analysis of the flawed logic in this Supreme Court decision, see Fischel (2010).

56. 42 USC § 14071(a)(3)(E)(2001).

57. Zilney and Zilney (2009).

58. Terry (2013); Zilney and Zilney (2009).

59. Author interview with Marshall.

60. Author field notes.

61. *U.S. v. Shields*, 649 F.3d 78, 89 (1st Cir. 2011).

62. Hanson and Thornton (2000, 131, 132).

63. Author interview with Aaron Barton, June 22, 2016.

64. Author interview with Weitl.

65. Hanson and Morton-Bourgon (2009).

66. *U.S. v. Sheradin*, 499 Fed. Appx. 305, 307 (4th Cir. 2012).

67. *U.S. v. Perez*, 752 F.3d 398, 411 (4th Cir. 2014).

68. On the role of criminal history in offender risk assessment, see Harcourt (2007); Lynch and Bertenthal (2016).

69. SVP evaluation of Jordan Lowe by Dr. Edward Spencer, 46, 50. On file with author.

70. SVP evaluation of Jordan Lowe by Dr. Edward Spencer, 47.

71. Author interview with Travis.

72. Author interview with Karen Franklin, August 30, 2016.

73. Author interview with Wilson.

74. Ewald (1991); Rose, O'Malley, and Valverde (2006).

75. Douglas and Wildavsky (1982); Ericson and Doyle (2003).

76. Moore and Valverde (2000); Valverde (2003).

77. Valverde, Levi, and Moore (2005, 87).

CONCLUSION

1. Fligstein, Brundage, and Schultz (2017).

2. Savelsberg (1994, 938–39).

3. Stampnitzky (2013).

4. On "lay experts" in health social movements, see Cambrosio, Limoges, and Hoffman (1992); Epstein (1996).

5. Stryker (1989; 1994).

6. Vogler (2016).

7. Omi and Winant (1964, 61).

8. Duggan (2003).

9. Puar (2007).

10. Wynter (2003).

11. Crenshaw (1995).

12. Vogler (2019).

13. See Halperin and Hoppe (2017).

14. Foucault (1990).

15. Benjamin (2019); Chun (2009); Coleman (2009).

16. Stoler (1995).

17. Stoler (1987, 200).

18. On the ways technology can promulgate pernicious racial stereotypes, see Benjamin (2019).

19. Magnet (2011).

20. Available at https://www.theguardian.com/technology/2018/jul/07/artificial-intelligence-can-tell-your-sexuality-politics-surveillance-paul-lewis (accessed August 2, 2019).

21. Muhammad (2011).

22. Levin (2018).
23. Fussell (2017).
24. Kalhan (2013).

APPENDIX TWO

1. Doing a general keyword search for words such as sexual, sex offender, or sexual offender returned more cases than LexisNexis could process, and I therefore had to adapt my search methods. I found that using the "core terms" search feature resulted in a more manageable number of cases that were also more relevant.

2. My coding method is similar to that described by Stryker (1996).

REFERENCES

Abrams, Philip. 1988. "Notes on the Difficulty of Studying the State." *Journal of Historical Sociology* 1 (1): 58–89.

Acker, J. R. 1990. "Social Science in Supreme Court Criminal Cases and Briefs: The Actual and Potential Contribution of Social Scientists as Amici Curiae." *Law and Human Behavior* 14 (1): 25–42.

Adams, Jimi, and Ryan Light. 2015. "Scientific Consensus, the Law, and Same Sex Parenting Outcomes." *Social Science Research* 53: 300–10.

Ahlmeyer, S., P. Heil, B. McKee, and K. English. 2000. "The Impact of Polygraphy on Admissions of Victims and Offenses in Adult Sexual Offenders." *Sexual Abuse* 12 (2): 123–38.

Alanko, Katarina, Annika Gunst, Andreas Mokros, and Pekka Santtila. 2016. "Genetic Variants Associated with Male Pedophilic Sexual Interest." *Journal of Sexual Medicine* 13 (5): 835–42.

Alder, Ken. 2007. *The Lie Detectors: The History of an American Obsession.* New York: Free Press.

Alexander, Jeffrey. 2004. "Cultural Pragmatics: Social Performance between Ritual and Strategy." *Sociological Theory* 22: 527–73.

Alexander, Michelle. 2010. *The New Jim Crow: Mass Incarceration in the Age of Colorblindness.* New York: New Press.

Amnesty International. 2013. "Making Love a Crime: Criminalization of Same-Sex Conduct in Sub-Saharan Africa." London: Amnesty International.

Andersen, Ellen Ann. 2005. *Out of the Closets and into the Courts: Legal Opportunity Structure and Gay Rights Litigation.* Ann Arbor: University of Michigan Press.

Anderson, Benedict. (1983) 1991. *Imagined Communities: Reflections on the Origin and Spread of Nationalism.* London: Verso.

Anderson, Margo, and Stephen Fienberg. 1999. *Who Counts? The Politics of Census-Taking in Contemporary America.* New York: Russell Sage Foundation.

Anker, Deborah, and Sabi Ardalan. 2012. "Escalating Persecution of Gays and Refugee Protection." *NYU Journal of International Law and Politics* 44: 528–58.

Appadurai, Arjun. 1996. *Modernity at Large: Cultural Dimensions of Globalization.* Minneapolis: University of Minnesota Press.

Association for the Treatment of Sexual Abusers (ATSA). 2014. "Practice Guidelines for the Assessment, Treatment, and Management of Male Adult Sexual Abusers." Beaverton, OR.

Badgett, M. V. Lee, and Randall Sell. 2018. "A Set of Proposed Indicators for the LGBTI Inclusion Index." New York: UNDP.

Baker, Tom, and Jonathan Simon, eds. 2002. *Embracing Risk: The Changing Culture of Insurance and Responsibility*. Chicago: University of Chicago Press.

Bal, Roland. 2005. "How to Kill with a Ballpoint: Credibility in Dutch Forensic Science." *Science, Technology & Human Values* 30 (1): 52–75.

Ball, C. 2014. *Same-Sex Marriage and Children: A Tale of History, Social Science, and Law*. New York: Oxford University Press.

Balmer, Andrew S., and Ralph Sandland. 2012. "Making Monsters: The Polygraph, the Plethysmograph, and Other Practices for the Performance of Abnormal Sexuality." *Journal of Law and Society* 39 (4): 593–615.

Barbaree, H. E., M. C. Seto, C. M. Langton, and E. J. Peacock. 2001. "Evaluating the Predictive Accuracy of Six Risk Assessment Instruments for Adult Sex Offenders." *Criminal Justice and Behavior* 28 (4): 490–521.

Beauchamp, Toby. 2018. *Going Stealth: Transgender Politics and U.S. Surveillance Practices*. Durham, NC: Duke University Press.

Beck, Ulrich. 1992. *Risk Society: Towards a New Modernity*. London: Sage.

Belleau v. Wall 811 F.3d 929 (7th Cir. 2016).

Benjamin, Ruha. 2019. *Race after Technology*. Cambridge: Polity.

Berg, Laurie, and Jenni Millbank. 2009. "Constructing the Personal Narrative of Lesbian, Gay and Bisexual Asylum Claimants." *Journal of Refugee Studies* 22 (2): 195–223.

Berger, Susan A. 2009. "Production and Reproduction of Gender and Sexuality in Legal Discourses of Asylum in the United States." *Signs* 34 (3): 659–85.

Bernstein, Elizabeth. 2010. "Militarized Humanitarianism Meets Carceral Feminism: The Politics of Sex, Rights, and Freedom in Contemporary Antitrafficking Campaigns." *Signs* 36 (1): 45–71.

Billips v. Virginia 48 Va. App. 278 (Va. 2007).

Blair-Loy, Mary. 2001. "Cultural Constructions of Family Schemas: The Case of Women Finance Executives." *Gender & Society* 15 (5): 687–709.

Bloor, David. (1976) 1991. *Knowledge and Social Imagery*. Chicago: University of Chicago Press.

Boccaccini, M. T., K. A. Rufino, R. L. Jackson, and D. C. Murrie. 2013. "Personality Assessment Inventory Scores as Predictors of Misconduct among Sex Offenders Civilly Committed as Sexually Violent Predators." *Psychological Assessment* 25 (4): 1390–95.

Bourdieu, Pierre. 1987. "The Force of Law: Toward a Sociology of the Juridical Field." *Hastings Law Review* 38: 805–53.

Bourdieu, Pierre. 1994. "Rethinking the State: Genesis and Structure of the Bureaucratic Field." *Sociological Theory* 12(1):1–18.

Boutilier v. INS, 387 U.S. 118 (1967).

Bowker, Geoffrey, and Susan Leigh Star. 1999. *Sorting Things Out: Classification and Its Consequences*. Cambridge, MA: MIT Press.

Brandzel, Amy. 2005. "Queering Citizenship? Same-Sex Marriage and the State." *GLQ* 11 (2): 171–204.

Brint, Steven. 1994. *In an Age of Experts: The Changing Role of Professionals in Politics and Public Life*. Princeton, NJ: Princeton University Press.

Brown v. Watters 599 F.3d 602 (7th Cir. 2010).

Burick, Lawrence. 1968. "An Analysis of the Illinois Sexually Dangerous Persons Act." *Journal of Criminal Law, Criminology, and Police Science* 59 (2): 254–66.

Cambrosio, Alberto, Camille Limoges, and Eric Hoffman. 1992. "Expertise as a Network." In *The Culture and Power of Knowledge*, ed. Nico Stehr and Richard Ericson, 341–62. Berlin: Walter de Gruyter.

Camic, Charles, Neil Gross, and Michèle Lamont, eds. 2011. *Social Knowledge in the Making*. Chicago: University of Chicago Press.

Canaday, Margot. 2003. "'Who Is a Homosexual?': The Consolidation of Sexual Identities in Mid-Twentieth-Century American Immigration Law." *Law & Social Inquiry* 28 (2): 351–86.

Canaday, Margot. 2009. *The Straight State: Sexuality and Citizen*. Princeton, NJ: Princeton University Press.

Cantor, James, Ray Blanchard, Bruce Christensen, Robert Dickey, Philip Klassen, A. Beckstead, Thomas Blak, and Michael Kuban. 2004. "Intelligence, Memory, and Handedness in Pedophilia." *Neuropsychology* 18 (1): 3–14.

Cantú, Lionel. 2005. "Well-Founded Fear: Political Asylum and the Boundaries of Sexual Identity in the U.S.-Mexico Borderlands." In *Queer Migrations: Sexuality, U.S. Citizenship, and Border Crossings*, ed. Eithne Luibhéid and Lionel Cantú Jr., 61–74. Minneapolis: University of Minnesota Press.

Cantú, Lionel. 2009. *The Sexuality of Migration*. New York: New York University Press.

Carrillo, Héctor. 2002. *The Night Is Young: Sexuality in Mexico in the Time of AIDS*. Chicago: University of Chicago Press.

Carrillo, Héctor. 2010. "Immigration and LGBT Rights in the USA: Ironies and Constraints in US Asylum Cases." In *Routledge Handbook of Sexuality, Health and Rights*, ed. Peter Aggleton and Richard Parker, 444–52. London: Routledge.

Carroll, Patrick. 2006. *Science, Culture, and Modern State Formation*. Berkeley: University of California Press.

Chapkis, Wendy. 2003. "Trafficking, Migration, and the Law: Protecting Innocents, Punishing Immigrants." *Gender & Society* 17 (6): 923–37.

Chapkis, Wendy. 2005. "Soft Glove, Punishing Fist: The Trafficking Victims Protection Act of 2000." In *Regulating Sex*, ed. Elizabeth Bernstein and Laurie Schaffner, 51–66. New York: Routledge.

Chauncey, George. 1993. "The Postwar Sex Crime Panic." In *True Stories from the American Past*, ed. William Graebner, 160–78. New York: McGraw-Hill.

Chauncey, George. 1994. *Gay New York: Gender, Urban Culture, and the Making of the Gay Male World, 1890–1940*. New York: Basic Books.

Chun, Wendy Hui Kyong. 2009. "Introduction: Race and/as Technology; or, How to Do Things to Race." *Camera Obscura* 24 (1): 7–35.

Clemens, Elisabeth, and James Cook. 1999. "Politics and Institutionalism: Explaining Durability and Change." *Annual Review of Sociology* 25: 441–66.

Cole, Simon. 2000. "From the Sexual Psychopath Statute to 'Megan's Law': Psychiatric Knowledge in the Diagnosis, Treatment, and Adjudication of Sex Criminals in New Jersey, 1949–1999." *Journal of the History of Medicine and Allied Sciences* 55 (3): 292–314.

Cole, Simon. 2001. *Suspect Identities: A History of Fingerprinting and Criminal Identification*. Cambridge, MA: Harvard University Press.

Coleman, Beth. 2009. "Race as Technology." *Camera Obscura* 24 (1): 177–207.

Collins, Harry, and Robert Evans. 2007. *Rethinking Expertise*. Chicago: University of Chicago Press.

Cossman, Brenda. 2007. *Sexual Citizens: The Legal and Cultural Regulation of Sex and Belonging*. Stanford, CA: Stanford University Press.

Crenshaw, Kimberlé. 1995. "Mapping the Margins: Intersectionality, Identity Politics, and Violence against Women of Color." In *Critical Race Theory: The Key Writings That Formed the Movement*, ed. Kimberlé Crenshaw, Neil Gotanda, Gary Peller, and Kendall Thomas, 357–83. New York: New Press.

Daston, Lorraine, and Peter Galison. 2007. *Objectivity*. New York: Zone Books.

Daubert v. Merrell Dow Pharmaceuticals, 509 U.S. 579 (1993).

D'Emilio, John. 1983. "Capitalism and Gay Identity." In *The Lesbian and Gay Studies Reader*, ed. Henry Abelove, Michele Aina Barale, and David Halperin, 467–76. New York: Routledge.

D'Emilio, John, and Estelle Freedman. 1988. *Intimate Matters: A History of Sexuality in America*. New York: Harper and Row.

de Orio, Scott. 2017. "The Creation of the Modern Sex Offender." In *The War on Sex*, ed. David Halperin and Trevor Hoppe, 247–67. Durham, NC: Duke University Press.

Desrosières, Alain. 1998. *The Politics of Large Numbers: A History of Statistical Reasoning*. Cambridge, MA: Harvard University Press.

Diamond, Lisa. 2008. *Sexual Fluidity: Understanding Women's Love and Desire*. Cambridge: Harvard University Press.

Diamond, Lisa, and Clifford Rosky. 2016. "Scrutinizing Immutability: Research on Sexual Orientation and U.S. Legal Advocacy for Sexual Minorities." *Journal of Sex Research* 53 (4–5): 363–91.

Doren, Dennis. 2002. *Evaluating Sex Offenders: A Manual for Civil Commitments and Beyond*. Thousand Oaks, CA: Sage.

Douard, John, and Pamela Schultz. 2013. *Monstrous Crimes and the Failure of Forensic Psychiatry*. New York: Springer.

Douglas, Mary. 1992. *Risk and Blame: Essays in Cultural Theory*. New York: Routledge.

Douglas, Mary, and Aaron Wildavsky. 1982. *Risk and Culture: An Essay on the Selection of Technological and Environmental Dangers*. Berkeley: University of California Press.

Drescher, Jack. 2015. "Out of DSM: Depathologizing Homosexuality." *Behavioral Sciences* 5: 565–75.

Duggan, Lisa. 2003. *The Twilight of Equality: Neoliberalism, Cultural Politics, and the Attack on Democracy*. Boston: Beacon Press.

Emigh, Rebecca Jean. 2002. "Numeracy or Enumeration?" *Social Science History* 26 (4): 653–98.

Emigh, Rebecca Jean, Dylan Riley, and Patricia Ahmed. 2016. *Antecedents of Censuses from Medieval to Nation States*. New York: Palgrave.

English, Kim. 1998. "The Containment Approach: An Aggressive Strategy for the Community Management of Sex Offenders." *Psychology, Public Policy, and Law* 4 (1/2): 218–35.

Epps, Brad, Keja Valens, and Bill Johnson González, eds. 2005. *Passing Lines: Sexuality and Immigration*. Cambridge, MA: Harvard University Press.

Epstein, Steven. 1996. *Impure Science: AIDS, Activism, and the Politics of Knowledge*. Berkeley: University of California Press.

Epstein, Steven. 2007. *Inclusion: The Politics of Difference in Medical Research*. Chicago: University of Chicago Press.

Epstein, Steven, and Héctor Carrillo. 2014. "Immigrant Sexual Citizenship: Intersectional Templates among Mexican Gay Immigrants to the USA." *Citizenship Studies* 18 (3–4): 259–76.

Epstein, Steven, and Laura Mamo. 2017. "The Proliferation of Sexual Health: Diverse

Social Problems and the Legitimation of Sexuality." *Social Science & Medicine* 188: 176–90.

Ericson, Richard V. 2007. *Crime in an Insecure World*. Cambridge: Polity.

Ericson, Richard V., and Aaron Doyle, eds. 2003. *Risk and Morality*. Toronto: University of Toronto Press.

Esacove, Anne. 2013. "Good Sex/Bad Sex: The Individualised Focus of US HIV Prevention Policy in Sub-Saharan Africa, 1995–2005." *Sociology of Health & Illness* 35 (1): 33–48.

Espeland, Wendy, and Mitchell Stevens. 1998. "Commensuration as a Social Process." *Annual Review of Sociology* 24: 313–43.

Ewald, Francois. 1991. "Insurance and Risk." In *The Foucault Effect: Studies in Governmentality*, ed. Graham Burchell, Colin Gordon, and Peter Miller, 197–210. Chicago: University of Chicago Press.

Ewick, Patricia, and Susan Silbey. 2003. "Narrating Social Structure: Stories of Resistance to Legal Authority." *American Journal of Sociology* 108: 1328–72.

Eyal, Gil. 2006. *The Disenchantment of the Orient: Expertise in Arab Affairs and the Israeli State*. Stanford, CA: Stanford University Press.

Eyal, Gil. 2013. "For a Sociology of Expertise: The Social Origins of the Autism Epidemic." *American Journal of Sociology* 118 (4): 863–907.

Eyal, Gil, and Larissa Buchholz. 2010. "From the Sociology of Intellectuals to the Sociology of Interventions." *Annual Review of Sociology* 36:117–37.

Ezrahi, Yaron. 1990. *The Descent of Icarus: Science and the Transformation of Contemporary Democracy*. Cambridge, MA: Harvard University Press.

Faigman, David, Elise Porter, and Michael Saks. 1994. "Check Your Crystal Ball at the Courthouse Door, Please: Exploring the Past, Understanding the Present, and Worrying about the Future of Scientific Evidence." *Cardozo Law Review* 15: 1799–829.

Falk, P. J. 1994. "The Prevalence of Social Science in Gay Rights Cases: The Synergistic Influences of Historical Context, Justificatory Citation, and Dissemination Efforts." *Wayne Law Review* 41: 1–69.

Fassin, Didier, and Estelle D'Halluin. 2005. "The Truth from the Body: Medical Certificates as Ultimate Evidence for Asylum Seekers." *American Anthropologist* 107 (4): 597–608.

Fausto-Sterling, Anne. 2000. *Sexing the Body: Gender Politics and the Construction of Sexuality*. New York: Basic Books.

Feeley, Malcom, and Jonathan Simon. 1992. "The New Penology: Notes on the Emerging Strategy of Corrections and its Implications." *Criminology* 30 (4): 449–74.

First, Michael. 2014. "DSM-5 and Paraphilic Disorders." *Journal of the American Academy of Psychiatry and the Law* 42 (2): 191–201.

Fischel, Joseph. 2010. "Transcendent Homosexuals and Dangerous Sex Offenders: Sexual Harm and Freedom in the Judicial Imaginary." *Duke Journal of Gender Law & Policy* 17: 277–311.

Fischer, Frank. 2009. *Democracy and Expertise: Reorienting Policy Inquiry*. Oxford: Oxford University Press.

Fiske, Susan, and E. Borgida. 2008. "Providing Expert Knowledge in an Adversarial Context: Social Cognitive Science in Employment Discrimination Cases." *Annual Review of Law and Social Science* 4 (1): 123–48.

Fligstein, Neil, Jonah Brundage, and Michael Schultz. 2017. "Seeing Like the Fed: Culture, Cognition, and Framing in the Failure to Anticipate the Financial Crisis of 2008." *American Sociological Review* 82 (5): 879–909.

Foucault, Michel. 1977. *Discipline and Punish*. New York: Vintage.

Foucault, Michel. 1980. *Power/Knowledge: Selected Interviews and Other Writings, 1972–1977*. New York: Pantheon.

Foucault, Michel. 1990. *The History of Sexuality*. Vol. 1. New York: Vintage.

Foucault, Michel. 1997. *Society Must Be Defended: Lectures at the College de France, 1975–1976*. New York: Picador.

Foucault, Michel. 2007. *Security, Territory, Population: Lectures at the College de France, 1977–1978*. New York: Picador.

Fourcade, Marion. 2009. *Economists and Societies: Discipline and Profession in the United States, Britain, and France*. Princeton, NJ: Princeton University Press.

Frances, Allen, and Michael First. 2011. "Paraphilia NOS, Nonconsent: Not Ready for the Courtroom." *Journal of the American Academy of Psychiatry and the Law* 39 (4): 555–61.

Freedman, Estelle. 1987. "'Uncontrolled Desires': The Response to the Sexual Psychopath, 1920–1960." *Journal of American History* 74 (1): 83–106.

Frickel, Scott, and Kelly Moore, eds. 2006. *The New Political Sociology of Science: Institutions, Networks, and Power*. Madison: University of Wisconsin Press.

Friedland, Roger, and Robert Alford. 1991. "Bringing Society Back In: Symbols, Practices and Institutional Contradictions." In *The New Institutionalism in Organizational Analysis*, ed. Walter W. Powell and Paul J. DiMaggio. Chicago: University of Chicago Press.

Frye v. United States, 293 F. 1013 (D.C. Cir. 1923).

Fuechtner, Veronika, Douglas Haynes, and Ryan Jones, eds. 2018. *A Global History of Sexual Science, 1880–1960*. Berkeley: University of California Press.

Fussell, Sidney. 2017. "AI Experts Say ICE's Predictive 'Extreme Vetting' Plan Is 'Tailor-Made for Discrimination.'" *Gizmodo*, November 16. https://gizmodo.com/ai-experts-say-ices-predictive-extreme-vetting-plan-is-1820505745.

George, M. A. 2016. "The Custody Crucible: The Development of Scientific Authority about Gay and Lesbian Parents." *Law & History Review* 34: 487–529.

Gieryn, Thomas. 1999. *Cultural Boundaries of Science: Credibility on the Line*. Chicago: University of Chicago Press.

Glenn, Evelyn Nakano. 2010. "Constructing Citizenship: Exclusion, Subordination, and Resistance." *American Sociological Review* 76 (1): 1–24.

Golan, Tal. 2004. *Laws of Men and Laws of Nature*. Cambridge, MA: Harvard University Press.

Goldberg, Stephen. 1994. *Culture Crash: Law and Science in America*. New York: New York University Press.

Goldberg, Suzanne. 2002. "On Making Anti-Essentialist and Social Constructionist Arguments in Court." *Oregon Law Review* 81: 629–62.

Gookin, Kathy. 2007. "Comparison of State Laws Authorizing Involuntary Commitment of Sexually Violent Predators." Olympia: Washington State Institute for Public Policy.

Group for the Advancement of Psychiatry. 1977. "Psychiatry and Sex Psychopath Legislation: The 30s to the 80s." New York: Group for the Advancement of Psychiatry.

Grubin, Don, and Robert Prentky. 1993. "Sexual Psychopath Laws." *Criminal Behaviour and Mental Health* 3 (4): 381–92.

Hacking, Ian. 1995. "The Looping Effects of Human Kinds." In *Causal Cognition: An*

Interdisciplinary Debate, ed. Dan Sperber, David Premack, and Ann James Premack, 351–83. Oxford: Oxford University Press.

Halmenschlager v. Holder, 331 Fed Appx. 612 (10th Cir. 2009).

Halperin, David, and Trevor Hoppe, eds. 2017. *The War on Sex*. Durham: Duke University Press.

Haney López, Ian. 2006. *White by Law: The Legal Construction of Race*. New York: New York University Press.

Hannah-Moffat, Kelly, Paula Maurutto, and Sarah Turnbull. 2009. "Negotiated Risk: Actuarial Illusions in Probation." *Canadian Journal of Law and Society* 24: 391–409.

Hanson, R. K., and K. E. Morton-Bourgon. 2009. "The Accuracy of Recidivism Risk Assessments for Sexual Offenders: A Meta-Analysis of 118 Prediction Studies." *Psychological Assessment* 21 (1): 1–21.

Hanson, R. Karl, and David Thornton. 2000. "Improving Risk Assessments for Sex Offenders: A Comparison of Three Actuarial Scales." *Law and Human Behavior* 24 (1): 119–36.

Harcourt, Bernard. 2003. "The Shaping of Chance: Actuarial Models and Criminal Profiling at the Turn of the Twenty-First Century." *University of Chicago Law Review* 70 (1): 105–28.

Harcourt, Bernard. 2007. *Against Prediction: Profiling, Policing, and Punishing in an Actuarial Age*. Chicago: University of Chicago Press.

Harris, G. T., and M. E. Rice. 2003. "Actuarial Assessment of Risk among Sex Offenders." In *Sexually Coercive Behavior: Understanding and Management*, ed. Robert A. Prentky, Eric S. Janus, and Michael C. Seto, 198–210. Baltimore: Johns Hopkins University Press.

Hassani v. Mukasey, 301 Fed. Appx. 602 (9th Cir. 2008).

Hathaway, James C. and Michelle Foster. 1991. *The Law of Refugee Status*. Cambridge: Cambridge University Press.

Hebenton, Bill, and Toby Seddon. 2009. "From Dangerousness to Precaution: Managing Sexual and Violent Offenders in an Insecure and Uncertain Age." *British Journal of Criminology* 49: 343–62.

Hegarty, Peter. 2003. "Homosexual Signs and Heterosexual Silences: Rorschach Research on Male Homosexuality from 1921 to 1969." *Journal of the History of Sexuality* 12 (3): 400–423.

Heimer, Carol. 2001. "Cases and Biographies: An Essay on Routinization and the Nature of Comparison." *Annual Review of Sociology* 27: 47–76.

Herdt, Gilbert. 2009. *Moral Panics, Sex Panics: Fear and the Fight over Sexual Rights*. New York: New York University Press.

Hernandez-Montiel v. INS, 225 F.3d 1084 (9th Cir. 2000).

Hilgartner, Stephen. 2000. *Science on Stage: Expert Advice as Public Drama*. Stanford, CA: Stanford University Press.

Hooker, Evelyn. 1957. "The Adjustment of the Male Overt Homosexual." *Journal of Protective Techniques* 21: 18–31.

Hoppe, Trevor. 2014. "From Sickness to Badness: The Criminalization of HIV in Michigan." *Social Science & Medicine* 101: 139–47.

Hoppe, Trevor. 2016. "Punishing Sex: Sex Offenders and the Missing Punitive Turn in Sexuality Studies." *Law & Social Inquiry* 41 (3): 573–94.

Hoppe, Trevor. 2017. *Punishing Disease: HIV and the Criminalization of Sickness*. Berkeley: University of California Press.

Huber, Peter. 1991. *Galileo's Revenge: Junk Science in the Courtroom*. New York: Basic Books.

Hull, Kathleen. 2017. "The Role of Social Science Expertise in Same-Sex Marriage Litigation." *Annual Review of Law and Social Science* 13: 471–91.

Human Rights Watch. 2009. "'Not Worth a Penny': Human Rights Abuses against Transgender People in Honduras." New York: Human Rights Watch.

INS v. Cardoza-Fonseca 480 U.S. 421 (1987).

Janus, Eric S. 2006. *Failure to Protect: America's Sexual Predator Laws and the Rise of the Preventive State*. Ithaca, NY: Cornell University Press.

Janus, Eric S., and Paul Meehl. 1997. "Assessing the Legal Standard for Predictions of Dangerousness in Sex Offender Commitment Proceedings." *Psychology, Public Policy, and Law* 3: 33–64.

Janus, Eric S., and Robert Prentky. 2003. "Forensic Use of Actuarial Risk Assessment with Sex Offenders: Accuracy, Admissibility and Accountability." *American Criminal Law Review* 40: 1443–502.

Jasanoff, Sheila. 1990. *The Fifth Branch: Science Advisers as Policymakers*. Cambridge, MA: Harvard University Press.

Jasanoff, Sheila. 1995. *Science at the Bar: Law, Science, and Technology in America*. Cambridge, MA: Harvard University Press.

Jasanoff, Sheila. 2002. "Science and the Statistical Victim: Modernizing Knowledge in Breast Implant Litigation." *Social Studies of Science* 32 (1): 37–69.

Jasanoff, Sheila, ed. 2004. *States of Knowledge: The Co-Production of Science and Social Order*. London: Routledge.

Jasanoff, Sheila. 2005. *Designs on Nature: Science and Democracy in the United States and Europe*. Princeton: Princeton University Press.

Jasanoff, Sheila. 2008. "Making Order: Law and Science in Action." Pp. 761–86 in *Handbook of Science and Technology Studies, 3rd edition*, edited by Edward Hackett, Olga Amsterdamska, Michael Lynch, and Judy Wajcman. Cambridge: MIT Press.

Jenkins, Philip. 1998. *Moral Panic: Changing Concepts of the Child Molester in Modern America*. New Haven, CT: Yale University Press.

Joppke, Christian. 2007. "Transformation of Citizenship: Status, Rights, Identity." *Citizenship Studies* 11 (1): 37–48.

Jordan-Young, Rebecca M. 2011. *Brain Storm: The Flaws in the Science of Sex Difference*. Cambridge, MA: Harvard University Press.

Jumper, Shan, Mark Babula, and Todd Casbon. 2012. "Diagnostic Profiles of Civilly Committed Sexual Offenders in Illinois and Other Reporting Jurisdictions: What We Know So Far." *International Journal of Offender Therapy and Comparative Criminology* 56 (6): 838–55.

Kalhan, Anil. 2013. "Immigration Policing and Federalism through the Lens of Technology, Surveillance, and Privacy." *Ohio State Legal Journal* 74: 1106–65.

Kansas v. Crane 534 U.S. 407 (2002).

Kansas v. Hendricks 521 U.S. 346 (1997).

Kendall, Kathleen. 2005. "Beyond Reason: Social Constructions of Mentally Disordered Female Offenders." In *Women, Madness, and the Law: A Feminist Reader*, ed. Wendy Chan, Dorothy E. Chunn, and Robert Menzies, 41–57. London: GlassHouse.

Kertzer, David, and Dominique Arel, eds. 2002. *Census and Identity: The Politics of Race, Ethnicity, and Language in National Censuses*. Cambridge: Cambridge University Press.

King, Christopher, Lindsey Wiley, Eve Brank, and Kirk Heilbrun. 2014. "Disputed Paraphilia Diagnoses and Legal Decision Making: A Case Law Survey of Paraphilia NOS, Nonconsent." *Psychology, Public Policy, and Law* 20 (3): 294–308.

Knighton, Jefferson, Daniel Murrie, M. T. Boccaccini, and Darrel Turner. 2014. "How Likely Is 'Likely to Reoffend' in Sex Offender Civil Commitment Trials?" *Law and Human Behavior* 38 (3): 293–304.

Knorr Cetina, Karin. 1999. *Epistemic Cultures: How the Sciences Make Knowledge.* Cambridge, MA: Harvard University Press.

Kornbluh, Felicia. 2011. "Queer Legal History: A Field Grows Up and Comes Out." *Law and Social Inquiry* 36 (2): 537–59.

Krafft-Ebing, Richard von. 1965. *Psychopathia Sexualis.* New York: Stein and Day.

Kunzel, Regina. 2008. *Criminal Intimacy: Prison and the Uneven History of Modern American Sexuality.* Chicago: University of Chicago Press.

Kunzel, Regina. 2017. "Sex Panic, Psychiatry, and the Expansion of the Carceral State." In *The War on Sex*, edited by David Halperin and Trevor Hoppe, 229–46. Durham, NC: Duke University Press.

Lalumière, Martin, Ray Blanchard, and Kenneth Zucker. 2000. "Sexual Orientation and Handedness in Men and Women: A Meta-Analysis." *Psychological Bulletin* 126 (4): 575–92.

Lancaster, Roger. 2011. *Sex Panic and the Punitive State.* Berkeley: University of California Press.

Landau, Joseph. 2004–2005. "'Soft Immutability' and 'Imputed Gay Identity': Recent Developments in Transgender and Sexual Orientation–Based Asylum Law." *Fordham Urban Law Journal* 32: 237–63.

Lara-Millan, Armando. 2017. "States as a Series of People Exchanges." In *The Many Hands of the State: Theorizing Political Authority and Social Control*, ed. Kimberly J. Morgan and Ann Shola Orloff, 81–102. Cambridge: Cambridge University Press.

Latour, Bruno. 2010. *The Making of Law: An Ethnography of the Conseil d'État.* Cambridge: Polity.

Latour, Bruno, and Steve Woolgar. 1979. *Laboratory Life: The Construction of Scientific Facts.* Princeton, NJ: Princeton University Press.

Laumann, Edward O., John H. Gagnon, Robert T. Michael, and Stuart Michaels. 1994. *The Social Organization of Sexuality: Sexual Practices in the United States.* Chicago: University of Chicago Press.

Lee, Sharon. 1993. "Racial Classifications in the U.S. Census: 1890–1990." *Ethnic and Racial Studies* 16: 75–94.

Lempert, R. 2013. "Growing Up in Law and Society: The Pulls of Policy and Methods." *Annual Review of Law and Social Science* 9 (1): 1–32.

Leon, Chrysanthi S. 2011. *Sex Fiends, Perverts, and Pedophiles: Understanding Sex Crime Policy in America.* New York: New York University Press.

Levenson, Jill S. 2004. "Reliability of Sexually Violent Predator Civil Commitment Criteria in Florida." *Law and Human Behavior* 28 (4): 357–68.

Levenson, Jill S., and J. W. Morin. 2006. "Factors Predicting Selection of Sexually Violent Predators for Civil Commitment." *International Journal of Offender Therapy and Comparative Criminology* 50: 609–29.

Levi, Ron, and Mariana Valverde. 2001. "Knowledge on Tap: Police Science and Common Knowledge in the Legal Regulation of Drunkenness." *Law and Social Inquiry* 26 (4): 819–46.

Levin, Sam. 2018. "US Government to Use Facial Recognition Technology at Mexico Border Crossing." *Guardian*, June 5. https://www.theguardian.com/technology/2018/jun/05/facial-recognition-us-mexico-border-crossing.

Levit, N. 2010. "Theorizing and Litigating the Rights of Sexual Minorities." *Columbia Journal of Gender and Law* 19: 21.

Lewis, Rachel. 2014. "'Gay? Prove It': The Politics of Queer Anti-Deportation Activism." *Sexualities* 17 (8): 958–75.

Longino, Helen. 2013. *Studying Human Behavior: How Scientists Investigate Aggression and Sexuality*. Chicago: University of Chicago Press.

Loveman, Mara. 2005. "The Modern State and the Primitive Accumulation of Symbolic Power." *American Journal of Sociology* 110 (6): 1651–83.

Loveman, Mara. 2014. *National Colors: Racial Classification and the State in Latin America*. Oxford: Oxford University Press.

Luibhéid, Eithne. 2002. *Entry Denied: Controlling Sexuality at the Border*. Minneapolis: University of Minnesota Press.

Lynch, Michael. 2004. "Circumscribing Expertise: Membership Categories in Courtroom Testimony." In *States of Knowledge: The Co-Production of Science and Social Order*, ed. Sheila Jasanoff, 161–80. London: Routledge.

Lynch, Michael, Simon Cole, Ruth McNally, and Kathleen Jordan. 2008. *Truth Machine: The Contentious History of DNA Fingerprinting*. Chicago: University of Chicago Press.

Lynch, Michael, and Sheila Jasanoff. 1998. "Contested Identities: Science, Law and Forensic Practice." *Social Studies of Science* 28 (5–6): 675–86.

Lynch, Mona. 2002. "Pedophiles and Cyber-Predators as Contaminating Forces: The Language of Disgust, Pollution, and Boundary Invasions in Federal Debates on Sex Offender Legislation." *Law and Social Inquiry* 27 (3): 529–57.

Lynch, Mona. 2019. "The Narrative of the Number: Quantification in Criminal Court." *Law & Social Inquiry* 44 (1): 31–57.

Lynch, Mona, and Alyse Bertenthal. 2016. "The Calculus of the Record: Criminal History in the Making of US Federal Sentencing Guidelines." *Theoretical Criminology* 20 (2): 145–64.

Magnet, Shoshana Amielle. 2011. *When Biometrics Fail: Gender, Race, and the Technology of Identity*. Durham, NC: Duke University Press.

Mansnerus, Laura. 2017. "For What They Might Do: A Sex Offender Exception to the Constitution." In *The War on Sex*, edited by David Halperin and Trevor Hoppe, 268–90. Durham, NC: Duke University Press.

Marouf, Fatma. 2008. "The Emerging Importance of 'Social Visibility' in Defining a 'Particular Social Group' and Its Potential Impact on Asylum Claims Related to Sexual Orientation and Gender." *Yale Law & Policy Review* 27: 47–106.

Marx, Anthony. 1998. *Making Race and Nation: A Comparison of the United States, South Africa, and Brazil*. Cambridge: Cambridge University Press.

Matter of Acosta. 1985. United States Board of Immigration Appeals.

McAdam, Doug. 1982. *Political Process and the Development of Black Insurgency, 1930–1970*. Chicago: University of Chicago Press.

McGee v. Bartow, 593 F.3d 556 (7th Cir. 2010).

McGrath, Robert, Georgia Cumming, Brenda Burchard, Stephen Zeoli, and Lawrence Ellerby. 2010. *Current Practices and Emerging Trends in Sexual Abuser Management: The Safer Society 2009 North American Survey*. Brandon, VT: Safer Society Press.

McKinnon, Sara. 2016. *Gendered Asylum*. Urbana: University of Illinois Press.

McLawsen, Julia, Mario Scalora, and Charles Darrow. 2012. "Civilly Committed Sex Offenders: A Description and Interstate Comparison of Populations." *Psychology, Public Policy, and Law* 18 (3): 453–76.

Merry, Sally Engle. 2016. *The Seductions of Quantification: Measuring Human Rights, Gender Violence, and Sex Trafficking*. Chicago: University of Chicago Press.

Mertz, Elizabeth. 2008. *The Role of Social Science in Law*. Burlington, VT: Ashgate.

Millbank, Jenni. 2009. "From Discretion to Disbelief: Recent Trends in Refugee Determinations on the Basis of Sexual Orientation in Australia and the United Kingdom." *International Journal of Human Rights* 13 (2): 391–414.

Miller, Banks, Linda Camp Keith, and Jennifer S. Holmes. 2015. *Immigration Judges and US Asylum Policy*. Philadelphia: University of Pennsylvania Press.

Miller, Clark A. 2008. "Civic Epistemologies: Constituting Knowledge and Order in Political Communities." *Sociology Compass* 2 (6): 1896–919.

Mitchell, Timothy. 1999. "Society, Economy, and the State Effect." In *State/Culture: State Formation after the Cultural Turn*, ed. George Steinmetz, 76–97. Ithaca, NY: Cornell University Press.

Mol, Annemarie. 2002. *The Body Multiple*. Durham, NC: Duke University Press.

Moore, Dawn, and Mariana Valverde. 2000. "Maidens at Risk: Date Rape Drugs and the Formation of Hybrid Risk Knowledges." *Economy and Society* 29 (4): 514–32.

Moran, P. 1999. "The Epidemiology of Antisocial Personality Disorder." *Social Psychiatry and Psychiatric Epidemiology* 34 (5): 231–42.

Mossaad, Nadwa. 2016. "Annual Flow Report: Refugees and Asylees 2014." Washington, DC: Office of Immigration Statistics.

Muhammad, Khalil. 2011. *The Condemnation of Blackness: Race, Crime, and the Making of Modern Urban America*. Cambridge, MA: Harvard University Press.

Mukerji, Chandra. 1989. *A Fragile Power: Scientists and the State*. Princeton, NJ: Princeton University Press.

Mukerji, Chandra. 2009. *Impossible Engineering: Technology and Territoriality on the Canal du Midi*. Princeton, NJ: Princeton University Press.

Murray, David A. B. 2014. "The (Not So) Straight Story: Queering Migration Narratives of Sexual Orientation and Gendered Identity Refugee Claimants." *Sexualities* 17 (4): 451–71.

Nagel, Joane. 2003. *Race, Ethnicity, and Sexuality: Intimate Intersections, Forbidden Frontiers*. New York: Oxford University Press.

Nathan, Debbie, and Michael Snedeker. 1995. *Satan's Silence: Ritual Abuse and the Making of a Modern American Witch Hunt*. New York: Basic Books.

Nelson, Robert, Ellen Berrey, and Laura Beth Nielsen. 2008. "Divergent Paths: Conflicting Conceptions of Employment Discrimination in Law and the Social Sciences." *Annual Review of Law and Social Science* 4 (1): 103–22.

Nobles, Melissa. 2000. *Shades of Citizenship: Race and the Census in Modern Politics*. Stanford, CA: Stanford University Press.

Norton, Aaron T. 2013. "Surveying Risk Subjects: Public Health Surveys as Instruments of Biomedicalization." *BioSocieties* 8 (3): 265–88.

Odeshoo, Jason. 2004. "Of Penology and Perversity: The Use of the Penile Plethysmograph on Convicted Child Sex Offenders." *Temple Political & Civil Rights Law Review* 14: 1–44.

Omi, Michael, and Howard Winant. 1994. *Racial Formation in the United States*. 2nd ed. New York: Routledge.

Organization for Refuge, Asylum and Migration. 2010. "Testing Sexual Orientation: A Scientific and Legal Analysis of Plethysmography in Asylum & Refugee Status Proceedings." San Francisco: ORAM.

Packard, Richard, and Jill S. Levenson. 2006. "Revisiting the Reliability of Diagnostic Decisions in Sex Offender Civil Commitment." *Sex Offender Treatment* 1 (1): 1–15.

Pascoe, Peggy. 2009. *What Comes Naturally: Miscegenation Law and the Making of Race in America.* Oxford: Oxford University Press.

People v. Hayes (In re Hayes), 747 N.E.2d 444 (Ill. App. Ct., 2001).

People of Illinois v. Simons 213 Ill. 2d 523 (2004).

People v. Superior Court (Ghilotti), 44 P.3d 949 (Cal. 2002).

Poeppl, Timm, Joachim Nitschke, Pekka Santtila, Martin Schecklmann, Berthold Langguth, Mark Greenlee, Michael Osterheider, and Andreas Mokros. 2013. "Association between Brain Structure and Phenotypic Characteristics in Pedophilia." *Journal of Psychiatric Research* 47 (5): 678–85.

Polletta, Francesca. 2006. *It Was Like a Fever: Storytelling in Protest and Politics.* Chicago: University of Chicago Press.

Polletta, Francesca, Pang Ching Bobby Chen, Beth Gharrity Gardner, and Alice Motes. 2011. "The Sociology of Storytelling." *Annual Review of Sociology* 37:109–30.

Porter, Theodore. 1995. *Trust in Numbers: The Pursuit of Objectivity in Science and Public Life.* Princeton, NJ: Princeton University Press.

Powell, Brian, N. Quadlin, and O. Pizmony-Levy. 2015. "Public Opinion, the Courts, and Same-Sex Marriage: Four Lessons Learned." *Social Currents* 2 (1): 3–12.

Prentky, Robert, Howard Barbaree, and Eric Janus. 2015. *Sexual Predators: Society, Risk, and the Law.* New York: Routledge.

Puar, Jasbir. 2007. *Terrorist Assemblages: Homonationalism in Queer Times.* Durham, NC: Duke University Press.

Puri, Jyoti. 2016. *Sexual States: Governance and the Struggle over the Antisodomy Law in India.* Durham, NC: Duke University Press.

Quinsey, V. L. 2010. "Coercive Paraphilic Disorder." *Archives of Sexual Behavior* 39: 405–10.

Ramji-Nogales, Jaya, Andrew I. Schoenholtz, and Philip G. Schrag. 2009. *Refugee Roulette: Disparities in Asylum Adjudication and Proposals for Reform.* New York: New York University Press.

Rayner, Steve. 1992. "Cultural Theory and Risk Analysis." In *Social Theories of Risk*, ed. Sheldon Krimsky and Dominic Golding, 83–115. Westport, CT: Greenwood Press.

Raynor, Peter, and Sam Lewis. 2011. "Risk-Need Assessment, Sentencing and Minority Ethnic Offenders in Britain." *British Journal of Social Work* 41: 1357–71.

Razkane v. Holder, 562 F.3d 1283 (10th Cir. 2009).

Reddy, Sita. 2002. "Temporarily Insane: Pathologising Cultural Difference in American Criminal Courts." *Sociology of Health & Illness* 24 (5): 667–87.

Reding, Andrew. 2003. *Sexual Orientation and Human Rights in the Americas.* New York: World Policy Institute.

Reyes-Sanchez v. United States AG, 369 F.3d 1239 (11th Cir. 2004).

Rip, Arie, and Peter Groenewegen. 1989. "Les faits scientifiques à l'épreuve de la politique." In *La science et ses réseaux*, ed. Michel Callon, 149–72. Paris: La Découverte.

Rojas v. INS, 937 F.2d 186 (5th Cir. 1991).

Rosario, Vernon. 2002. *Homosexuality and Science: A Guide to the Debates.* Santa Barbara: ABC-CLIO.

Rose, Nikolas. 2002. "At Risk of Madness." In *Embracing Risk: The Changing Culture of Insurance and Responsibility*, ed. Tom Baker and Jonathan Simon, 209–37. Chicago: University of Chicago Press.

Rose, Nikolas, Pat O'Malley, and Mariana Valverde. 2006. "Governmentality." *Annual Review of Law and Social Science* 2 (1): 83–104.

Rubin, Gayle. 1984. "Thinking Sex: Notes for a Radical Theory of the Politics of Sexuality." In *Pleasure and Danger*, ed. Carol Vance, 267–319. New York: Routledge.

Ryo, Emily. 2016. "Detained: A Study of Immigration Bond Hearings." *Law & Society Review* 50 (1): 117–53.

Sarat, Austin, Lawrence Douglas, and Martha Merrill Umphrey, eds. 2007. *How Law Knows*. Stanford, CA: Stanford University Press.

Savelsberg, Joachim. 1994. "Knowledge, Domination, and Criminal Punishment." *American Journal of Sociology* 99 (4): 911–43.

Savic, Ivanka, and Per Lindstrom. 2008. "PET and MRI Show Differences in Cerebral Asymmetry and Functional Connectivity between Homo- and Heterosexual Subjects." *Proceedings of the National Academy of Sciences* 105 (27): 9403–8.

Savin-Williams, Ritch, and Geoffrey Ream. 2007. "Prevalence and Stability of Sexual Orientation Components during Adolescence and Young Adulthood." *Archives of Sexual Behavior* 36 (3): 385–94.

Schiltz, Kolja, Joachim Witzel, Georg Northoff, Katerin Zierhut, Udo Gubka, Hermann Fellmann, Jörn Kaufmann, Claus Tempelmann, Christine Wiebking, and Bernhard Bogerts. 2007. "Brain Pathology in Pedophilic Offenders Evidence of Volume Reduction in the Right Amygdala and Related Diencephalic Structures." *Archives of General Psychiatry* 64 (6): 737–46.

Scott, James C. 1998. *Seeing Like a State*. New Haven, CT: Yale University Press.

Seto, M. C., J. P. Fedoroff, J. M. Bradford, N. Knack, N. C. Rodrigues, S. Curry, B. Booth, J. Gray, C. Cameron, D. Bourget, S. Messina, E. James, D. Watson, S. Gulati, R. Balmaceda, and A. G. Ahmed. 2016. "Reliability and Validity of the DSM-IV-TR and Proposed DSM-5 Criteria for Pedophilia: Implications for the ICD-11 and the Next DSM." *International Journal of Law and Psychiatry* 49 (Pt. A): 98–106.

Seto, M. C., and M. Kuban. 1996. "Criterion-Related Validity of a Phallometric Test for Paraphilic Rape and Sadism." *Behaviour Research and Therapy* 34 (2): 175–83.

Seto, M. C., and M. L. Lalumière. 2001. "A Brief Screening Scale to Identify Pedophilic Interests among Child Molesters." *Sex Abuse* 13: 15–25.

Seto, Michael. 2012. "Is Pedophilia a Sexual Orientation?" *Archives of Sexual Behavior* 41: 231–36.

Sewell, William. 1992. "A Theory of Structure: Duality, Agency, and Transformation." *American Journal of Sociology* 98 (1): 1–29.

Shah, Nayan. 2012. *Stranger Intimacy: Contesting Race, Sexuality, and the Law in the North American West*. Berkeley: University of California Press.

Shapin, Steven. 1994. *A Social History of Truth: Civility and Science in Seventeenth-Century England*. Chicago: University of Chicago Press.

Shapin, Steven. 1995. "Cordelia's Love: Credibility and the Social Studies of Science." *Perspectives on Science* 3 (3): 76–96.

Shapin, Steven, and Simon Schaffer. 1985. *Leviathan and the Air-Pump: Hobbes, Boyle, and the Experimental Life*. Princeton, NJ: Princeton University Press.

Silbey, Susan S. 2008. "Introduction." In *Epistemological, Evidentiary, and Relational Engagements*. Vol. 1 of *Law and Science*, , ed. Susan S. Silbey. Burlington, VT: Ashgate.

Silbey, Susan, and Patricia Ewick. 2003. "The Architecture of Authority: The Place of Law in the Space of Science." In *The Place of Law*, ed. Austin Sarat, Lawrence Douglas, and Martha Merrill Umphrey, 77–108. Ann Arbor: University of Michigan Press.

Simon, Jonathan. 1998. "Managing the Monstrous: Sex Offenders and the New Penology." *Psychology, Public Policy, and Law* 4 (1/2): 452–67.

Simon, Jonathan. 2007. *Governing through Crime: How the War on Crime Transformed American Democracy and Created a Culture of Fear.* Oxford: Oxford University Press.

Skerry, Peter. 2000. *Counting on the Census? Race, Group Identity, and the Evasion of Politics.* Washington, DC: Brookings Institution Press.

Small, Jamie. 2015. "Classing Sex Offenders: How Prosecutors and Defense Attorneys Differentiate Men Accused of Sexual Assault." *Law & Society Review* 49 (1): 109–41.

Smith, Dorothy. 1984. "Textually Mediated Social Organization." *International Social Science Journal* 36 (1): 59–75.

Smith, Dorothy E. 2005. *Institutional Ethnography: A Sociology for People.* Lanham, MD: AltaMira Press.

Smith v. Doe, 538 U.S. 84 (2003).

Sohoni, Deenesh. 2007. "Unsuitable Suitors: Anti-Miscegenation Laws, Naturalization Laws, and the Construction of Asian Identities." *Law & Society Review* 41 (3): 587–618.

Solomon, Shana, and Edward Hackett. 1996. "Setting Boundaries between Science and Law: Lessons from *Daubert v. Merrell Dow Pharmaceuticals, Inc.*" *Science, Technology & Human Values* 21 (2): 131–56.

Somerville, Siobhan. 2000. *Queering the Color Line: Race and the Invention of Homosexuality in American Culture.* Durham, NC: Duke University Press.

Somerville, Siobhan. 2005. "Queer Reading of the 1952 U.S. Immigration and Nationality Act." In *Queer Migrations: Sexuality, U.S. Citizenship, and Border Crossings*, edited by Eithne Luibhéid and Lionel Cantú Jr., 75–91. Minneapolis: University of Minnesota Press.

Southam, Keith. 2011. "Who Am I and Who Do You Want Me to Be? Effectively Defining a Lesbian, Gay, Bisexual, and Transgender Social Group in Asylum Applications." *Chicago-Kent Law Review* 86: 1363–87.

Stampnitzky, Lisa. 2013. *Disciplining Terror: How Experts Invented 'Terrorism.'* Cambridge: Cambridge University Press.

Star, Susan Leigh. 1985. "Scientific Work and Uncertainty." *Social Studies of Science* 15: 391–427.

Steinmetz, George, ed. 1999. *State/Culture: State-Formation after the Cultural Turn.* Ithaca, NY: Cornell University Press.

Steptoe, George, and Antoine Goldet. 2016. "Why Some Young Sex Offenders Are Held Indefinitely." The Marshall Project. https://www.themarshallproject.org/2016/01/27/why-some-young-sex-offenders-are-held-indefinitely.

Stern, P. 2010. "Paraphilic Coercive Disorder in the DSM: The Right Diagnosis for the Right Reasons." *Archives of Sexual Behavior* 39: 1443–47.

Stoler, Ann Laura. 1987. "Racial Histories and Their Regimes of Truth." *Political Power and Social Theory* 11: 183–206.

Stoler, Ann Laura. 1995. *Race and the Education of Desire: Foucault's History of Sexuality and the Colonial Order of Things.* Durham, NC: Duke University Press.

Stryker, Robin. 1989. "Limits on Technocratization of the Law: The Elimination of the

National Labor Relations Board's Division of Economic Research." *American Sociological Review* 54 (3): 341–58.

Stryker, Robin. 1994. "Rules, Resources, and Legitimacy Processes: Some Implications for Social Conflict, Order, and Change." *American Journal of Sociology* 99 (4): 847–910.

Stryker, Robin. 1996. "Beyond History versus Theory: Strategic Narrative and Sociological Explanation." *Sociological Methods and Research* 24 (3): 304–52.

Stryker, Robin. 2000. "Legitimacy Processes as Institutional Politics: Implications for Theory and Research in the Sociology of Organizations." *Research in the Sociology of Organizations* 17: 179–223.

Sutherland, Edwin. 1950. "The Diffusion of Sexual Psychopath Laws." *American Journal of Sociology* 56: 142–48.

Terry, Jennifer. 1999. *An American Obsession: Science, Medicine, and Homosexuality in Modern Society*. Chicago: University of Chicago Press.

Terry, Jennifer. 2000. "'Unnatural Acts' in Nature: The Scientific Fascination with Queer Animals." *GLQ* 6 (2): 151–93.

Terry, Karen J. 2013. *Sexual Offenses and Offenders: Theory, Practice, and Policy*. Belmont, CA: Wadsworth.

Thompson, Debra. 2016. *The Schematic State: Race, Transnationalism, and the Politics of the Census*. Cambridge: Cambridge University Press.

Timmermans, Stefan, and Steven Epstein. 2010. "A World of Standards but Not a Standard World: Toward a Sociology of Standards and Standardization." *Annual Review of Sociology* 36: 69–89.

Tolman, Arielle. 2018. "Sex Offender Civil Commitment to Prison Post-*Kingsley*." *Northwestern University Law Review* 113 (1): 155–96.

Tong, Dean. 2007. "The Penile Plethysmograph, Abel Assessment for Sexual Interest, and MSI-II: Are They Speaking the Same Language?" *American Journal of Family Therapy* 35: 187–202.

United Nations High Commissioner for Refugees. 2008. "UNHCR Guidance Note on Refugee Claims Relating to Sexual Orientation and Gender Identity."

United States v. Rhodes 552 F.3d 624 (7th Cir. 2009).

US Citizenship and Immigration Services (USCIS). 2011. "Guidance for Adjudicating Lesbian, Gay, Bisexual, Transgender, and Intersex Refugee and Asylum Claims."

US Department of State. 2011. *Country Reports on Human Rights Practices, Mexico*. Washington, DC: U.S. Department of State.

US Department of State. 2013. *Country Reports on Human Rights Practices, Jordan*. Washington, DC: U.S. Department of State.

U.S. v. McLaurin 731 F.3d 258 (2nd Cir. 2013).

U.S. v. Perez, 752 F.3d 398 (4th Cir. 2014).

U.S. v. Shields, 649 F.3d 78 (1st Cir. 2011).

Valverde, Mariana. 2003. *Law's Dream of a Common Knowledge*. Princeton, NJ: Princeton University Press.

Valverde, Mariana, Ron Levi, and Dawn Moore. 2005. "Legal Knowledges of Risk." In *Law and Risk*, ed. Law Commission of Canada, 86–120. Vancouver: UBC Press.

Vance, Carol, ed. 1984. *Pleasure and Danger: Exploring Female Sexuality*. New York: Routledge.

Vaughan, Diane. 1999. "The Role of the Organization in the Production of Techno-Scientific Knowledge." *Social Studies of Science* 29 (6): 913–43.

Vogler, Stefan. 2016. "Legally Queer: The Construction of Sexuality in LGBQ Asylum Claims." *Law & Society Review* 50 (4): 856–89.

Vogler, Stefan. 2019. "Determining Transgender: Adjudicating Gender Identity in U.S. Asylum Law." *Gender & Society* 33 (3): 439–62.

Wacquant, Loïc. 2009. *Punishing the Poor: The Neoliberal Government of Social Insecurity.* Durham, NC: Duke University Press.

Waidzunas, Tom. 2013. "Intellectual Opportunity Structures and Science-Targeted Activism: Influence of the Ex-Gay Movement on the Science of Sexual Orientation." *Mobilization* 18 (1): 1–18.

Waidzunas, Tom. 2015. *The Straight Line: How the Fringe Science of Ex-Gay Therapy Reoriented Sexuality.* Minneapolis: University of Minnesota Press.

Waidzunas, Tom, and Steven Epstein. 2015. "'For Men Arousal Is Orientation': Bodily Truthing, Technosexual Scripts, and the Materialization of Sexualities through the Phallometric Test." *Social Studies of Science* 45 (2): 187–213.

Wald, Priscilla. 2008. *Contagious: Cultures, Carriers, and the Outbreak Narrative.* Durham, NC: Duke University Press.

Ward, Jane. 2015. *Not Gay: Sex between Straight White Men.* New York: New York University Press.

Wynter, Sylvia. 2003. "Unsettling the Coloniality of Being/Power/Truth/Freedom: Towards the Human." *New Centennial Review* 3 (3): 257–337.

Yoshino, Kenji. 2015. *Speak Now: Marriage Equality on Trial: The Story of Hollingsworth v. Perry.* New York: Crown.

Yung, Corey. 2010. "The Emerging Criminal War on Sex Offenders." *Harvard Civil Rights–Civil Liberties Law Review* 45: 435–81.

Zilney, Laura, and Lisa Anne Zilney. 2009. *Perverts and Predators: The Making of Sexual Offending Laws.* Lanham, MD: Rowman & Littlefield.

Zylan, Yvonne. 2011. *States of Passion: Law, Identity, and the Construction of Desire.* Oxford: Oxford University Press.

INDEX

www.ingramcontent.com/pod-product-compliance
Lightning Source LLC
Chambersburg PA
CBHW060030030426
42334CB00019B/2260